SOCIOLOGY, RACE AND ETHNICITY

SOCIOLOGY, RACE AND ETHNICITY
A Critique of American Ideological Intrusions upon Sociological Theory

HARRY H. BASH
University of Missouri–St. Louis

GORDON AND BREACH
New York   London   Paris

Copyright © 1979 by Gordon and Breach, Science Publishers, Inc.

Gordon and Breach, Science Publishers, Inc.
One Park Avenue
New York, NY10016

Gordon and Breach Science Publishers Ltd.
41/42 William IV Street
London WC2 4DF

Gordon & Breach
7-9 rue Emile Dubois
Paris 75014

Library of Congress Cataloging in Publication Data
Bash, Harry H
    Sociology, race, and ethnicity.

    Bibliography: p.
    Includes indexes.
    1.   Sociology — Methodology.   2.   United States —
Race relations.   3.   Assimilation (Sociology)   I.   Title.
HM24.B362   301   76—43589
ISBN 0—677—05390—8

to
MARGEL
and the
DADDE

Ce mot
ne se trouve encore dans aucun dictionnaire,
mais sans doute, dans l'avenir,
les traités de dénationalisation
formeront de vastes bibliothèques,
comme en forment aujourd'hui
les traités de stratégie, de tactique
ou les traités de droit.

JACQUES NOVICOW *La Dénationalisation*

Preface

This inquiry represents, in the strictest sense, a conceptual analysis. As such, it focuses attention upon the meeting ground for concerns with the "theory" of Methods and the "methods" of Theory.

Since the conceptual realm occupies a logical space somewhere between considerations designated as theoretical and those matters that are of a substantive character, concepts perform the vital service of stepping-stones that make the two-way passage between the empirical and the theoretical possible. Yet, indispensable as these footholds are for negotiating between the two, they can not be relied upon for providing safe passage. In the context of sociology, at least, such conceptual stepping-stones combine the tendency toward slipperiness with a disconcerting inclination to shift position. Consequently, they not only constitute a problem in their own right, but they engender difficulties that extend into both the theoretical and the empirical facets of sociological inquiry. It is our intention, therefore, to explore certain aspects of the conceptual realm, and thus illuminate this crucial, but less frequently highlighted area of sociological topography, where Theoretical endeavors intersect with the conventional concerns of Method.

Few substantive specializations in sociology are currently receiving more public or professional attention than the field of Minority Groups or, as it had for a long time been called, Racial and Ethnic Relations. Yet, despite a plethora of well-grounded empirical research, sociologists on the whole have failed, almost spectacularly, to anticipate the racial developments in America in the course of the last decade and a half.

Concerned citizens have charged, and specialists in this field have generally conceded (perhaps somewhat reluctantly but certainly quite belatedly), that much of what has been occurring in the *sociology* of race relations, bears little relevance to the unfolding *reality* of race relations.

This discontinuity between on-going events and a sociology purporting to interpret and inform these events, must be recognized as a logically predictable consequence of a much more fundamental failure to come to grips, at the most basic conceptual level, with the social realities of so-called race relations. The problem appears to be rooted in an elemental, but difficult step, requisite for the possibility of any science, that of transforming the materials of common-sense experience into an analytically adequate reconstruction of social reality. Since the sociologist is not only in, but *of* society, the attainment of a posture of detachment from popular *social* conceptions in order to achieve their *sociological re*construction constitutes and remains a special challenge for the process of conceptualization in sociology.

In the light of these considerations, it is our contention, and the guiding rationale for this study, that in the area of "racial" and ethnic relations, at least, sociological inquiry is seriously impeded by the "slippery" and "shifting" character of certain of its basic concepts; that for reasons that are more nearly ideological than either logical or empirical, one concept, that of assimilation, has been gradually accorded analytic priority over alternative modes of conceptualizing, particularly, "race" relations processes; that due to prevailing ambiguities that surround the process of conceptualizing in general, assimilation has, in addition, been uncritically transmuted from the level of a conceptual tool to a position that is perhaps more accurately described as an implicit theoretical presumption; and that this "Assimilationist Perspective," as we shall designate it, carries with it conceptual biases that compromise the sociological analysis of "race" relations, and provoke critical questions with regard to the normative or empirical character of the process of sociological theorizing.

We propose, therefore, in the ensuing inquiry, to divide our analytic sights and to train them, respectively, on the conduct of sociological conceptualizing in general, and on the concept of assimilation, as it has been adapted in the sociology of race and ethnic relations, in particular. Our concentration on the general issue will, hopefully, illuminate some difficulties that we believe to be obstructing a more relevant sociological engagement with the social problems of "racial" encounters. Conversely, our narrower focus on the concept of assimilation should contribute insights that will reflect back on the broader concern, and inform and disicipline the conduct of proper conceptualization in sociology. Perhaps most importantly, we hope to suggest modes of re-entry, that would permit this in many ways isolated specialized field to attain conceptual and theoretical reintegration with general sociology.

It shall always remain somewhat more true than its reiteration can ever render it trite, that an inquiry of this sort is not solely the product of the author's efforts alone. Some of my debts are acknowledged conventionally, but hardly discharged adequately, through bibliographic citations. In a more personal and immediate sense, acknowledgments are due Professors W. Wallace Weaver and Samuel Z. Klausner of the University of Pennsylvania. Each, after his fashion, has been helpful with suggestions, cautions, and points of critical comment. E. Digby Baltzell, also of the University of Pennsylvania, has not only been an inspiring mentor, a role-model of catholic and humane scholarship and, on a number of issues, a provocative intellectual foil, but also an admired friend. My debt to him is difficult to repay. I must also acknowledge a debt, of the most profound sort, that I owe Professor Joseph Schneider of Indiana University. It was he who first provoked my commitment to sociology, and it is to his hypercritical standards that I continue to regard my work as having to "measure up." If it does not, needless to say, it is neither he, nor my other intellectual creditors, who can be held culpable.

Additionally, I owe an incalculable debt to my wife, and sometime-sociologist, Carrie E. S. Bash. Hours that she might have spent more exhileratingly, she endured as a tolerant captive audience; she subordinated the pressures of her own work to the drudgeries of initial typings and multiple proof-readings; but most importantly, she was an encouraging supporter and a typically thoughtful critic. My debt to her remains unpayable.

The University of Missouri—St. Louis saw its way clear to granting me a sabbatical leave, thus affording me the time and the much appreciated tranquility for completing the study. Finally, my gratitude is extended to Ms. Chris Perniciaro. Not just a superbly professional typist, she has made me the beneficiary of her perspicacity, her fine sense of language, and her unfailing tolerance for my pernicious persnicketiness.

HARRY H. BASH

Table of Contents

PART I

Introduction

CHAPTER 1

The Special Problem
of Concepts in Sociology

I

The discipline of sociology has, in its comparatively short
career, and perhaps especially in the course of its American
elaboration, undergone a number of changes in developmental emphasis. The resulting preoccupations, however, are
more than a mere series of ephemeral or trivial intellectual
diversions, but reflect instead a coherent growth trend that is
in most respects not significantly different from that experienced by other sciences.

Thus, there is general agreement that after an initial phase
of massive European influence, a distinctly American sociology began to form, one that reflected much of the reforming
zeal, "individualism," and belief in Progress that characterized American culture in general. This period was followed
by a retrenchment from what today appears as facile
optimism, and American sociology turned inward toward a
concern with its empirical foundations and a preoccupation
with sharpening its descriptive and analytic tools. Having, it
would seem, achieved a greater confidence in its empirical
apparatus, the discipline appeared ready to readdress, on a
modest scale, some of its broader issues. Thus, the next
developmental phase of American sociology involved
an attempted rapprochement with its theoretical superstructure.[1]† While this phase can hardly be said to have run

---

† Numbered footnotes are collected at the end of each chapter.

3

its course, the influence of governmental, foundation and, increasingly, corporate demands upon its promise had, in the course of the 1950s, injected another major focal concern into the sociological enterprise. This concern is reflected in the theme of the 1962 meetings of the American Sociological Association: "The Uses of Sociology."[2]

This brief overview of the changing emphases in the development of American sociology is intended to suggest that these changes are not simply fortuitous. Rather, their sequence indicates, at each stage, a continuing responsiveness to difficulties that became evident in the course of the preceding phase, as well as a sensitivity to factors that impinged on the sociological enterprise from the social world outside.

We are concerned, in this chapter, with the special problem that sociology faces with respect to its conceptual tools. Such a concern has, of course, not been entirely lacking in past sociological endeavors, but its evidence has been intermittent and the problem has, in part, been ceded to the attention of the philosophers of (social) science. However, as a result of complications encountered in the aforementioned sociological efforts toward empirical-theoretical integration, and in response to difficulties experienced in navigating between the "purity" of sociological research and the "practicality" of its application to on-going social problems, the concern with concepts has acquired a new urgency. We shall first direct our attention, therefore, to the problem of scientific concepts in general, and to the special problem of sociological concepts in particular.

II

The process of conceptualizing within the strategy of research, particularly in the social sciences, has always constituted a critical area of logical ambiguity and methodological laxity. It is precisely in this conceptual realm, that much of the criticism that is leveled at sociology, by outsiders as well as those within the profession, finds its most sensitive target (see Merton, 1968: 168). It is difficult, indeed, to overestimate the importance of the process of concept formation and specification, since it serves as a vital link in the reciprocal relationship between valid empirical research and viable theorizing. No matter, therefore, how meticulously the processing of data, and how judiciously the theoretical elaborations are carried out, the overall scientific endeavor is necessarily compromised if it tolerates a lack of circumspection in the mediating conceptual sphere.

There is little need, here, to attest to the considerably sophisticated disciplining guidelines, that encourage methodological rigor and statistical precision in the conduct of the empirical research. The sociological literature abounds with tributes, frequently expressed in the form of left-handed compliments such as Mannheim's (1934:30), that extol the facility of American sociology for ingenuity and exactitude in deriving and manipulating data for specified ends. In this realm, at least, even the most devout positivist must concede some scientific legitimacy to the discipline of sociology.

Sociological theorizing, also, is subject to systematic ground rules with respect to the formulation of theory and to theory validation. Theory building, when conducted competently, proceeds within a framework of logical canons through which a set of laws and definitions, deductively interrelated, are concatenated into an axiomatic system (Hochberg, 1959: 427). The complementary problem of determining the validity of theories is similarly guided by procedures, adapted from the major philosophic conceptions of truth, such as norms of correspondence, norms of coherence and pragmatic or functional norms (Kaplan, 1964: 311-322). While neither the norms governing theory construction, nor those guiding the validation of theories, are always rigorously adhered to in the actual conduct of sociological theorizing, the point is that logical structures and methodical procedures for theorizing do exist. Both in the handling of data and, admittedly on a more modest scale, in theoretical endeavors, the sociological enterprise can thus lay claim to systematic procedural guidelines.

No such situation can be said unequivocally to prevail with respect to the treatment of concepts. At best, the

scientific adoption and implementation of concepts in sociology must be regarded as exhibiting a relatively primitive
state of development. Clearly, this bears further examination,
especially in a discipline that is notoriously sensitive with
respect to its methodological foundations.[3]

Inasmuch as concepts do occupy such a strategic position
at the juncture of empirical and theoretical endeavors, the
relative lack of rigor governing their use in sociology has led
to a frequently expressed line of reasoning, which it would be
well to dispose of at the outset of our discussion.

It is not unusual to find skepticism regarding the possibility of rigorous conceptualization in sociology lying at the
heart of the recurring controversy that surrounds the status
of sociology as a genuine science. A serious concern with the
problematics of concepts is, of course, justified and potentially
constructive. Yet, when such a concern is turned into an
argument for withdrawing the stamp of scientific legitimacy
from sociology, then its proponents must be suspected of
misunderstanding the nature of both sociological concepts,
and of science.

In part, the confusion with respect to concepts derives
from the type of analytic units that sociology typically
employs as empirical referents for its conceptual tools. These
units of analysis generally encompass collective phenomena
which, following Durkheim (1938: 97-112) and, more
recently, Mandelbaum (1955), are treated as specific realities,
with characteristics that must be logically distinguished
from those of the individual elements on which they are
predicated. While the analytic treatment of such collective
entities poses logical and methodological difficulties for
the sociologist (Warriner, 1956; Mandelbaum, 1955), as
well as ontological and epistemological problems for the
philosopher of (social) science (Berger and Luckman, 1966:
13ff; Gellner, 1959), to the uninitiated layman the treatment
of such entities appears thoroughly "abstract" and "unscien-
tific." Unable to emancipate himself from the popular psychological tradition of regarding only the individual, immediate,
tangible case as "real," he is bound, in Wilson's (1966: 695)
terms, to the "myopia of a raw empirical nominalism."

Popular misunderstandings aside, problems associated with conceptualization in sociology must be regarded as genuine; but they do not constitute a sufficient warrant for denying scientific validity to sociological inquiry. While this issue can be expected to erupt sporadically in the semi-popular press,[4] there is no need to resurrect it here, for the argument is an essentially spurious one. It rests on a confused understanding of the nature of science, and specifically on a still prevalent tendency to base the scientific status of a discipline on the character of its substantive content, rather than on the logic of its analytic strategy. The resolution of the argument turns on the extent to which an inquiry models its procedures in conformity with the ideal of "the" scientific method. However, if the test of a "genuine science" is to be absolute conformity to, rather than an approximation of that ideal, then, as Nagel (1961: 449) points out in discussing the social sciences, "apparently none but a few branches of physical inquiry merit the honorific desgination."

If the problematic nature of conceptualization in sociology does not constitute a legitimate basis for challenging sociology's scientific standing, it does, nevertheless, reflect a marked contrast to the status of conceptualization in the natural sciences. No useful purpose is served by obscuring the undeniable differences between the relative denotative and connotative specificity of conceptual tools in the latter disciplines, and the lack of such clarity that characterizes the conceptual equipment of sociology.

This difference is attributable in large part to the fact, seemingly unique to the social sciences, that man is a participating agent in the phenomena which his researches are designed to interpret. Most simply stated, the problem arises out of the proximity, experienced in essentially psychological terms, between the all-involving world of social events and the detachment-demanding strategy for their dispassionate analysis and interpretation.

To the skeptical layman, this proximity appears as a virtual congruence between the subject-matter of sociology and the substance of social life. Yet, the two are hardly identical categories of cognition, since the former constitutes a selective, rational, *secondary* reconstruction of reality, while the latter is comprised of the essential properties of primary psycho-social experience. The problem lies in the apparent difficulty in recognizing that distinctive levels of abstraction are involved. The inability to discriminate between knowledge and the objects of knowledge is an affliction restricted neither to the ancients nor, for that matter, to the layman.[5] We shall have occasion, in Chapters 4 and 5, to return to this issue.

The issue clearly signifies a problem of the greatest consequence to the sociologist. His inescapable dual role as sociological analyst and as social participant invites a facile transfer of perceptual as well as conceptual conventions from the world of social events to the discipline seeking to interpret it. There is an ever-present tendency for a popular vocabulary to be absorbed into his professional terminology, only to be refracted back onto the social world from which it originated, although now bearing the seal of legitimacy as "sociological" concepts. The warrant for such concepts generally rests on the belief that they have been carefully defined (specified) or the fact that they have been formulated in, for example, scalable (operationalized) terms. Alternatively, their legitimacy is predicated upon their effectiveness in representing, or for inferring, empirical phenomena (instrumentalism).[6] Yet typically, such concepts represent little more than refined terminological transfers from their common-sense usage in the social world to the analytic operations of sociology. Were sociological conceptualization to involve no more than this, then it would reduce sociology to the functions of a factually sound and well-articulated journalism, to a discrete text-book accounting of contemporary history.[7]

This imperialistic inclination of appropriating *social* perceptions and harnessing them to the performance of *sociological* operations is as wide-spread, as it is scientifically untenable. The point is that such terminological transfers are not simply translational in effect. If they were, then sociological analysis would lose its *raison d'être*, and would be adequately supplanted by social commentary. As we intend to show, these transfers compromise scientific aims since they carry over into sociology the shifting, perspectivistic, ideologically encumbered meanings that flavor the social idiom.[8] What is required for sociological analysis is not a transfer of social perceptions and common-sense conceptual categories, but rather their transfiguration or reconstruction.

Sociology is, of course, not unique in this respect, for every science proceeds through a conceptual reconstruction of the phenomena within its substantive purview. At the very least, this means that direct sense experience must be reworked from the common-sense "logic" through which it is apprehended, into a reconstructed logic that permits scientific analysis.[9] While, in notable contrast to the natural sciences, this prerequisite still remains largely a matter of aspiration in sociology, it is important to reiterate that this differential development in the sciences can not be directly attributable to any pecularity in sociology's subject matter.

Before proceeding to a closer examination of the peculiar difficulties experienced by sociology, it is useful to look for a moment at the common developmental problems encountered by all sciences.

III

Regardless of what type of phenomenon happens to capture the investigator's curiosity, the emergence of a science out of its antecedent mode of inquiry is typically marked by a newly-attained capacity for detachment. Such a detachment entails, at least within the limits of relevance, a willing suspension of the obvious, traditional, orthodox habits of organizing experience, that are embedded in a common-sense view of the world. In place of the conventional view, a novel conceptualization of the apperceptual material is substituted, and this logical reconstruction is frequently so radical, as to stigmatize its author as a heretic in the eyes of whatever established authority happens to feel disconcerted by its implications. Whether in celestial or terrestial physics, in chemistry or biology, as Herbert Butterfield illustrates so effectively in his lectures addressed to this point, the composite event known as "the scientific revolution" resulted from those pivotal moments in each discipline, when "men not only solved a problem but had to alter their mentality in the process, or at least discovered afterwards that the solution involved a change in their mental approach" (Butterfield, 1961: viii). The same process of reapprehending the prevailing orthodoxies, operates not only in the emergence of a science, but also frequently in developments leading up to an impending scientific "breakthrough." "Change is brought about, not by new observations or additional evidence in the first instance, but by transpositions that were taking place inside the minds of the scientists themselves . . . which virtually means putting on a different kind of thinking-cap for the moment" (Butterfield, 1961: 1).

This vital capacity for donning a "different kind of thinking-cap" is, of course, predicated on the aforementioned faculty for detachment from the objects of inquiry. Without this ability for relinquishing, at least partially and temporarily, certain of the Baconian Idols,[10] a scientific, as distinct from a common-sense mode of knowing is effectively precluded. Since, however, it not only informs the scientific enterprise as an institution, but must also permeate the personal working habits of the individual scientist, such a detachment from common-sense perspectives involves cultural as well as psychological dimensions.

Culturally, at least, this detachment must be regarded as something of an accomplished fact, at least insofar as it relates to the events embraced by the natural sciences. The scientific ethos appears thoroughly embedded in the thought-ways of mid-twentieth century Western civilization. It arose as a by-product of a gradual evolution in man's assessment of his place in the scheme of things. In the context of this protracted ferment of ideas, a wholly new type of *Weltanschauung* emerged, one which necessarily preceded even the possibility of a science. The gradual emancipation from a classical conception of the Eternal Order, which it behoved man to discern so that he might conform with it, has been too well documented to require elaborate exposition here.[11] Briefly, it entailed a radical shift from a sacred view of man as participating in, and obliged to conform to the Eternal Order, to a naturalistic view, in which man sees his task as one of discovering the laws that govern a secularized natural order, and so manipulating these laws as to transform the world to the satisfaction of his changing needs.

Thus Carl Becker, in his lectures on the eighteenth-century *Philosophes*, contrasts the earlier commitment to theology, philosophy and deductive logic as "the three stately entrance ways to knowledge erected in the Middle Ages," with the gradual enthronement, by the time of the nineteenth century, of history, science and techniques of observation and measurement. "In the hands of St. Thomas, philosophy, with deductive logic as its instrument of precision, was a method of building a rational world, *its aim being to reconcile experience with revealed truth*" (Becker, 1932: 20, italics added). Under the guidance of the modern approach to knowing, "*our supreme object is to measure and master the world* rather than to understand it" (1932: 16-17, italics added).

Since our interest here lies in tracing man's increasing capacity for detachment from the world in which he participates, the notable change underlying the transition is the complete reversal that has come to characterize the normative role defining man's posture toward that world. The classical tradition prescribed *conformity* in order to effect an integrating identity with the objective world of events; the modern pattern supports a *confrontation* of the phenomenal world for the, at least potential, purpose of transforming it. Knowledge, Francis Bacon had insisted, is power, and it is only a short logical (or, should we say, *ideo*logical) step to Marx's anti-Idealist dictum that "the philosophers have only *interpreted* the world, in various ways; the point, however, is to *change* it."[12] With each step toward the secularization of physical, chemical and, later, biological orders of phenomena, the way was paved for their rationalization and ultimate treatment in scientific terms — and from there to their politicalization and treatment in manipulative terms.

Clearly, no such confrontation of on-going events is possible without the observer's prior personal separation, or psychic detachment, from these events.[13] While in the individual case, this detachment is of course an essentially psychological operation, it acquires, with the institutionalization of science and its subsequent popularization, a facilitating cultural base. There is little question that today, insofar as physical, chemical or biological events are concerned, man's relationship toward these phenomena reflects a posture of "psychic distance." This posture is indeed so widely and easily assumed in Western culture, as to be taken for granted, even among laymen. Any resurgence, for example, of such man-and-nature-merging religions as animism or totemism would find little meaningful linkage, or, in terms of Benedict's conception, would be wholly incommensurable[14] with the interlocking institutional patterns of the contemporary Western culture system.[15] Indeed, at the risk of belaboring the point, fetishism offers a telling illustration. Once an elaborately institutionalized religious practice among a number of tribal societies it is, in contemporary Western civilization, so devoid of a cultural base as to be relegated to the casebooks of individual psycho-*pathology*.

This has been an admittedly cursory glance at the change in man's relationship toward nature that is associated with the emergence of a scientific world view. In no way do we wish to minimize the still very real creative effort that "putting on a different kind of thinking-cap" demands of the natural scientist. The point is, that a natural-scientific *re*construction of reality from its popular common-sense construction is vastly facilitated once the prevailing culture supports a widely diffused view of man as detached from, rather than supernaturally bound to, or physically merged with, the processes of nature. The types of substantive inquiry with which the natural scientist is concerned are thus no longer significantly complicated by the notion that man is a participating agent in the phenomena that his researches lay claim to interpreting. Stated in somewhat more Comtean language, the natural sciences have effectively purged themselves of their metaphysical preconceptions, and their positivist stage of development has, to a considerable extent, penetrated the thoughtways of popular culture.

IV

If we now turn our attention back to the field of sociology, we are faced with a somewhat different situation than that characterizing the current status of the natural sciences. Whether or not one is prepared to accept Comte's notion of the hierarchy of the sciences and his "Law of Three Stages" as a logically or empirically satisfactory account of historical evolution in the modes of knowing, there is no dispute that questions dealing with specifically social phenomena are only among the most recent concerns to be pursued within a format of logico-empirical (scientific) inquiry. This late emergence of sociology as a scientific discipline must be attributed to the same set of circumstances that impede, or at least complicate, its conceptual development: the difficulties encountered in achieving a (socio)logical reconstruction of social reality.

We insisted earlier, that the explanation for sociology's less than refined conceptual development lies not with any allegedly extrascientific conduct of inquiry that sociologists have, on occasion, been charged with employing; nor do we believe it to rest with any essential pecularity that distinguishes social phenomena *per se* from the phenomena associated with the natural order of events. Rather, we suggest, the explanation must be sought in the *quality of relationship* between the sociologist and the substance of social life. If the sociologist finds an effective detachment from commonly-shared social experience difficult to attain, if sociology strains at a scientific reconstruction of social reality, then the character of man's *involvement* in society poses problem dimensions that are not similarly encountered in man's (mere) *participation* in nature.

Unlike the kind of continuity, if not perhaps even mutual reinforcement, that has come to prevail between the natural sciences and Western culture, the relationship between sociology and the general culture base does not, as yet, bear evidence of any significant measure of integration. The discontinuity, in fact, is rather pronounced, and is indicated by the widely diffused and variously grounded misgivings that laymen express toward sociological inquiry and its conclusions.[16]

One form of this distrust, arising from a belief that the complexity and variability of social phenomena renders them invulnerable to explication by scientific analysis, can be met on rational grounds, and most basic sociology texts make efforts to dispel it.[17] This issue is a mere technical one, and can be resolved to the extent that analytic procedures, not fundamentally different from those used in other sciences, can be effectively communicated. The point is that, thanks largely to the pioneering work of the natural sciences, the popular culture does encompass an adequate technical base in which sociological research techniques may be anchored. At worst, sociologists and uninitiated laymen simply part company on the more subtle points, with the former regarding them as challenging opportunities for, and the latter relegating them as hopelessly immune to, scientific analysis.

A different kind of uneasiness about the sociological enterprise, one that is not so readily surmounted, takes us closer to the nub of the difficulties that plague properly sociological conceptualization. It grips not only the uninitiated layman along with the humanist-intellectual, but touches also the sociologist at those junctures in scholarship where superficial professionalism does not suffice to sustain him. The problem at issue reflects less of a technical naiveté, than it does, perhaps, a kind of generalized mystique that permeates the culture in which the sociologist not merely participates, but which, in a significant sense, animates him. It is in this connection, that the quality of relationship between the sociologist and substance of social life becomes a complicating factor.

The kind of phenomena that have, in modern times, become the substantive concerns of the natural sciences, were initially outside of culture. Indeed, the history of civilization may be read as the progressive incorporation of nature into culture, which proceeded, adhering to Comte's account, through the conceptualization of natural phenomena first in theological, then in metaphysical, and finally in positive terms. If this conception is granted, then natural science is seen to act as an agent for the methodical demystification and the gradual enculturation of previously extra-cultural phenomena.

In contrast to the incorporative growth of the natural sciences, in the course of which culture might be seen as progressively extended outward to embrace "nature," sociology's development involves a turning inward upon the culture, a digestive rather than an ingestive operation, a rationalization of phenomena that had already been culturally encompassed. Accordingly, the challenge of sociology takes the form of socio-cultural introspection and the demythification of culture itself.

The distinctive terms *demystification* and *demythification* are used here quite deliberately, since they are indicative of the popular image of what natural science and sociology, respectively, are about. Where natural science is seen as penetrating the *mysteries* of nature, sociology is popularly regarded as a debunking enterprise which seeks to empty social life of its comforting *myths*. Quite understandably, the exploring of mysteries "out in nature" is as widely met with approval, as the exploding of myths within culture is viewed with apprehension. At the risk of courting the reductionist fallacy, the position of sociology respecting the "Ethnos" may find its analogue in the clinical relationship between psycho-analysis and the Ego. Where psycho-analytic insights provoke defense-mobilizing responses when focused on the constructed rationalizations of the Ego, sociological inquiry is met with uneasiness when it seeks to penetrate and interpret the accreted myths that function as legitimations and justifications in culture.[18]

We would argue, then, that despite the widely diffused scientific (properly: technological) ethos that characterizes contemporary culture and serves as an institutional base for natural science, the scientific study of society is accorded less hospitality, and is still regarded as vaguely suspect. The target of sociological inquiry — social structure and social process — is still deemed relatively inviolable, even if its sanctity is experienced so intuitively as to defy lucid exposition, much less sound justification. If sociology amounted to nothing more than disciplined social surveying, then without doubt it would be comfortably accommodated in a book-keeping, inventory-ridden culture.[19]

Of course, sociology is not to be equated with *social* research or *social* analysis. The conclusive descriptions that constitute the end-product of social research serve only as raw data for sociological analysis; and the social reality described conclusively by social research becomes sociologically problematic. Where social research identifies, details and elaborates social reality *in terms* of the premises lodged in prevailing culture, sociological inquiry, aiming at the interpretation of social reality, is constrained to disregard these premises or, at best, to treat them as hypothetical rather than axiomatic.[20] It is precisely here, therefore, that a reconceptualization of common-sense experience affords the potential for the interpretation of that experience, and that a sociological reconstruction of social reality becomes imperative. It should now be readily apparent that this intellectual step can not be taken, unless the sociologist can emancipate himself from the confines of a common-sense ordering of social experience, and is able to refocus upon it from a posture of detachment.

The putting on of "a different kind of thinking-cap" entails difficulties for the sociologist to which the contemporary[21] natural scientist is rarely subjected any longer. The (natural) scientific revolution is accomplished — a sociological one is not. The natural sciences today enjoy a supportive cultural base, and their technological fruits are generally applauded; sociology lacks a comparably facilitating culture base, and social engineering is widely viewed with apprehension.[22] While, to be sure, the narrow technical dimensions of sociological inquiry, commonly referred to as "methods," may be consonant with a technologically receptive culture, sociology's conceptual dimensions, prerequisite to the possibility of sociological theory, are not commensurate with the general culture. They strain, and even transgress the definitions that are culturally imposed on social experience. This can not, of course, be otherwise. If there is to be a science of society, and if the aforementioned confusion between knowledge and the objects of knowledge is to be avoided, then sociological conceptualizations of observed events must, like conceptualizations in the natural sciences, transcend their conventional social definition. The difference is one of levels, and the levels of analysis and interpretation transcend the level of experience.

We have endeavored to show, through the foregoing discussion, that in a very specific sense an essential discontinuity must be maintained between a prevailing culture and a properly sociological enterprise; it is needed in order to impede the temptation of slipping from a world of everyday social perception to the "altered mentality" that marks the sociological workshop without assuming the transitional "thinking-cap." Once this objectively necessary discontinuity is acknowledged, however, it becomes important to follow through by recognizing its subjective concomitant. As in the case of the more familiar migration movements across political boundaries that separate incommensurable culture areas, the discontinuity identified here becomes the basis for a parallel disjunction of a more psychic character, which affects those who attempt to navigate between the level of social experience and that of its interpretation. The sociologist is not only an active, but an *involved* participant in the events on which he trains his analytic sights; he is not only socially *in*, but culturally *of*, and to some extent psychologically *enmeshed* with the phenomena he seeks to study. In th language of C. Wright Mills (1959: 8ff), the "public issues" of social structure that engage his sociological imagination, tend to be transmutations of the "personal troubles" of his private milieu. The special problem of the sociologist thus rests in the quality of relationship he maintains with the substance of social life, and it arises out of the peculiar proximity between his roles as social creature and social critic.[23]

The sociological utility of the notion of role has been

amply demonstrated by its adoption as a fundamental tool
for conceptualizing variations in social conduct through their
linkage with social statuses.[24] In the present context, it serves
to illuminate the complications that result when the juxtaposed statuses of social participant and sociological analyst
give the appearance of being collapsed through their joint
occupancy by a single individual. Such status-straddling
reveals these statuses as bearing a curious relationship to one
another: being, at once, difficult to reconcile, and yet leaving
the sociologist, who plays both roles, hard-put to separate
them effectively. When played properly, the roles are not
notable, as we have tried to show in the preceding pages, for
their complementarity; on the other hand it is difficult, on
partially psychological grounds, to relinquish one role when
assuming the other.[25]

We shall examine this problem, with a focus on its consequences for the conduct of sociological inquiry, somewhat
more closely in a later chapter. At this point, it is sufficient
to suggest that the sociologist experiences one form, of what
is generally discussed under the notion of "role-strain": "the
felt difficulty in fulfilling role obligations" (Goode, 1960:
483). If the sociologist encounters greater difficulties, than
his natural science colleague, in "putting on a different kind
of thinking-cap," we are led to identify the obstacle in the
combined effects of two considerations: his deep personal
enmeshment in his role as social participant, and his obligation to embrace the discontinuity that estranges this role
from that of the detached sociological analyst.[26]

V

We have attempted to introduce through this discussion
some of the difficulties involved in the formulation of
properly sociological concepts. As is the case with other
scientific disciplines, the possibility of sociology turns on
the ability of man to transcend the common-sense perceptions and definitions of reality that inhere in and are
supported by culture, and in their place create a novel,

scientific reconstruction of that reality. Failing this achievement, a piece of research may be *social*, but it can not be
properly considered *sociological*.

Critical as this distinction is, among laymen it may appear
trivial and go widely unrecognized, while among sociologists
it should be elemental, yet is not infrequently ignored. The
occasional conscious temptation to neglect it, or the probably more wide-spread innocent tendency to do so, suggest
the primacy of the sociologist's role of participant in the
world of social events, over his professional role of disengaged interpreter of those events. Clearly, as sociologist,
he can not abdicate either role — he is obliged to compartmentalize them — yet as we have tried to show, their
combined assumption tends to generate role-strain. One
understandingly tempting resolution of the strain, to merely
allude at this time to a problem that we shall examine more
closely later on, lies in reducing the "sociological imagination" to terms that are culturally more familiar. This may,
given the individualistic presumption that pervades the
American ethos, assume the form of psychological reductionism; but, in any case, it diminishes the promises of sociology
to the prosaics of common-sense. While role-strain may
thereby indeed be reduced, the practice would not only beg
the sociological issue, but would in fact compromise the role
of sociologist and thus effectively preclude the discipline of
sociology.

Durkheim's perhaps more quoted than observed caution
against reducing social facts to psychological variables, has
come to overshadow his comparable concern that sociological
conceptions not be reduced to social ones. Reflecting on the
nature of scientific work, he declares (1938: 43-44):

It needs concepts that adequately express things as they actually are,
and not as everyday life finds it useful to conceive them. Now those
concepts formulated without the discipline of science do not fulfil
this condition. Science, then, has to create new concepts; it must dismiss all lay notions and the terms expressing them, and return to sense
perception, the primary and necessary substance underlying all concepts. From sensation all general ideas flow, whether they be true or
false, scientific or impressionistic. The point of departure of science,

or speculative knowledge, cannot be different from that of lay, or practical, knowledge. It is only beyond this point, namely, in the manner of elaboration of these common data, that divergences begin.

This crucial point of distinguishing between social and sociological concepts should not be obscured by the (retrospectively) naive empiricism in which the issue, here, appears to be couched. Indeed, it may be that this very type of "rampant empiricism," as Bierstedt (1974: 133-149) characterizes it in an early critical essay, has contributed precisely toward confounding social and sociological concepts, particularly in an American sociological zeal for emulating the natural sciences. The Durkheimian notion that science "needs concepts that adequately express things as they are" is simply no longer tenable; and the assertion that "the point of departure of science, or speculative knowledge, can not be different from that of lay, or practical knowledge" appears, today, simplistic and, if salvageable at all, must be hedged with so many qualifications as to recommend its merciful abandonment. These are parts of the epistemological legacy of our positivistic tradition, which includes, according to Anthony Giddens (1976: 727):

the empiricist notion that there exists a neutral or theory-free observation language, in terms of which observations of objects or events can be made and generalizations inductively established, and the thesis that such a model, derived initially from natural science, is appropriate for the study of social phenomena, so that we may consider sociology a "natural science of society."

The relations between social and sociological concepts, just where their "divergences begin" and, specifically, just how scientific or sociological concepts are appropriately devised, are matters that are neither satisfactorily resolved nor frequently addressed.

   The problem of the relationship between the empirical datum and its properly sociological conceptualization remains a serious issue, and we shall take up its further examination in subsequent chapters. In the following chapters, however, we will turn to the more specific task of tracing the development and the application of one particular concept in sociology, that of *assimilation*.

Notes

1. The stages traced here are not a matter of controversy, and are described in most introductory texts and introductions to sociological theory. For a concise presentation, see Hinkle and Hinkle (1954).
2. Fifty-seventh Annual Meeting of the American Sociological Association, Washington, D.C., August 29 to September 1, 1962. The importance attributed to this theme is underscored by the recommendation of the Association's Committee on Publications, that plans be approved for a volume on "Uses of Sociology," to be edited by Paul Lazarsfeld, with William H. Sewell and Harold L. Wilensky. See the Committee report: *American Sociological Review*, 27 (December, 1962), p. 921. The book has since been published, as recommended, as *The Uses of Sociology* (Lazarsfeld, et al., 1967).
3. This sensitivity has not diminished notably since Henri Poincaré remarked that in contrast to physicists who have a subject matter, sociologists engage almost exclusively in discussions of method. Cited in Alex Inkeles (1964: 29).
4. See for example the "charge" by Russell Kirk and Robert K. Merton's "defense," which appeared in the pages of the *New York Times Magazine*, reprinted in Milton L. Barron (1964: 29-35, 35-40).
5. See for example Ernest Nagel's comments in "An Alternative to Marxism," in Nagel (1956: 417).
6. It is worth pursuing the discussion of three variant types of semantic empiricism in their relevance to the legitimation of scientific concepts in Kaplan (1964: 36-44).
7. The conception of sociology as a vehicle for engaging in this type of contemporary history is, of course, not novel. It threads its way throughout the nineteenth and early twentieth century German controversy concerning the nature of history as a branch of knowledge. The extreme position was epitomized on the Comtean, positivistic side, by Ranke's famous dictum that the task of historians lies in establishing *"wie es eigentlich gewesen ist"* (how it essentially happened). On the other side were the "imaginative reconstructionists," exemplified by Droysen, but probably epitomized by Dilthey. The resulting bitter, and extended, *"Methodenstreit"* spilled over into other social disciplines, and

inevitably had its repercussions in sociology. It is traced most lucidly in Cahnman's scholarly essay "Weber and the Methodological Controversy," in Cahnman and Boskoff (1964: 103-127). The effect, if not the intention, of viewing sociology as a journalistic form of doing contemporary history will be considered later in this study, in it specific bearing on the sociology of racial and ethnic relations (see 149-151, *infra* and Ch. 7, note 1).

8. The reverse situation, of laymen employing the technical vocabulary of sociology to express social meanings, results at worst in generally harmless malapropisms. Thus, resentment is popularly expressed over the "sociological" decisions handed down by the Supreme Court (when their *social* as distinct from their legal foundations are being challenged); or, socially undesirable conditions such as juvenile delinquency or drug-addiction are popularly referred to as "sociological" problems, rather than social problems; and occasionally a novelist is lauded for his sensitive "sociological" portrait of a protagonist and his milieu.

9. This distinction follows in essence what Kaplan has referred to, respectively, as "logic-in-use" and "reconstructioned logic." See Kaplan (1964: 8ff).

10. Of the four species of Idols, Bacon identified, probably the Idols of the Cave, of the Market, and of the Theater are the most pertinent. For a thoughtful analysis of these Idols, particularly in their relevance to the sociology of knowledge, see Gunter W. Remmling (1967: 118-127).

11. Perhaps more effectively than Butterfield's book, referred to above, Alfred North Whitehead's Lowell Lectures of 1925 portray the changing mentality that led to the scientific cosmology. See Whitehead (1925); see also Harry Elmer Barnes and Howard Becker (1938: I, Chapters VII and IX).

12. See the *eleventh* of the "Theses on Feuerbach" in Marx (1959: 245, italics in original).

13. The process finds it social-psychological counterpart in Mead's distinction of the "Me" from the "I," and in Cooley's analogy of the "Looking-Glass Self." Both constitute a detached facet of an analytically dichotomized self, i.e. an objective vantage point for a subjective ego assessment. See George H. Mead (1934: 173-178); Charles Horton Cooley (1902: 151ff).

14. See Ruth Benedict (1959), Chapter VII, and *passim*. Of similar relevance here is Sumner's notion of the "strain toward consistency" which he sees evidenced among the folkways and the institutions of a given society. See William Graham Sumner (1940: 5-6).

15. While such a resurgence appears most unlikely in the context of religion, a not dissimilar impulse in that direction is, nevertheless, reflected in the contemporary Ecology Movement. In this case, however, the issue is compelled by the pressures of technology

rather than the mandates of theology, and thus resonates more readily with the current culture base.

16. See for example Merton's description of the typical public response to sociological inquiry, which views the sociologist's role as virtually limited to the alternatives of "bore" or "heretic." Robert K. Merton (1959: xv-xvi).

17. For a representative set of seven such "major objections to the possibility of social science," see Ralph Ross (1962: 68-79).

18. With respect to this subject, compare the consideration of the "debunking motif" in sociology, in Peter L. Berger (1963: 38-42).

19. A sociology harmlessly engaged in "out-house counting" can be dismissed as ludicrous, or tolerated as trivial; a compilation of census data, or the result of opinion surveys can be ignored as fallible, or welcomed as a guide to the economic or political market place; and an inventory of community deficiencies or resources may be disregarded, or valued as informative. In any case, such essentially journalistic or actuarial undertakings are not likely to pose a threat to contemporary myths. Rather than serving to undermine them, they tend to buttress them by occasionally illuminating their fissures that want patching. In other words, social surveys and "Study Commissions" are more typically the strategies of "Liberal" Reform, than of "Radical" Reconstruction.

20. The distinction drawn here between sociological inquiry and social research, while perhaps not acceptable to all, is not to be read as a denigration of the latter. It is compatible with the views of Lazarsfeld, hardly known for his hostility to social research, as expressed in his 1962 Presidential Address to the American Sociological Association. See Paul F. Lazarsfeld (1962).

21. This is not to say that the early, pioneering natural scientists, prior to the "legitimation" of the scientific revolution, did not share certain of these difficulties.

22. This apprehension is not necessarily restricted to laymen. Just as few philosophers, today, seriously cherish a Platonic Utopia in which philosophers rule as kings, and natural scientists would similarly decline H. G. Wells' vision of a world administered by scientists, so sociologists are disposed to be leery of Comte's dream of a sociocracy, ministered by a sociological priesthood. If anything, they tend to cling to the monasticism of the Ivory Tower.

23. The term "critic" is freighted with a number of meanings. It is used here in its "neutral" sense of designating one who employs reasoned and judicious evaluation in assessing an event. The congruence of this meaning with that which describes the basic role of the "intellectual," is thus fully intended. It is precisely the critical posture of the sociologist-as-intellectual, as distinct

from the sociologist-as-technician, that occupies our interest in this discussion.

24. The seminal, and still authoritative formulation of this conception is found in Ralph Linton (1936: Chapter VIII). Its relevance to our appraisal of the sociologist's position has been subsequently enhanced by Merton's contribution of the term "role-set" (as distinguished from "multiple roles"), referring to "that complement of role relationships which persons have by virtue of occupying a particular social status." See Robert K. Merton (1968: 423ff). See also Merton (1957).

25. Difficult as it may be, according to Dick Atkinson, sociologists have succeeded all too well. The consequence, he charges, is an established orthodoxy in which the layman "does not recognize himself in the sociologists' explanations. He feels, often quite rightly, that he could tell the expert 'a thing or two' about the way people really live and die" (Atkinson, 1972: 2).

26. A comparison with Spencer's effort to identify the special difficulties facing sociology may be of interest. He ascribes these difficulties to (a) the intrinsic nature of sociology's subject-matter, (b) man's nature as observer of this subject-matter, and (c) the relation of man *vis à vis* sociology's subject-matter. Our own concerns have centered mainly on the last of these problems. Spencer's points are summarized in Chapter IV, and respectively elaborated in Chapters V, VI and VII in Herbert Spencer (1966).

PART II

*The Natural History of
Assimilation*

CHAPTER 2

The Concept of Assimilation in the Sociology of Racial and Ethnic Relations

I

In the introductory chapter, we tried to show that there are special difficulties that attach to the process of conceptualizing in sociology; that these difficulties constitute a critical impediment to effective sociological inquiry; and we tried to indicate something of the character of these difficulties, and to offer some perspective on the factors out of which they appear to arise. In order to pursue this line of inquiry more productively, we propose now to concentrate our attention toward an intensive analysis of one particular sociological concept. This should not only afford us a more concrete basis for assessing conceptual difficulties in sociology, but it will also lay down the ground-work for tracing their ramifications into issues of broader methodological import and their special bearing on the sociology of, so-called, race relations.

The concept we have selected for intensive scrutiny is the notion of assimilation. This choice is not arbitrary. Assimilation recommends itself as an exceptionally instructive case-in-point for the problem we have chosen to explore, since it combines the virtues of longevity and extensive usage as a concept in sociology, and because it has come to assume, as we intend to show, a peculiarly equivocal position in the sociology of minority group relations. This latter

27

development is, however, of relatively recent origin, and a brief historical over-view is required, to support our choice of assimilation as warranting special attention.

Paralleling their chronic prominence as social problem conditions in American *society*, the processes reflected in the encounters of racial, ethnic and religious minorities with the white, Anglo-Saxon, Protestant "host" society have traditionally constituted a major concern in American *sociology*. Such group relationships are so inextricably a part of the American experience, that their influence permeates every substantive field of sociological inquiry.

To acknowledge this pervasive motif in the American discipline is, of course, not to belittle the attention directed toward comparable group relationships by earlier, as well as more recent, European social theorists and sociologists. From Gobineau, Gumplowicz and Ratzenhofer, to Durkheim, Weber and Simmel, the European literature reflects clear evidence of efforts to come to grips, in analytic terms, with problems seen as arising from the contacts of racially and ethnically distinct groupings. Moreover, the work of European scholars has served, in the area of "race relations" no less than in sociology in general, to influence and guide the thinking of early American sociologists in their approaches to these phenomena. Typically, these approaches adapted such basic interactive processes as competition and cooperation, conflict, accommodation and assimilation to an analysis of the distinctively American patterning of racial and ethnic relations.

However, particularly in recent decades and especially in American sociology, approaches to race relations have followed a line of development that made the assimilative process a central preoccupation in both theoretical and empirical endeavors. The relative decline of analytic attention that was consequently paid to alternative social processes in the race relations field turned out, it appears, to be only a relatively minor by-product of the gradual assumption of assimilation to a position of priority as a conceptual tool. Much more significantly, this development had proceeded to a point by the mid-1960s, where assimilation had come to transcend the role typically associated with *concepts* in the conduct of inquiry. From the probing and relatively modest function of informing the collection and interpretation of data, the notion of assimilation had been transmuted to a position where it virtually carried the burdens associated with theoretical or explanatory functions on its own, already frail, conceptual shoulders. On the basis of the established literature through 1970, and to a considerable extent since then, the predominating American sociological approach to race relations reflects a celebration of "assimilation" as a reigning "theoretical" principle. Not only does this development represent a clear departure from traditional European sociological orientations as well as a divergence, of admittedly lesser proportion, from earlier American perspectives, but it provokes some vital questions regarding normative factors in sociological conceptualizing and theorizing.

In the light of these considerations, the selection of the assimilation concept for intensive analysis appears to hold particular promise for illuminating our broader conceptual concerns. The favorable attention which assimilation has been accorded over other social processes, and its elevation from the realm of concepts to a loftier theoretical sphere, constitute changes that must be attributed to the joint influence of the evolving history of (scientific) ideas, and the unfolding of American social events. Importantly, these changes took place against a backdrop of general ambiguity within the discipline and lack of consensus among sociologists, regarding the appropriate relationship between sociology and social life. We shall begin, therefore, to clarify and substantiate our contentions by tracing some antecedent intellectual traditions, the gradual diminution of sociological concerns with conflict, and the growing preoccupation with the notion of assimilation.

II

The impressive developments that marked the progress of the biological sciences during the nineteenth century made their impact not only on the prevailing popular and intellectual varieties of social thought, but inevitably left their impression on the emerging modes of sociological thinking. The promising application of Darwinian evolutionary conceptions to social processes occuring among and, on a grander scale, between the peoples of European societies, provided the authority for raising "struggle" and "conflict" (or at the very least, "competition") to a position of primary importance within the taxonomy of group interactions.

Gobineau, interpreting the revolutionary upheavals that plagued the traditional orders in France and other European countries, had already, in the intellectual footsteps of Boulainvilliers and the historian Thierry, defined the contending factions in racial terms.[1] Now, Social Darwinism offered the kind of directional guidelines, within which these seemingly idiosyncratic racial struggles could be ordered into a scheme of human phylogeny, extrapolated into a logic of history, generalized into a theory of social dynamics and, finally, transmuted into a Law of Progress.

The combined influences of Racial Determinism and Social Darwinism led to a kind of sociological perspective that was perhaps most saliently expressed in the work of Ludwig Gumplowicz (1883). For Gumplowicz, conflict was the essential and irremediable form of relationship characterizing contacts between groups that did not share common blood-bonds. This *Rassenkampf* may result either in extermination, or in subjugation of the defeated race, and Gumplowicz regarded the state as the political instrument created by the victor for continued subordination and exploitation of the vanquished, and for their eventual assimilation (1899: 116ff, 150-154).

Gumplowicz's conception evidences a striking congruity with Marx's view of the political state as the exploitative instrument of the ruling class, but distinguishes itself significantly by a difference in premises regarding the source of the antagonisms that animate contending groups. Marx envisioned the basis of the struggle as resting in incompatible *class* interests, defined in strictly social structural terms, while Gumplowicz ascribed it to *racial* animosities, arising from inherent incompatibilities that have their roots in the assumed polygenetic origin of groups. Interesting, and consequential for subsequent developments, as these distinctive conceptions are, the important point for our purpose here is, of course, that Marx too maintained that "the history of all hitherto existing society is the history of class *struggles*" (Marx and Engels, 1959: 7, italics added).

Gustav Ratzenhofer also regarded conflict as the basic process governing the relationships between groups, which he viewed as differentiated on the criterion of kinship or consanguinity.[2] Unlike Gumplowicz, however, he perceived a rhythm of alternating struggles and consolidations, resulting over time in increasingly more comprehensive and integrated population groups, or social structures.[3] It is interesting to note that the notion of "kinship" when used as an organizing principle for "blood-bonds," constitutes a subtle alteration from the structuring of such bonds in simple *racial* terms. Without relinquishing the underlying theme of a common, shared heritage which the notion of blood-bonds implies, the emphasis is significantly shifted from a heritage of common racial origins to a consanguine heritage of shared familial traditions — from an unequivocally biogenetic bond to one that accommodates socio-cultural interpretation. While conflict, rooted in man's biological drives and projected into his social relations, is still regarded as primary in structuring those relationships, Ratzenhofer acknowledged the important operation of other, more socially determined processes, which were later to be differentiated and conceptualized into accommodative, cooperative and assimilative patterns.[4]

The kind of theorizing that emerged from such focal emphases on competitive struggles as the essence of all social process, was thus carried on both within the Social Darwinist tradition and, as we suggested in the case of Marx's formulation, apart from that tradition. Ratzenhofer represents a figure of some importance not because he symbolizes a break with Social Darwinist traditions, but because he constitutes a transitional figure in whose work, particularly through his use of the notion of "interests," the glimmer of a *social* basis for the analysis of social phenomena may be perceived.

Seen from the vantage point of retrospection, the shift in thought was one of a gradual retrenchment from the bio-logic that posited "human nature" as a causal-explanatory device for observed social events, in favor of a growing and, indeed, radical suspicion that the explanations might be more profitably pursued through the assumption of a *socio*-logic. Yet, it was to be a while before the biological predilections would be entirely abandoned, much less repudiated, in socio-logical inquiry. In the emerging American sociology, racial (i.e. biogenetic) attempts at explanation seemed eminently congenial particularly to the Southern milieu,[5] and unassail-able when linked with the Social Darwinist persuasion. It was not until the third decade of the twentieth century that, quoting van den Berghe (1967: 3), "in reaction against the patently pseudo-scientific notions of nineteenth-century European and American racists and social Darwinists, a new orthodoxy developed," that of assiduously demonstrating social environment to be the more relevant explanatory locus for socially meaningful individual or group differences. Espe-cially in American sociology, explicitly biological modes of explanation henceforth all but disappeared.

It is worth noting however, that in both European and American sociological development, an echo of the more general biological heritage lingers on even today in societal models that are fashioned in organismic analogy, and in theoretical stances that support functional modes of analysis. Indeed, after several decades of almost contemptuous abandonment, there is a resurgent effort in the 1970s to root modern sociological analysis in a sound biological base.[6]

Irrespective, however, of the waxing or waning of one or another of the broad explanatory frames through which group relations patterns were to be understood, patterns of conflict and struggle retained a prominent place in European sociological concerns. This emphasis on conflict in its theoretical linkage both to Marxian and to Social Darwinist conceptions, found its way into the development of Ameri-can sociology by the beginning of the twentieth century. Its interpolation into the then still rather amorphous American perspective must be attributed largely to Albion Small.[7]

However, another important European tradition of theorizing needs to be identified here, one that was to have a more lasting influence on American sociology than either Social Darwinism or Historical Determinism.[8] Certainly since Durkheim, social theorists had become increasingly more sensitive to the fallacious appropriation of facts from one level of observation for the explanation of phenomena at another level. Durkheim's caution (1938: 110), that "the determining cause of a social fact should be sought among the social facts preceding it, and not among the states of the individual consciousness," seemed equally applicable as a general admonition to the sociological Social Darwinists and to the sociological Marxists. The former were inclined to construct social theories out of facts drawn from the sub-social world of biology, while the latter sought to reduce a supra-social logic of history to a theory of society.

Yet, significantly, Durkheim's warning was not explicitly directed toward those who would either biologize or historicize the study of societal phenomena. The more serious threat to the emerging identity and developing viability of sociology seemed to be posed by the logically much more proximate discipline of psychology.

The situation facing sociology as an emerging intellectual perspective was very similar to that of a "deviationist" socio-political movement. Typically, the struggle for identity of such a movement is marked by the direction of its most vituperative polemics toward its closest ideological neighbors — just as the parent-movement, in protecting its orthodoxies, reserves its most aggressive defense devices, no matter how hair-splitting the issue, for the ideological "revisionists" rather than for those who stand in diametric opposition.[9]

Thus Durkheim felt obliged to argue, emphatically and repeatedly, that collective phenomena have a reality of their own; that as social entities, they are as real *at their particular phenomenal level*, as the concrete reality that conventional intellectual habits had seen fit to confer upon the more familiar physical and psychic elements, of which these entities are composed (1938: xliii-lvii, 1-13). The risk that Durkheim assumed, of being charged with committing the extravagance of sociologism, was undoubtedly a calculated one, and his arguments were reiterated in specific response to those who would psychologize sociology out of a tenuously established existence.

Nevertheless, the distinction between the "psychic" and the "social" remained difficult to articulate and even harder to maintain in practice, and the problem is reflected in a continuing controversy surrounding sociological nominalism and sociological realism.[10] The thoughtways of contemporary psychology did penetrate the defenses that Durkheim and other sociologists had erected, and with them came some of the biological presumptions with which they tended to be freighted.

Conspicuous among these, and of course pertinent to our interests here, was the injection of psychology's own pre-occupation with phenomena of conflict, and its frequently biologically-grounded inquiry into their origins. We need hardly recall that psychology was, itself, only recently emancipated from the formal hegemony of biology. Moreover, those of its interests that ranged closer to the somatic end of the Mind-Body dichotomy, remained inseparably merged with the physiology branch of the parent-discipline. It is not at all surprising, therefore, that the early psychological study of conflict (translated as "hostility" or "aggression") focused on "human nature" as its facilitating structure, and came to rest on "instinct" as its causal impetus. The influence of these notions reverberated throughout much of sociology in the latter part of the nineteenth century, and Durkheim's apprehensions with respect to psychological reductionism in sociology turned out not only to have been largely justified, but they were compounded by inclinations toward biological reductionism.

The net effect of all this was, that a concern with conflict, already supported by Social Darwinist and Historical Determinist influences in sociology, was additionally reinforced by the weight that a psychologically-tinged orientation exerted within the sociological enterprise.

Georg Simmel occupies a prominent position in the tradition of theorists who attempted to construct a science of society that would stray neither toward the direction of bio-psychological reductionism, nor that of historicism. His sociological perspective led him to concentrate particularly on the *forms* of association, the empirically observable modes of interaction through which society could be said to have a unity above and beyond the individuals who constitute it. Simmel regarded conflict or opposition so typical a pattern in inter-group and intra-group dynamics, that he is generally classified among the "conflict theorists" in sociology.[11] In contrast with the Social Darwinists and the Marxists, Simmel was less interested in identifying the forces animating bio-logical evolution or historical development, than he was in discovering the forms of interaction that shape, sustain or modify group structures.

Through this in-a-certain-sense ahistorical perspective, Simmel viewed conflict simply as an important form of rela-tionship among a number of typically social patterns. Arising out of opposing social interests, it bears no implications for a grand design impelled by either involuntary genetic impulse or impersonal cosmic guidance. Moreover, his conception of conflict as a form of interaction within a strictly social con-text, led Simmel to view the outcomes of struggle along a continuum, ranging from annihilation or submission at one end, to unity or greater cohesiveness among the contending factions at the other (Simmel, 1964: 25ff; Spykman, 1965: 112-127). Much like Durkheim (1938: 65-75) had observed with reference to crime in society, Simmel (1964: 17-18, 96-107) recognized that conflict was not only a normal pro-cess arising out of social life, but that within limits, it carried with it (positively) functional consequences for the group structure.

Simmel was of course not the only European social theorist who saw conflict as a strictly social phenomenon. Max Weber (1949: 26-27), too, regarded conflict as integral to social life, but unlike Simmel, he did not concede to it a primary significance in group relations. In Weber's analysis, the social basis of conflict takes on an additional meaning. He does not merely, as did Simmel, regard conflict as an *objec-tive social* fact, divorced from its biological and historical manifestations on which the Social Darwinists and the nineteenth century Marxists, respectively, had built their arguments. Developing out of the objectively opposed interests typical in social life, conflict acquires its significantly *social* character for Weber through the *subjective meanings* which social definitions impose both on the antagonists' conduct, and on the ends toward which that conduct is directed (Weber, 1947: 80ff).

In summary, our interest in the antecedents to what later appeared as an American sociological preoccupation with assimilation, has led us to trace briefly the kind of emphases, along with their intellectual roots, that were prominent in European social theorizing during the second half of the nineteenth century. The early tendency to explain social life on the basis of biological and evolutionary assumptions, propelled the notion of conflict into a position of central importance among social theorists. However, the Social Darwinist perspective, although widely adopted, was not the only intellectual current that inclined scholars toward a conflict orientation in social theorizing. A similar focus on social conflict, but devoid of a biological rationale, resulted from a number of theories of history, particularly those of the Marxist variety. Yet, as we noted, the biological tradition was reasserted through the assumptions that early psychology carried into the formative sociological enterprise, and the stress on conflict was thus reinforced, although here more often on the basis of instinctual, than on evolutionary, premises. Thus whether society was visualized as the stage upon which biological drives were acted out or, alternatively, as the arena in which historical destinies ran their course, conflict was regarded as the central reality that patterned group relations.

Toward the end of the nineteenth century, both the Social Darwinist and the Historical Determinist influences on social theorizing had begun to diminish. The work of Durkheim, Simmel and Weber has retained its relevance to current sociological thought precisely because of the pioneering efforts of these men toward establishing the *social basis* of social phenomena. Yet, the concern with conflict, not as pronounced in Durkheim or perhaps even Weber as we suggested it was in the work of Simmel, was still evident.

We wish now to turn our attention to the influence that these European thought traditions exerted on the emerging American sociology of the twentieth century, and to trace the diminishing role that the notion of conflict came to play in the course of its development.

III

Albion Small, to whom we referred earlier, represents an important figure in early American sociology for at least two reasons. He was instrumental, probably more so than any sociologist of his generation, in transmitting European social theory into American sociological scholarship; and he served, though his translations and his own writings, as a synthesist for the Social Darwinist and the emerging socio-logical orientations that we traced above. The influence of Ratzenhofer, representing the former tradition, and that of Simmel, reflecting the latter, is traceable and acknow-ledged throughout Small's works.[12] It is notable, however, that the synthesis which Small effected clearly lent greater weight to its sociological elements. Small was quite selective in what he adapted from Ratzenhofer, and although his debt is substantial, what he chose to accept was all but severed from the latter's Darwinian premises.

Most significant from our point of view, is the importance that Small placed on social conflict. Yet, while he may be justifiably classified loosely among the "conflict theorists," he did not regard conflict as a necessarily primary or ubi-quitous fact of social life. He expressed considerable support for Ratzenhofer's conception of an alternating rhythm of struggle and consolidation in society, asserting that "Social-ization, indeed, is the transformation of conflict into cooperation" (Small, 1905: 499). However, his departure from Ratzenhofer, and at the same time his affinity to Simmel, rested on his insistence that conflict is to be under-stood in *social* terms, and grows out of socially structured opposing interests.

Perhaps in an effort to uproot the strains of Social Darwinism that prevailed also in American sociology (and had
their probably most prominent American spokesman in his
contemporary, William Graham Sumner), Small linked the
future development of American sociology to a rigorous
analysis of *social processes* (1905: ix).

It was Edward A. Ross, whom Small cited approvingly as
having been ". . . the first in English to put much stress on
the term 'process' as a scientific social category" (1924:
23n). Ross insisted that if we hope to engage in a serious
study of society, ". . . we must ascend to that primordial fact
known as the *social process*" (Ross, 1905: 91), and he specified and analyzed some thirty-seven of these, identifying
them as basic units of sociological investigation. It became
fairly apparent, even to Ross himself, that the distinctions
he drew between these processes rested more often on
semantic than on empirical differences, and he subsequently
pared his classification down to a smaller number of types.
Nevertheless, such dissociative social processes as "opposition," "competition," "conflict," and "adaptation" (i.e.
accommodation), figure prominently in his typology.

Possibly the most outstandingly influential textbook
published in American sociology is Robert E. Park and
Ernest W. Burgess' *Introduction to the Science of Sociology* (1921). If any one book can be so described, then surely
this volume represents a definitive statement and codification
of American sociology up to the time of its publication, and
its influence on texts published over more than three subsequent decades is difficult to dispute. In Park and Burgess, the
extensive lists of differentiated social processes that Ross and
others had advanced, are distilled into "four great types of
interaction" (1921: 507), and this classification has substantially prevailed as an ordering principle until the present day.
In their formulation, Park and Burgess linked the four social
processes of Competition, Conflict, Accommodation and
Assimilation to the social structures with which they were
regarded as typically related (1921: 511).

Competition	—	the Economic Equilibrium
Conflict	—	the Political Order
Accommodation	—	Social Organization
Assimilation	—	Personality and the Cultural Heritage

It is notable that Park, whose formal sociological training was, admittedly, restricted to a few years at the University of Berlin where he attended Simmel's lectures (Park, 1950: vi), placed considerable stress on conflict in his other writings.[13] However, in the Park and Burgess text, the four social processes, in their linkage with the respective social structures, are depicted on a basis approximating parity (1921: Chapters VIII to XI).

Park and Burgess' book, apart from representing a benchmark in American sociology, also occupies a pivotal position in the developmental history of the discipline. With — it would be extravagant to say *as a result of* — its publication, American sociology may well be said to have come into its own, and to embark on a line of development that all but ignored European scholarship. Totally ignored it was not. But American sociologists, generally, were inhibited by their monolingual constraint, and even when Talcott Parsons (1937) was to "translate" such theorists as Durkheim and Weber for them, it was not a faithful rendering, but rather a noble exegesis that molded their work into congeniality with the American intellectual and conceptual idiom. Importantly, the appearance of Park and Burgess' book also signified the culmination of an intellectual heritage that included a long-standing European and a significant American focal concern with conflict in social theorizing, and its replacement by a growing preoccupation with assimilation. Again, to attribute this shift to Park and Burgess would be an over-statement, and the more fundamental reasons have to be sought, as we shall do, elsewhere. Park and Burgess were influential however, as we indicated above, in "clearing the field" and establishing the "four great types of interaction," and in presenting them as essentially co-equal social processes in society. But from then on, concern with the process of

conflict diminished, and for the subsequent three decades
conflict theorizing, as well, virtually disappeared from
American sociology.

Among sociologists interested in the problems of racial
and ethnic relations, some sought to discover patterns that
would permit generalizations in the form of "race relations
cycles."[14] But even here, to the extent that conflict was
recognized as typically following the initial stage of contact,
it was treated as relatively insignificant and transitory. In
broadest terms, and perhaps astonishingly this includes the
area of inter-group relations, American sociology had ceased
viewing society as an on-going conflict system in which conflicting interest groups act out their socially structured
antagonisms. A new perspective, one in which assimilation
played an increasingly more important role, began to replace
the earlier American, heavily European influenced, conflict
orientation (see Coser, 1956: 20ff). By 1950, this trend in
theorizing had drifted so far from the tradition of Small,
Ross and Park, that Jessie Bernard (1950) was moved to ask
"Where is the Modern Sociology of Conflict?," charging that
it remained precisely where Simmel had left it.

IV

Bernard's hortatory question was prompted by a sociology
that was not only in demonstrable retreat from an analytic
concern with the social process of conflict, but one that had
increasingly turned to the notion of assimilation in its assessment of the patterns of American ethnic relations. In seeking
to account for this shift in the allocation of analytic attention, several plausible, although not necessarily mutually
exclusive, lines of explanation suggest themselves.

Inasmuch as concepts typically represent abstractions from
observed events, it is entirely possible that the American
experience with respect to immigrant as well as resident
ethnic and racial populations became, in fact, overwhelmingly assimilative in character. If this can be demonstrated,
then the *empirical* realities would not only warrant, but

perhaps dictate their sociological conceptualization and justify their extensive analytic treatment, in assimilative terms. Alternatively, the explanation for the shift may proceed from the recognition that concepts properly sustain a linkage with some entirely independent theoretical frame from which they not only derive their meaning, but in terms of which they may have been formulated as purely logical constructions. Accordingly, *theoretical* rather than empirical considerations would account for the predilection for assimilative conceptions. Closely related, but significantly distinct from this latter alternative, is the possibility that *extra-sociological* factors, *ideological* and *normative* in character, intervened in the sociological reconstruction of social reality, thus making the analytic process of negotiating from the social objects of knowledge to their sociological comprehension scientifically suspect.

With respect to the first of these possibilities, any attempt to account for the shift in analytic interest from conflict to assimilation on strictly empirical grounds, appears to be exceedingly difficult to support on the basis of either the historical record, or of the conclusions of many of the "assimilation studies" themselves. Despite the romantic and rhetorically attractive Zangwillian metaphor of the "Melting-Pot" ideal, the American historical reality reflects at best an uneven mixture of only partial and selective assimilation on the one hand, and various forms of either voluntary or coerced lack of assimilation on the other.

In contrast to Europe, where the meetings of ethnically or racially distinctive peoples were typically accompanied by contentions over territorial *proprietorship*, in the New World this was rarely the case. Even the initial contacts between "settlers" and "aborigines," and the subsequent periodic re-enactment of these contacts westward across the continent, did not fit the European pattern precisely. While the Indian culture systems included a notion of peoplehood, i.e. of "nation" in its strict meaning, among hunters or the Plains Indians particularly, they did not universally support the normative conception of private territorial ownership on which the traditional European feudal, and the contemporary

Western concept of Nation-State rests.[15] Nevertheless, acknowledging the "frontier" relationship between whites and Indians as a perhaps uniquely contrary case, the pattern among racially and ethnically distinguishable populations in the settled region of North America did not recapitulate this aspect of the European tradition. It is thus hardly surprising, that the type of rationale that supported Gumplowicz's conflict theorizing seemed inappropriate to the American experience.

The empirical impropriety of a Gumplowiczian conflict conception does not, however, justify the abandonment of all conflict theorizing in this connection. Conflict certainly was not absent from the emerging patterns of ethnic and racial relations in nineteenth and twentieth century America. Rather, conflict tended to assume new dimensions and a new character, in as much as racial and ethnic patterns were now increasingly structured in relation to the developing American industrial order, instead of being conditioned by a European, pre-industrial conquest system of territorial proprietorship. If a racially-based Gumplowiczian conception of conflict did not appear applicable, perhaps a Marxian, class-structured version might prove more empirically supportable.

A loosely Marxian conception, or perhaps some native, more Americanized modalities of it, can indeed be found to have been advanced throughout American history from a variety of quarters. For the moment, however, our interest rests less with these interpretive perspectives, than with the ongoing events that prompted these interpretations. The meeting of ethnically and racially diverse peoples in an industrializing and concomitantly urbanizing America were, virtually without exceptions, encounters between "unequals." The patterns of their interrelationships tended to be shaped by their inclinations and abilities, respectively, to consolidate or enhance a position of superordinance, or to accept or overcome a relegation to subordinance (or at least avoid its most debilitating consequences).

Now, the introduction of the notions of superordinance and subordinance into the discussion of racial and ethnic relations constitutes a rather significant step, for it opens up new interpretive and explanatory possibilities. Specifically, it offers the advantage of neutralizing the kind of racial or biological assumptions that inhere in the Gumplowiczian *Rassenkampf* conception and, without necessarily precluding them, permits their transcendence in the direction of *social* assumptions. Viewed as mere descriptive and static structural concepts, superordinance and subordinance have a certain limited utility. As such, they provide a simple classificatory scheme for ordering and generalizing the distribution of inequality in numbers of societies and across historical periods; and as an orienting conceptualization, or model, they can serve to suggest the direction of theoretical development. But their significant analytic utility lies, as Simmel must be credited for showing, in their *processual* formulation as super- and subordination, rather than as structural categories, and in their historically-specific *inter*active relationship. Thus, the appearance of a one-sided influence exerted by the superior over the inferior must give way, according to Simmel (Spykman, 1965: 95-97), to a recognition of the fundamentally social and interactive relationship that obtains; and it also leads to the proposition, highly controversial and unpalatable in some quarters, that the subordinate actively (socially) participates in his own subordination.[16]

Implicit in this general conception, and of course this holds for any conception of social stratification systems (Davis and Moore, 1945: 243), is the recognition that *systemic* superordination and subordination represent processes of *institutionalized* inequality; that collective status differentiations are normatively regulated, and form legitimate and just structures of social inequality — in that society, and for the time being. This recognition, combined with that of the reciprocal relation between status categories, suggests what amounts to a basic sociological postulate: the relative advantage that one stratum holds over another is a function of its ability to perpetuate the relative disadvantage of the other — and depends on maintaining effective control over the prevailing structure of justifications and legitimations. Such control is of course never total, and always impermanent, particularly under the volatile conditions that characterize industrial societies.

Consequently, modern social "orders" constitute arenas in which the politics of status-preservation and interest-pursuits are carried on almost continuously, leading to group confrontations of one form or another, and in one institutional context or another, and rendering any established system of super- and subordination relatively tenuous and ephemeral. When, as in the United States, societies are laced with varieties of unassimilated ethnic and racial populations, additional dimensions are imposed on the minimal class-basis of such socio-political scrimmages, and they are, at least potentially, the more volatile.[17] Thus, the American experience offers a record of intriguing interplays between status-differentiating and status-equalizing interests. The net-effect has at times shifted in favor of the restrictive and exclusive tendencies among White-Anglo-Saxon-Protestant upper strata toward congealing caste-like structures, only to be contested by incursive pressures emanating from the lower strata, including ethnic and racial groups, and inclining the balance in the direction of a more fluid, boundary-vitiating open-class framework.[18]

With the exception of the very earliest settlers who largely isolated themselves into ethnically homogeneous enclaves, the succession of ethnically or racially distinct groups that came to America were increasingly subject to sets of strain-inducing conditions that seem to be a part of the industrializing process. Industry, it has been pointed out (Hughes and Hughes, 1952: 63; E. K. Francis, 1976: 119-126), is a great mixer of peoples, ensuring its requisite labor pool through the attraction or conscription of ethnically diverse populations to supplement its rarely adequate supply of indigenous workers. Yet, if the industrializing process creates the potential for either an enriching cultural pluralism or an assimilated homogeneity, it also undermines their realizations through its tendency to subordinate and segregate the ethnic populations. Segregation, for Hughes and Hughes (1952: 64),

. . . refers to some degree of functional separation of different kinds of people within a common system. Industry brings people together and sorts them out for various kinds of work; the sorting will, where the mixture is new, of necessity follow racial and ethnic lines. For cultures (and when races first meet they are always unlike in culture) differ in nothing more than in the skills, work habits, and goals which they instil into the individual. These differences may tend to disappear in the course of industrial experience, although segregation may tend to keep them alive in some modified form for a long time.

That these differences have indeed persisted, although in attenuating form, is attested by the significance that remains attached to "hyphenated Americanism." This significance is lost neither on those who impose ethnic labels, nor on those who are thus identified. An accumulating body of American stratification analyses, from community studies through statistics on income distribution, supports the broad generalization that with respect to inequalities in the distribution of life-chances and life-styles, ethnicity operates as a partial, although salient, ordering principle. It is also apparent, of course, that a group's priority in the succession of immigration waves to America correlates roughly with its relative position in the stratification hierarchy. It is fair to conclude, therefore, that ethnicity matters, although it tends to become of decreasing significance as an inhibiting factor for mobility, the longer the group has experienced participation in industrial American society.

The continued use of the term "ethnicity" constitutes, in and of itself, an acknowledgment that assimilation is, at best, not an accomplished fact; and to conceptualize ethnics in minority group terms is to recognize their relative exclusion from valued economic, political or social positions, or from normative opportunity structures leading to their attainment. Whatever success in mobility or effectiveness in assimilation[19] may have characterized some individual ethnic families, the ethnic populations with which they had been identified have typically experienced concerted, if not always calculated and programmatic pressures of exclusion from the dominant host society. The minority's response to these experiences has assumed a variety of forms, including at least submission, self-segregation or various covert and overt conflict reactions.[20]

In terms of our immediate interests here, it is clear that some assimilation has indeed occurred. In its grand design, the historical impression of American society suggests general movement in the direction of gradually attaining an all-inclusive sense of nationality — a sense of common people-hood. However, it is also abundantly evident that the process of assimilation is slow, it is temporally variable, it is proceed-ing unevenly across institutional spheres, and it is ethnically selective. That this "Melting-Pot" development is, at best, not strictly linear, is attested by the recent resurgences of "nationalism" among segments of at least Black, Chicano, Jewish, Irish, Polish and Italian Americans, thus suggesting a short-run, or ultimate, Pluralist scenario. A less recognized, and only infrequently acknowledged aspect of assimilation becomes apparent, when the process is regarded in its stratifi-cational context. As an eligibility price exacted for mobility claims pressed by ethnics, assimilation also serves as a dominant-group instrument for the continued subordination of those ethnics who can not or choose not to abjure their folkways — or who are summarily defined as unassimilable.[21]

In view of this latter facet of assimilation, and the patterns of intergroup relations it has engendered, it is difficult to argue that a massive sociological interest in assimilation, to the at least relative analytic neglect of concurrently operating intergroup processes, is justifiable — or explained — on purely empirical grounds.

The second line of explanation that might account for the pervasive sociological interest in assimilative processes at the expense of an earlier preoccupation with conflict, attri-butes the shift to the intrinsic dynamics of sociological theorizing. We suggested earlier, that concepts may be generated not only through abstraction from the substance of social experience, but may instead be constructed through a process of purely logical deduction from an independent body of theoretical premises. This mode of concept forma-tion is undoubtedly less frequently encountered in sociology than is the more empirically direct conceptualization of concrete observations, and when it is employed, then its scientific propriety is somewhat more doubtful than when it occurs in the context of more systematically developed natural sciences. The reasons for this are readily apparent, and indicate also why it would be difficult to argue that the predilection for assimilative processes is stimulated by essentially theoretical considerations.

An attempt to advance this line of reasoning necessarily presupposes the attainment of a relatively systematic, coherent body of theory, if not over-arching the discipline in general, then at least embracing a crucial portion of the pertinent sub-field — in this case racial or ethnic relations. In physics, for example, the state of theoretical integration has proceeded to a point where the notion of antimatter, to cite one particularly provocative concept, can be logically deduced with impressive elegance from an established theoretical structure. In sociology in general, the status of theory or, perhaps we should say, the states of theories, and even the adequacy of its "theory language" (Lachenmeyer, 1971) have hardly attained a comparable measure of specification or systematization. In the area of racial and ethnic relations in particular, the question is not even one of the degree to which theoretical integration has been achieved, but whether the field has in fact attained,[22] or indeed should ever expect to attain, even the basic theoretical prerequisites for systematic theory. Thus, reviewing the accumulated research of the decade 1945-1955, Robin M. Williams pointed to the dearth of theory in this field, and suggested that the very treatment of the subject as a special sub-area of sociology is an acknowledgment of the as yet characteristic concreteness and empirico-descriptive emphasis of its contemporary research (Williams, 1957: 424).[23] He went on to express the thought that "it would be an edifying but unhappy irony if the sociology of race and cultural relations turned out to be, itself, provincial and isolated" (425). Williams' premonition proved insightful and received a somewhat firmer expression in the form of van den Berghe's conviction in 1967, that "the failure to arrive at a theory of race relations may simply reflect the fact that the subject has no theoretical leg to stand on" (van den Berghe, 1967: 6). He goes on to assert that "race is only an interesting special case in a broad range of similar phenomena, hence has little claim for autonomous theoretical status" (*loc. cit.*).

Whether or not the paucity of low order or highly abstract theory is a debility resulting from the parochial manner in which the field may have been analytically structured, the fact of a poverty of theory in the sociology of racial and ethnic relations is difficult to dispute. That the field has not generated an integrated body of reasonably systematic theory, is *beyond* dispute. Short of such an achievement, the possibility that fruitful concepts might be logically deduced with any methodological legitimacy from an independent theoretical frame is highly dubious, and such an expectation would have to be considered premature.

We are led to conclude, therefore, just as we were with respect to the preceding explanation pointing to empirical factors, that the shift from analytic concerns with conflict to those of assimilation in the sociology of racial relations can not be attributed to purely theoretical considerations of the discipline. The remaining possibility, that the explanation rests neither in the empirical nor in the theoretical realms, but rather in matters that are essentially extraneous to the sociological enterprise, will be explored in the following chapter.

V

The venerable and pervasive tradition of conflict thinking in European political theory and classical sociology was, to a considerable extent, accommodated within the elaboration of early sociological development in the United States. In the works of the founders of the American discipline, conflict is prominently represented among the important patterns of group interaction, and Park and Burgess included it in their typology of social processes and developed the notion in its connections with political structures in society.

Gradually, however, as the American discipline evolved through the 1930s and on, it diverged increasingly from the European heritage and followed its own line of development.

As Hinkle and Hinkle (1954: 18ff), as well as others have pointed out, American sociology entered a period of intense introspection, concentrating on purging itself of its more speculative, melioristic and metaphysical habits and encumberances. Efforts were directed toward strengthening the discipline's scientific foundations by proceeding inductively from empirical phenomena, and toward enhancing its scientific respectability by adapting and innovating rigorous techniques for quantitative description and statistical analysis and inference.

In the course of these developments, concerns with conflict theory and the empirical analysis of conflict phenomena diminished to a point of virtual disappearance. Of the three remaining social processes of competition, accommodation and assimilation which Park and Burgess had identified in their influential paradigm, it was the last which, especially in the study of racial and ethnic relations, seemed uniquely apropos and commanded the preponderance of research attention.

A justification for the virtual abandonment of concerns with conflict in favor of assimilation analyses, would have to rest on either empirical considerations, or in aspects of the theoretical elaboration of the discipline. Since American sociology, during this period, particularly favored empiricism and inductive procedures, it would be reasonable to expect that the analytic interest in assimilation processes was in large part a reflection of what was actually occurring in American society; that, conversely, the decline of conflict thinking and conflict analysis simply followed from an absence or diminution of conflict behavior among the prevailing patterns of inter-group relations. Significantly, but hardly surprisingly, the historical as well as contemporary evidence does not bear out these expectations. To some limited extent, and in a manner that does not easily permit unqualified generalization, assimulation did indeed seem to be occurring. At the same time, however, it would have constituted a falsification of social reality to claim that conflict was either absent, or demonstrably diminishing.

An examination of the alternative possibility, that the

trend toward assimilation studies may have been impelled by logical extension from a powerful theoretical apparatus that served to guide the direction of race and ethnic relations research, yields a similarly unsatisfactory explanation. Clearly, this alternative is predicated upon an established corpus of relatively systematic abstract theory to which, we have tried to show, the field is simply not able to lay claim. No doubt this relative absence of theory can be traced in part to the predominantly empirico-descriptive research emphasis, which the special field of race and ethnic relations shared with American sociology in general for at least some twenty years following World War One. Beginning with the thirties, however, a gradual theoretical resurgence appeared in general sociology, and the development of general sociological theory has advanced to the stage where today some very tentative attempts toward theoretical integration can be discerned.

In contrast, the substantively specialized field of race and ethnic relations, apart from having yielded a multiplication of empirical research, has failed to develop beyond the state of virtual impotence with regard to theory that had characterized it since the thirties. It is not injudicious to assert that there simply is no special theory of race and ethnic relations extant today. The scatter of theoretical nodules that serve to hold together some of the research proliferation *within* the various sub-specialties in the field, is not indigenous to the field but rather represents an eclectic borrowing from general sociological theory and, significantly, from the funds of theory in psychology and anthropology. There appears to be little that is intrinsically sociological, to justify the perpetuation of race and ethnic relations as a substantive specialty in the field of sociology. On the other hand, there is a great deal to recommend the area's re-integration with general sociology, and the reconceptualization of its content as, at best, a special instance of more general sociological categories.

While the broader implications of this have a central bearing upon the general problem under consideration, the immediate point here is that the extensive analytical pre-occupation with assimilation is not attributable to a logical derivation from some established structure of race relations theory. The answer thus lies neither in the empricial realities undergirding sociological endeavors, nor in legitimately theoretical superstructures that embrace them, and has to be sought somewhere else. Specifically, it must be traced to the process of conceptualization *per se*: to the logical and empirical constraints that properly guide it, and to the broader ideological milieu that inclines to intrude on it.

Notes

1. Arthur de Gobineau's *Essay on the Inequality of the Human Races* was published in France between 1853 and 1855. An excerpted translation, seemingly selected for its most virulent "racist" implications, first appeared in the United States in 1856. See William Stanton (1960: 175, 235n). For a more general discussion of the impact of racial theories in America from the Colonies through the mid-1950s, see Thomas F. Gossett (1963).

2. The most extensive statement of Ratzenhofer's sociology, in English, has been rendered by Albion Small, although its fidelity to the original may be somewhat marred by the interpolation of Small's own thoughts. What Ratzenhofer describes as a resulting race-differentiation, is more a community of interests than a unity of racial identities. See Albion W. Small (1905: 190-191, 254-255).

3. See Small (1905: 192ff). For a comparison of Gumplowicz and Ratzenhofer, see Floyd N. House (1936: 163-178).

4. The basis for the subsequent articulation of these social processes appears throughout Ratzenhofer's work. See Small (1905: 245, 189-394 *passim*).

5. More significant, perhaps, than the racial explanations that characterized this early sociology, were the social inferences which they invited with respect to Negro inferiority as an opportune rationale for slavery. For a prime example, see George Fitzhugh (1854).

6. This resurgence is actually fed concurrently from two directions. In biology, Edward O. Wilson (1975) has reopened the issue through his highly controversial volume; in sociology, with no less controversy, Pierre L. van den Berghe (1975) is among those who seek to revitalize a bio-social rapprochement. The controversy is aired through a lively debate provoked by a challenging lead article, followed by critical comments and a rejoinder, in a

recent issue of *The American Sociologist*. See "Exchange" (1977: 56-80).

7. In addition to Small's *General Sociology*, see also: *Origins of Sociology* (1924) and "The Present Outlook of Social Science" (1913). Small also translated Georg Simmel, "Superiority and Subordination as Subject-Matter of Sociology" (1896) and Georg Simmel, "The Sociology of Conflict" (1904).

8. For the argument that, in the final analysis, Marx's contributions must be viewed, particularly in their sociological relevance, not in their widely accepted recognition as economic determinism, but rather as a form of historical determinism, see Bash (1964).

9. For a discussion of this mechanism as an offensive strategy used by Communists to annihilate rival left-wing movements, or to prevent the translation of radical objectives into shallow liberal reforms, see Philip Selznick (1960: 225-242). In this particular regard, see also Mannheim (1936: 239). For a description of these processes in the face of threatening assimilation among the ultra-orthodox Hasidic Jews, see also Solomon Poll (1962: 37-51). Here, the mechanism serves not as a radical offensive strategy, but as one of conservative defense.

10. For an attempt to resolve the controversy at the methodological level, see Robert Bierstedt (1959).

11. See for example Irving Louis Horowitz (1962). Martindale, on the other hand, conspicuously ignores Simmel in his chapter on "Sociological Conflict Theories." In a subsequent discussion of Simmel, he asserts that in his "reduction of society to individual behaviors, Simmel stands sharply opposed . . . to conflict theory" (Martindale, 1960: 246). The issue may well turn on whether conflict is construed in terms of a relatively voluntaristic *social* process, or as an impersonal, structurally-generated *societal* process.

12. As was suggested earlier, his interpretation of Ratzenhofer in *General Sociology* is frequently difficult to disentangle from his own posture; and his several translations of Simmel's work in the *American Journal of Sociology* betray his affinity for, and debt to Simmel's sociology.

13. See for example, Robert E. Park, "The Social Function of War" (1941).

14. For a critical discussion of the "race relations cycles" of Park, Bogardus, W. O. Brown, C. E. Glick and Stanley Lieberson, see Brewton Berry (1965: 129-134). See also Banton (1967: 75-76) for a critical discussion of the general notion of "race relations cycles" and its correspondence to real events.

15. This aspect of the "culture conflict" between white settlers and Native Americans has not been widely explored by sociologists, although it occasionally crops up as a nagging grievance in the periodic collisions between Tribal Councils or dissident factions

and the Bureau of Indian Affairs or the Department of the Interior. For discussions by anthropologists of American Indians' conceptions of territorial proprietorship, see Lowie (1948: 140); Wissler (1957: 158, 185-187); and Driver (1961: 244-261).

16. Simmel's initial discussion of superordination and subordination focuses primarily on "the leader and his followers" and, in that context, tends to be couched in the language of *individual* superiority and submission. Nevertheless, his subsequent development of the topic indicates clearly that his arguments not only permit extension, but are intended to carry over to such processes between hierarchically structured groups.

17. A more recent case-in-point is that of England, where traditional class-cleavages have been complicated and exacerbated by the influx of non-white peoples from the Commonwealth over the last few decades.

18. For a provocative study of the historical interplay between "caste tendencies" and "democratic" counter-tendencies in American society, see E. Digby Baltzell (1964).

19. At least in American society, mobility and assimilation have tended to be functionally interrelated, such that either may serve as facility for the other. Typically, the prerequisite for upward mobility has been the loss of ethnic identifiability which, for ethnics, may have exacted a psychic price of ruptured ethnic identity.

20. For an interesting discussion of mobility alternatives open to ethnics, and the respective costs entailed, see Norbert F. Wiley (1967).

21. This conception is consistent with the "theory" of assimilation that Gordon has described as "Anglo-Conformity." See Milton M. Gordon (1964: 88-114).

22. The claim that the field is devoid of theory may appear surprising, but can hardly be considered controversial. It has been either asserted or strongly suggested by numerous authorities in their assessments of the race and ethnic relations literature in sociology. See E. B. Reuter (1945: 455-456, 460); E. Franklin Frazier (1947: 265-271, *passim*); Louis Wirth (1949: 399-400); Louis Wirth (1950: 125); Maurice Freedman (1954: 343, 352); George E. Simpson and J. Milton Yinger (1959: 376-377); Frank R. Westie (1964: 576-580); Tamotsu Shibutani and Kian M. Kwan (1965: 14-15); Hubert M. Blalock (1967: vii). Michael Banton (1967: 62); Sami Zubaida (1970: 1); E. K. Francis (1976: xii); among others.

23. For an assessment that differs somewhat from that of Williams, regarding "the slow pace of theoretical development" in this field, see Peter I. Rose (1968: 57).

CHAPTER 3

The Concept of Assimilation: Its Genealogy and its Ambiguities

I

In the preceding chapter, we sought to show that of all the social processes that, in principle, might enter into the patterning of racial and ethnic group relations, it was the assimilative process that seemed to command the major share of research attention among American sociologists for nearly thirty years following the mid-thirties. Neither the on-going reality of empirical events, nor an impelling derivation from some established structure of race relations theory, can be regarded as accounting adequately for this almost single-minded interest.

In some respects, the situation is reminiscent of the considerable period of developmental immobility into which certain areas of sociology had worked themselves some decades earlier, through their stubborn preoccupation with the notion of "instincts." Not being subject to primary observation from human behavior, much less from the more abstract flow of actual social events, the popularity of instinct as a concept would be difficult to explain on empirical grounds. Neither could prevailing sociological theory[1] be appealed to for an acceptable explanation of the receptiveness that sociology had accorded to the notion of instinct as a key concept for the study of social behavior. Early in the ensuing controversy over instinct in which sociology became embroiled (see House, 1936: 241), Ellsworth Faris expressed what must be regarded as its definitive resolution. In criticizing instinct theorists, among whom he singled out particularly William McDougall, he referred to them as "professional mythologists" who uncritically accepted as facts what were, after all, only explanatory assumptions (Faris, 1921: 184-185) or hypothetical inferences (193). Nearly two decades later, and speaking of concepts in general, Herbert Blumer pointed out that in human behavior, merely physical activity can easily be handled conceptually; but the genuinely social component of it is necessarily conceptualized judgmentally and as an inference (Blumer, 1940: 714-716). Therefore, he concluded, we must safeguard ourselves by viewing concepts as hypothetical (719).

There are several lessons to be learned from this controversy over instincts, but central to them must surely be the caution that concepts are not to be treated as though they were sacrosanct and autonomous entities. Indispensable to the scientific enterprise as concepts are, they are nevertheless dependent, and their subordination is very acutely two-directional, subjecting them to the exigencies of empirically observed fact as well as to the contingencies of logically structured theory. Whatever range of freedom prevails in the conceptual ordering of facts is necessarily conditioned by the logical demands of theoretical structures; while flights of logical ingenuity at the theoretical end of concept construction must be disciplined by the sobrieties of empirical warrant.

Faris' critique of sociological approaches to the notion of instinct carries some fairly clear implications with respect to the fallacy of reification. There is, however, a broader point at issue, one that perhaps becomes more easily apparent in retrospect, as the controversy itself recedes into history. The notion of instinct in sociology is not likely to have arisen independently (even as an inference) from observed social behavior, but rather entered the discipline through its socio-psychological door by way of its anterior usage in instinct psychology, which in turn represents an inheritance of the concept from biology. Accordingly, the

notion of instinct is demonstrably alien to sociology. Of
course, its status as an alien term makes it neither unique nor,
in itself, suspect. There is, to be sure, the problem of
ambiguity which Cooley found so disconcerting with respect
to "heredity." "How can we differentiate the biological and
social processes when nearly all the words in general use may
mean either?" (Cooley, 1966: 207). However, transcending
mere nomenclature, the more substantial problem arises from
the fact that apart from being alien, it is also, in the controversial sense of that word, illegitimate, in as much as it can
not be demonstrated to have either issued from, or to be
comparable with, properly *sociological* theory. The notion of
instinct is irreconcilable with sociological theory because the
two represent fundamentally different universes of discourse
that attach to distinct analytic levels, and a sociology
founded on instinct would have simply reduced itself out of
existence.[2]

The sociological flirtation with the notion of instinct is
instructive because it affords an insight into the consequences
that can attend the transplantation of a concept into a discipline in which it does not serve as a direct observational
term,[3] and in which it also fails to establish a theoretical
linkage, or systemic meaning (Kaplan, 1964: 57). Unrestrained
by either empirical foundations at one end or a theoretical
frame at the other, the concept tends to be invested with
inflated explanatory power, which at least in this case, leads
to a circular or closed, and thus sterile "explanatory" system.

In the previous chapter we sought to explain the extensive
sociological interest in the notion of assimilation in the area
of race and ethnic relations. The empirical substructure, we
suggested, did not offer sufficient warrant for its pre-emin-
ence over other social processes, nor could we account for it
adequately by appealing to the discipline's theoretical superstructure. Turning from assessing its popularity to exploring
its genealogy, we therefore propose now to direct our attention specifically to the mediating realms of concepts, proper.
More precisely, we are led to inquire into some rather
general, but frequently unacknowledged, factors that attend
the introduction of terms into scientific usage; to consider

the circumstances under which the notion of assimilation, specifically, made its appearance in the sociological enterprise; and to trace and assess the extensions and intensions of meaning with which assimilation, as a concept, came to be invested.

II

Since we are interested here in tracing the circumstances attending the adoption of the assimilation idea into the sociology of race and ethnic relations, it is important to acknowledge two methodologically sound processes, either of which may lead to the accretion of a body of scientific concepts. Thus, the formulation of concepts may occur initially through the introduction, from outside the discipline, of popular terms that designate and are direct indicators of the phenomena which constitute the empirical point of departure for scientific inquiry. Expressed in the language and from the point of view of contemporary philosophy of science, this is a process of transferring extra-logical (i.e. descriptive) primitives from the natural language, for use in the constructed language of science.[4] The subsequent methodological problem confronting science, here, involves tying the observational term to a particular meaning structure, and the process of establishing a theoretical linkage typically necessitates a conceptual narrowing, sharpening or modulation of the original term.

Alternatively, the development of concepts may be generated from within the discipline itself, stimulated through essentially theoretical desiderata from which they are logically derived, and in terms of which they sustain their meaning.[5] The methodological challenge posed here lies in establishing a correspondence between these theoretically deduced constructs and their appropriate empirical referents. With respect to sociology, either procedure, properly implemented, can lead to what we described earlier as the sociological reconstruction of a common-sense, socially constructed reality.

These alternative modes of initiating scientific concept formation through either empirically inductive or theoretically deductive procedures, as it were, must of course be recognized as highly stylized and idealized versions of how terms are in fact introduced and elaborated in science.[6] Realistically, and this pertains to the social sciences in particular, the actual practice falls considerably short of such methodologically exemplary standards. Further, we ought to note, especially in sociology the opportunity for fabricating concepts from within the discipline through theoretical deduction is somewhat circumscribed, since this procedure clearly presupposes a fairly systematic body of abstract theory. While in general sociology such an attainment is at best a matter of contention, in the special area of race and ethnic relations, as we indicated in the preceding chapter, the consensus points to a virtual theoretical vacuum. On "theoretical" grounds, therefore, the incorporation of terms from outside the discipline appears as the more plausible process by which concepts are likely to have accrued in sociology.

However, even a casual consideration of some of the discipline's central concepts offers evidence that the technical language of sociology is largely an appropriated language. As we have had occasion to remark earlier, the discipline's professional language contains, and places considerable reliance, on terms that are paralleled in the vocabulary of the popular language.[7] Evidently, the natural language has served as a heavily exploited reservoir for the appropriation of terms into the technical language of sociology. By no means, however, has it constituted the discipline's only terminological resource. To some extent, and certainly with more far-reaching implications for the shape of its theory, sociology has also relied on the other major source for terminological borrowing: the technical languages of other, more established disciplines.

In the case of many, perhaps most, of the fundamental sociological terms, it is difficult to attribute their derivation unequivocally to either prior popular, or to earlier technical origins. More often, both sources have contributed to the introduction and the specification of their sociological usage. It is likely that the distinction is further obscured by the popularization of a narrowly defined technical meaning which the term first embodied in some other disciplinary context.

It is perhaps inevitable in a developing discipline, that terms are extensively appropriated from outside, for subsequent conceptualization within that discipline. Such borrowing might even be viewed as a felicitous alternative to an otherwise bewildering proliferation of neologisms and jargon. However unavoidable and perhaps even useful the process may be, it entails, in analogy with the Trojan Horse, certain hazardous consequences for the recipient discipline.

Thus, where the appropriation of terms involves the popular language, it carries with it a potential threat to the stability and even to the autonomy of sociology, and the problem emanates from some of the attributes that distinguish the donor language from the recipient language. The popular, conventional, or "natural" language is characteristically a vital "living" language, with an elastic vocabulary that is subject to connotative and even denotative modifications over time. On the other hand, the language of sociology, and of science in general, is an "artificial" language.[8] In its *ideal* construction, it is devoid of connotative vagaries, its observational terms, at least, are denotatively specific, and all terms, including theoretical terms, are characterized by semantic stability over time.[9] While the natural language displays historicity and invites etymological analysis of its evolving vocabulary, the constructed language of any of the various sciences is, although indeed historical in its accretion, in its purest form, subject only to a lexicology of its technical terms,[10] and to an accounting of its terminological additions or attritions.

The seeming contradiction, in the light of the foregoing, that our conceptual analysis of the notion of assimilation is leading us to undertake an at least partially etymological inquiry, merely serves to underscore that the preceding remarks pertain to an *ideal* form of constructed language, and that sociology still falls conspicuously short of such an

attainment.[11] The parallel presence of the assimilation term
in both the conventional social and the professional sociological languages invites a persisting threat of contamination,[12] and its sociological meaning remains susceptible to
any semantic shifts which the term may sustain in the
context of its vital popular usage.[13]

When we turn to the case of terminological appropriations
from another technical language, the problem becomes
primarily one of a challenge to the viability of legitimately
sociological theory, and by extension, again, to the autonomy of sociology itself. In the previous case, tendencies are
exerted for sociology to embrace prevailing *social* perceptions
and thus stand in danger of being coopted as an adjunct to
social commentary, or an accounting of contemporary
history. Here, in contrast, the hazard lies in being pre-empted
by other scientific disciplines, through sociology's uncritical
acceptance and inappropriate conceptualization of terms
whose authenticity, at a proper sociological level of analysis,
is open to serious question.

As Rudner (1966: 48ff) has pointed out, the borrowed
terms, in their original disciplinary context, may have been
formally integrated into a completely articulated deductive
system. In their transposition into sociology, however, they
are not automatically stripped of all their previous theoretical
implications and these concomitants are often, and unwittingly, imported as sub-rosa presuppositions. The problem is
not simply laid to rest by painstakingly defining the terms[14]
as they are to be employed in their new disciplinary context,
nor by investing them with denotative specificity.[15] Neither
of these obviously necessary, but perhaps deceptively
confidence-inspiring prerequisites for scientific analysis, is
sufficient for screening out the web of conceptual and
theoretical presuppositions, in which the terms are enmeshed.
In as much as they tend to go unrecognized, they insinuate
themselves into sociology under cover of the appropriated
terms, and become covertly established in the form of a
sociologically spurious explanatory system.[16] In the long run,
to be sure, the self-correcting impulse of scientific procedure
will tend to expose their counterfeit character. Meanwhile,

however, the weight of continuing empirical research tends to be additive rather than cumulative, and any advancement of real knowledge is, to that extent, suspended.

It becomes apparent therefore, that whether sociological terms are appropriated from another discipline, or whether they are borrowed from popular parlance, what is incorporated into the discipline through their introduction is more than a discrete, pristine vocabulary item. More realistically, what is being transposed from one language to another approximates an idiomatic expression, a term that is intimately enmeshed in the resource language's prevailing meaning structure. Intended or not, and recognized or not, the transfer of such a term becomes a "package-deal," an operation that involves more than its manifest content. Appropriations from the popular language entail a concomitant transfer of unstable connotative subtleties and, comparably, transpositions from the technical language of another scientific discipline mask a simultaneous infusion of inextricably linked, but typically inappropriate theoretical implications for sociology. The hazard, it should hardly be necessary to note, lies not so much in the fact that symbolic contexts typically accompany appropriated terms, but rather in that these concomitants intrude surreptitiously, and thus become ensconced in their new context as undiscerned biases. Such biases are not, properly speaking, theoretical biases, although they have theoretical implications in that they serve to stimulate and perpetuate flawed theory. We shall prefer to characterize them as *perspectivistic biases.* As such, they are considerably more resistant to neutralization than is flawed theory to rectification, and they are all the more mischievous in their effect since they tend to obscure the need, and to becloud the techniques, for proper theoretical re-orientation.

The ramifications of these difficulties in a Sociology of Race Relations are serious and far-reaching, and we shall pursue them in a later chapter. Now, bearing in mind the several considerations respecting the borrowing of terms, their sources, and their "idiomatic" character, we shall examine the case of "assimilation" specifically, and in some detail.

III

The adoption of, and indeed, the perceived need for the adoption of a term like "assimilation" arose logically from a growing recognition of dynamic process in society. We referred earlier to Albion Small, who perceived a "gradual shifting of effort from analogical representation of social structures to real analysis of social process," which marked "the central line in the path of methodological progress from Spencer to Ratzenhofer" (Small, 1905: ix). What Small was alluding to was a very modest but significant shift away from the stolidly conservative undertone that had marked the sociological enterprise from its inception. The conceptual building blocks of early sociology constituted a vocabulary of order and stability: community, authority, tradition, the Sacred, hierarchy, status, cohesion, adjustment, function, norm, symbol, ritual (see Nisbet, 1966: 17; Zeitlin, 1968: 53; Atkinson, 1972: 33, 147-148, and *passim*). Given such conceptual tools, it would have been most surprising had they not led to a preoccupation with the study of social structures — regardless of whether these were analogically represented in biological terms. More typically, of course, many were; and the vital functions implicit in an organismic conception, combined with the stimulus that evolutionary thought gave to concerns over the transformation of such structures, led to a growing interest in social process.

Small regarded Ross' *Foundations of Sociology* (1905) as a major contribution toward this shift, although he felt that his own *General Sociology*, which appeared only two months later, might not unfairly be described as a major treatise on the category of social process in its own right. Both books, Small points out, were anticipated by Ratzenhofer, although the term "social process" had, in the meanwhile, "been used in a semi-unconscious and amateurish way by a great many people" (Small, 1924: 23n).[17]

Yet, one would be remiss if one ignored the influence of Lester F. Ward in the increasingly central role that process came to play in American sociology and, with the specification of such processes, his effect both on the adoption and subsequent entrenchment of the notion of assimilation. Although, as Martindale (1960: 69ff) has shown, Ward was instrumental in the introduction of organicism in American sociology, through his formulation it acquired a dynamic, purposive and almost liberal tone which represented an at least partial, but entirely deliberate rejection of the conservative Spencerian version by which he had earlier been profoundly influenced (Martindale, 1960: 71-72; Hofstadter, 1959: 68). Organicism it remained nevertheless, and it therefore appears almost paradoxical that, as Hofstadter (1959: 78) has pointed out, the greater part of Ward's writings were directed toward the destruction of the tradition of biological sociology. The incongruity seems all the more striking, since the analogies and terms he employed were profusely, and on occasion pompously, derived from biology — as well as from any other likely discipline (see Vine, 1959: 71). Ward's debt to biology, in this regard, was indeed immense, and he transmitted this debt through his influence on other sociologists who subsequently concerned themselves with the study of social process. Thus, for example, Hinkle (1966: xv, xxiv) takes note of Cooley's use of a botanical model (sympodial branching) of social change, whose similarity to that of Ward, although unacknowledged, is unmistakable.

Actually, Ward's aim of divesting sociology of biological preconceptions was not really incompatible with his ubiquitous resort to complex biological analogies, or to comparably derived simpler concepts. With respect to the former, the point to note is that, in Ward's hands at least, what was being borrowed was illustratively culled from biology, but it was not employed *bio*logically; its intended function was stictly analogical, and not as a biological mold into which observations of social structure or social process were to be cast.[18] As regards his use of simpler concepts derived from biology, it was perhaps one of Ward's special skills that he could harness such borrowed terms to a sociological framework and, in their resulting application, to so transform them, as to endow them with an independent sociological legitimacy.

The notion of assimilation, in the development of Ward's system of sociology, is clearly revealed in its biological derivation, and Ward (1903: 106, 181, 308) makes this abundantly evident on occasions when he is not employing the term in a sociological application. To trace this derivation and to pursue Ward's transposition of "assimilation" from its formalization in biology to its incorporation into sociology, requires a brief consideration of the rationale that supports his conception of the "edifice of sociology."

Ward came to grasp what he hoped would ultimately be regarded as his major contribution as a scholar (1903: 204): a universal principle underlying all the phenomena of nature, for which he coined the term *synergy*. The term expresses the "twofold character of energy and *mutuality*, or the systematic and organic working together of the antithetical forces of nature" which also "implies some product, to distinguish it from simple activity" (171). For sociology, its relevance lies in accounting for the origin of society through the struggle of races, which "is simple and typical social synergy," or the particular way in which this "cosmic principle operates in the social world" (204).

Proceeding with an almost adulatory endorsement[19] of Gumplowicz' and Ratzenhofer's accounts of this racial struggle from conquest through its stages of resolution, Ward compares the process to the biological principle of karyokinesis as adapted by an early champion of sociological bio-organicism, Paul von Lilienfeld (see Martindale, 1960: 42, 79, 96). Ward's passage (1903: 205) warrants quoting:

Lilienfeld has likened the process which takes place through conquest to fertilization in biology, comparing the conquering race to the spermatozoa and the conquered race to the ovum, the former active and aggressive, the latter passive and submitting, resulting in a crossing of strains. Similarly Ratzenhofer compares this race amalgamation to conjugation in biology, and says that hordes and clans multiply by division. There certainly is a remarkable "analogy" between the process called karyokinesis in biology and that which goes on in societies formed by the conquest of a weaker by a stronger race. This process has been fully described and illustrated by Gumplowicz and Ratzenhofer, and they not only agree as to what the successive steps are but also as to the order in which they uniformly take place.

Once the conquest stage has run its course, Ward's principle of synergy assumes its genuinely social character and,
step by Gumplowiczian step, the "systematic and organic
working together of (heretofore) antithetical forces" culminates in the formation of a synthetic people with shared
national sentiments. Ward's statement is worthy of full
citation not only in the interest of economy of exposition,
but also because *imbedded in it lies the essence of what
remains, nearly seventy-five years later, the sum and substance of race relations theory*. Ward (1903: 208) wrote:

A people is a synthetic creation. It is not a mechanical mixture. It is
not either of the antagonistic races and it is not both of them. It is a
new product evolved out of these elements through precisely the same
process that goes on at every stage in cosmic evolution at which its
successive products appear . . . Two antagonistic races of nearly equal
social value, but one of which has by some means succeeded in sub-
jugating the other and is striving to secure the greatest return for the
cost involved in so doing. After a long trial of the stern policy of
repression the physically superior race tires of the strain and relaxes in
the direction of general law, of calling in the aid of the best elements
of the weaker race, and at length reaches the stage marked by the
formation of a state. At this stage in the process of social karyokinesis
the social idants mutually approach the equatorial plate and have
already commenced coquetting for a nearer approach. Concession and
resignation, compromise and mutual assistance, proceed apace. Ani-
mosity abates and toleration increases. A number of potent agencies
combine to accelerate the process. The most important of these is
interest. It is a truth of the deepest significance that *interest unites
while principle divides*.

Predicated on such "agencies" as interest, propinquity, and
associations based on personal qualities, a sentiment of affec-
tion for both people and territory crystallizes, marking the
attainment of patriotism, the conclusion of the process of
social karyokinesis. Ward continues (212): "The antagonistic
forces have spent themselves, social equilibrium is restored,
and one more finished product of social synergy is presented
to the world."

This entire process represents, for Ward, a "social assimilation" or a coalescence and continual conservation of social
structures. A contextual reading makes it quite clear that

simply as a term, "social assimilation" is not intended to
be a precise and crucially central organizing concept of
sociology, but instead a rather casual, incidental wording
introduced illustratively by way of analogy. Ward's preferred
concepts actually seem to be "social synergy," "social
karyokinesis" and even "socializing influence," all of which
are used, at various times, in approximate synonymity or
parallel meanings with "social assimilation." The choice of
this latter term to symbolize a vital social synthesizing
process, is perhaps best understood in Ward's system of
sociology as a heuristic device, intended, along with other
biological terminology (185), "not to lose sight for a moment
of the great unity that pervades all science."

Now, lest our consideration of Ward's sociology be construed as an identification of the original appearance of
"social assimilation" in the discipline, we should hasten to
correct that impression. Perhaps the most comprehensive and
definitive discussion of the meaning, the sociological
applications and the historico-social occurrences of social
assimilation up to that time, was published some two years
prior to Ward's book in a series of five articles which
appeared in sequential issues of the *American Journal of
Sociology* (Simons, 1901-1902).[20] Parts II through V of
Simons' essays are devoted to descriptive accounts of the
obstacles to and facilities for social assimilation, respectively,
in the Ancient World and the Middle Ages; the Modern World
including Russia; the United States with respect to immigrants; and with regard to Chinese, Negroes and Indians.

It is Part I, however, that is of special interest to us, and
there Simons ventures some generalizations about social
assimilation, which afford an insight into its approximate
sociological meaning and pertinence under then prevailing
usage. Thus, she points out that "the process of assimilation
is of a psychological rather than a biological nature, and
refers to the growing alike in character, thought and institutions, rather than to the blood-mingling brought about by
intermarriage" (1901: I, 801). Its two prerequisites are
"social," i.e. group contact, and "psychic," e.g. Giddings'
"consciousness of kind" (798-799); and the process may be

distinguished into "coercive assimilation" and "attractive assimilation" (808-815). Simons also suggests that perhaps the major and universal obstacle to assimilation resides in the "persistence of foreign languages" (822).

This last point was also singled out as a factor of prime significance by Weatherly in his treatment of social assimilation processes among several societal types distinguished by their forms of organization. Describing assimilation in contemporary national societies, he states that "the transformation is marked by a formal acceptance of certain new cultural elements, chief among which is usually reckoned language. The process [of assimilation] has been named by Novicow denationalization" (1911: 601-602).

That Lester Ward was not the first to inject "assimilation" into the sociological lexicon is hardly disputable. Ward's significance lies in the fact that he took a loose and somewhat intuitive notion — implicit or expressed under several designations and with varying degrees of ambiguity in the works of men like von Lilienfeld, Gumplowicz, Ratzenhofer, Tarde, Novicow, Durkheim, etc. — and formalized it into a major explanatory theme[21] which he wove coherently into his sociological system. That he should have seized upon the term "social assimilation" as one of his alternatives for articulating this principle is, as we have suggested, essentially coincidental. The principle itself, however, even down to its constituent elements, was destined for prominence in the subsequent development of sociology, and constituted, in the words of Floyd House, "a clear anticipation of Park and Burgess' treatment of similar topics" (1936: 233).

IV

If Ward fixed upon a widely-held but loosely-formulated *bio-social notion* and structured it, as we have suggested, into an overarching *psycho-social principle* of institutional development,[22] then it remained for Robert E. Park and Ernest W. Burgess to trim the explanatory implications from that principle, reduce it to the dimensions of an *analytic*

concept, and establish it as a fundamental category of social
process for American sociologists (see House, 1936: 299).

In an early essay, in which he acknowledged the borrowed
status of assimilation in sociology and, wisely, also recognized
the inevitable transfer of significations that accompany such
conceptual borrowing, Park (1950: 209) states:

Assimilation, as the word is here used, brings with it a certain borrowed
significance which is carried over from physiology where it is employed
to describe the process of nutrition. By a process of nutrition, somewhat similar to the physiological one, we may conceive alien peoples to
be incorporated with, and made part of, the community or state.

It is in the later and highly influential co-authored text,
that the treatment of assimilation comes to constitute a
vital juncture in the "natural history" of the assimilation
idea. Into it converged the various strains of signification and
differential application that had characterized its prior
usages, and from it issued a broad consensus regarding its
general meaning and, to a somewhat lesser degree perhaps,
agreement on its frame of reference in subsequent sociological endeavors.

Park and Burgess' definition of assimilation (1921: 735)
became the standard sociological definition:

Assimilation is a process of interpenetration and fusion in which
persons and groups acquire the memories, sentiments and attitudes of
other persons and groups, and, by sharing their experience and history,
are incorporated with them in common cultural life.

Consistent with this meaning, it was Personality and the
Cultural Heritage, which became the social structural anchor-
ages to which the assimilation process was deemed to be
directly attached (1921: 511).

If we acknowledge that Park and Burgess' formulation of
the assimilation concept and its designated structural linkage
laid down the framework for its subsequent treatment, we
cannot ignore that within these guidelines there remained
sufficient latitude for the emergence of some distressing and

persisting difficulties.

Perhaps among the last to seriously challenge Park and Burgess' reduction of the myriad of previously posited types of social relationships into the four great social processes of competition, conflict, accommodation and assimilation, was Edward Cary Hayes. Hayes (1925: 342n) proposed that in their place a taxonomy of thirteen "social relations" be once and for all established, and that the term "assimilation" be set aside in favor of a trilogy of Gabriel Tarde's much more illuminating, specific and inclusive concepts of "social suggestion," "sympathetic radiation" and "imitation" (334-335). The concept of assimilation, he argued, should not be discarded altogether, but should be reserved to designate "the result which follows in a large class of instances when social suggestion, sympathetic radiation and imitation have played their roles" (*loc. cit.*). Thus, while on the one hand raising into prominence, elaborating and extending the psychic, i.e. mental and emotional, attributes that lodge in Park and Burgess' formulation of the process, Hayes proposed, on the other hand, that "assimilation" be regarded not as a process, but as a result, a product, an outcome of a social relationship, in effect: a social structure. In a critical response to Hayes' article, House (1926: 629) conceded that "assimilation . . . can be taken either as an activity or as the result of an activity," but he defended Park and Burgess' typology of social processes, and reaffirmed the meaning which they had vested in "assimilation" (626-627):

There is to be observed in all communities, however, a process in which, through participation in common activities and through living together in relatively intimate relations — which is both cause and effect — persons develop an organic, sympathetic responsiveness to one another's claims and attitudes, so that their relations to one another no longer admit of description in terms of "organization" in any but the most nebulous and inclusive sense of the term. Through this process, which is termed "assimilation," the attitudes of one individual toward another become "personal," in the conventional sense of the term. A personal relationship in this sense of the term docs not necessarily involve like-mindedness; it involves mutual claims which are mutually recognized. Assimilation is a process in which persons come to, or continue to feel at home in each other's presence, in somewhat the same way in which a person comes to feel at home in a certain physical milieu.

The question of whether assimilation is to designate a process of becoming, or whether it is to refer to a state of affairs that marks the culmination of such processes, remains today as unsettled as it was then. Seemingly, the matter is arbitrary, and the decision as to which alternative meaning is actually adopted in a particular piece of research may simply be a condition of the type of available data. Where comparative data from several time periods permit longitudinal analysis, a conception of assimilation-as-process becomes feasible; where such data are lacking, an ahistorical view of assimilation-as-a-(relative)-state-of-affairs may be embraced.[23]

Turning from this particular ambiguity which mars "this bothersome concept," we shall now consider an aspect of vagueness that continues to haunt it.[24] The broad consensus, that we had said earlier issued from Park and Burgess' definition of assimilation, centered around its conception as an essentially *psychic* process. Thus, Hayes (1925: 334-335) had proposed the substitution of Tarde's trilogy of primarily mental and emotional categories. Park and Burgess (1921: 735) themselves, as had Simons (1901: 798-799) twenty years earlier, related assimilation functionally to Giddings' notion of "consciousness of kind"; similarly, Ward (1903: 101, 150) had strongly underscored the psychic factors that animate it; House shares with Park and Burgess a recognition of the element of "like-mindedness" that is included in assimilation, although they all hint that in advanced societies, this like-mindedness might be better understood as a sense of shared corporate identity, than as "being of a uniform mind" (Park and Burgess, 1921: 511, 735, 759; House, 1926: 626; Park, 1950: 204-206); and more recently, Shibutani and Kwan (1965: 21, 121, 504) have pointed out that "sociologists have long recognized that assimilation is a mental process, involving a drastic change of perspectives" and that it "is basically a psychological transformation" which occurs with "the displacement of reference groups." Yet, we must insist, while Park and Burgess certainly left the door open to the option of psychologizing the notion of assimilation, it was not they, and particularly not Park, who can be charged with picking up the option and venturing through.

Such documentations, ascribing essentially psychic, mentalistic, emotionally adjustive, personality transformative or similarly psychological attributes to the phenomena conceptualized as "assimilation," can easily be multiplied from the literature of more than sixty years of American sociology. In addition, "assimilation" is not infrequently employed in a manner so coterminous with the concept of "socialization," as to render the two virtually synonymous.[25]

The affinity between them is clearly attributable to the vagueness that characterizes assimilation as a concept in sociology. Lacking any rigorous specification of either intensions or extensions of meaning, it is devoid of definitional boundaries and therefore free to expand to the point of effective meaninglessness.[26] As illustrated with the case of socialization, it may thus also encroach upon another concept that is somewhat more precisely specified and circumscribed, and raise the potential of contamination and thereby lead to a blunting of the analytic utility of both.

An interesting and apposite case in point is offered by two otherwise entirely unrelated studies by Robert Nisbet (1945) and Roland L. Warren (1946). Each of the authors addresses himself, titularly, to the problem of "assimilation" and, coincidentally, both pursue the matter in the substantive context of the military setting. Nisbet's article describes the impending demobilization of the military (after World War II), and anticipates the problems that will be encountered when men are released *en masse* from military institutions into civilian society. The "coming problem of assimilation" must be met, Nisbet argues (268), through the establishment of psychological aid stations in order to prevent the chronic maladjustment of Ex-G.I.s to civilian life. "Assimilation" here, by any reading, refers to *psychological and emotional readjustment*. Where Nisbet's discussion involved "assimilation" problems attending military discharge, Warren's study examined the problem of "assimilation" *into* the armed services or, specifically, how "the Navy molded the behavior and attitudes of Reserve officers" (1946: 204n). His analysis leads Warren to the conclusion that "Assimilation, however satisfactory, was temporary; . . . the structure of assimilation weakened and crumbled at a rate with which discharge papers were hard put to it to keep up" (211). The meaning that is imputed into "assimilation" in Warren's usage bears no relationship to anything resembling psychological or emotional adjustment. The reader can not fail to recognize that the problem addressed here is one that is generally conceptualized in terms of "socialization" — (unsuccessful) socialization, if you will, into a military subculture.[27]

Neither of these examples of distinctive meanings that are indiscriminately embraced by the concept of assimilation, is at variance with the generally psychological character attributed to the processes thus conceptualized. However, an additional and clearly separable category of meaning came to be associated with the notion of assimilation, one that focused more specifically on life-styles, and was thus linkable to matters of ethnicity as that term is predominantly used. Particularly Warren's usage of assimilation signals another consequence of the concept's vague specification. If assimilation was to refer to the modification of sentiments, feelings, attitudes, memories, emotional states or even personality structures, its usage certainly also stretched to embrace processes by which the whole range of normative patterns are acquired or relinquished — in short, *cultural and sub-cultural adaptation.*

Commenting on the affinity between the study of culture and "what sociologists have discussed more abstractly as 'assimilation'," House (1936: 271-272) notes with what must seem, even forty years later, as something of an academic understatement: "Logical distinctions and relations between the concept of culture, with related and derivative concepts, and other sociological concepts and categories are still imperfectly defined." A brief review, beginning with 1930, of surely the most authoritative sources with respect to the established and legitimate meanings of sociological concepts, yields an overwhelming formal acknowledgement of assimilation as a profoundly cultural process. Thus Park, in a definitive statement in the *Encyclopedia of the Social Sciences*, recognizes that "as popularly used [assimilation] is a political rather than a cultural concept."[28] His ensuing discussion, however, reveals that in its sociological usage, cultural considerations figure prominently in the assimilation process. It refers to how diverse peoples "achieve a cultural solidarity," and "an immigrant is ordinarily considered assimilated as soon as he has acquired the language and the social ritual of the native community" (Park, 1930: 281). Fairchild, similarly, defines assimilation as "the process by which different cultures, or individuals or groups representing different cultures, are merged into a homogeneous unit" (Fairchild, n.d.: 276). Reminiscent of Novicow's discussion (1893: 125-253) of assimilation as denationalization, Fairchild (277) concludes that "in essence, assimilation is the substitution of one nationality pattern for another." Finally, in probably the most recent definitive statement on the concept, Robert E. L. Faris (1964: 38) writes that "assimilation denotes the process in which one set of cultural traits is relinquished and a new set acquired, through communication and participation."

We might also note that leading contemporary text-books in the sociology of racial and ethnic relations tend to ascribe a broadly cultural meaning to assimilation, although, as in the more definitive sources cited above, allusions to psychological meanings are typically retained, if not always explicitly stated.[29]

Now, we have been tracing, in the last several pages, the rather tenuous congeries of meanings imputed to assimilation, meanings which seem to hold the concept in a vacillating suspension between the polarities of psychological adjustment and cultural adaptation. Yet, it is necessary to acknowledge a third and additionally complicating meaning pattern that emerges, somewhat haphazardly, out of the discussions of assimilation. Buried in the conceptualization of assimilation as a psychic process, as well as in that of assimilation as a cultural process, lies a shadowy conception of assimilation as a categorically *social* process. Simons (1902: V, 544), for example, alluded to something more than a psychological adjustment or a cultural adaptation, when she pointed to the "exclusion of the negro [sic] from desirable social, business and political positions" as a hinderance to assimilation. The process of social integration into group structures is suggested more explicitly, when Reuter (1941: 55) defines assimilation as "the fact of full group membership and the means by which the condition comes about." Even in some of Park's many statements on the subject, a conception of assimilation as a social convergence and integration of groups is all but formally stated, especially in his essay on "Racial Assimilation in Secondary Groups" (1950: 204-220; see also 1950: 76-77).

Again, to argue that in these, and other similar instances, there is a clearly articulated conception of assimilation as a *social* process, distinct from its psychological or cultural counterparts, would be a gross misrepresentation. The point is that in virtually every discussion of assimilation, the nuances of each of the meanings are discernible or may be imputed, although the explicit emphases tend to fix on one or another, most typically the *psychological* or *cultural* ones. The situation indicates clearly that there is a serious problem of meaning-boundaries. Its vague specification endows the concept with an elasticity, such that it stretches to accommodate assimilation as *psychological adjustment*, as *cultural adaptation* and as *social structural integration*. As a strictly *social* process, assimilation has suffered comparative neglect, and probably in good part, its clearer emergence has been inhibited by the fact that the notion of social process, itself, occupies something of an awkward position among sociological concepts. We don't wish to get side-tracked here into a problem that deserves a separate analysis of its own, but in order to illuminate the problem at hand, we do need to point to some of its more obvious difficulties.

There appears to be no serious problem with the notion of social process in its most typical application, such as when the concept "social *process*" is juxtaposed to the concept "social *structure*." Nor is there much difficulty in the alternative emphasis, when "*social* process" is referred to, in contradistinction to, for example, *"biological* process." When, however, we are faced with differentiating between *psychological, cultural* and *social* processes, the problem assumes a fuzzier texture. To be sure, we distinguish conceptually between the psychological and the cultural, but as processes, are they not both "social" in character or context? On the other hand, if the study of psychological process is the acknowledged province of psychology, while cultural processes are pre-eminently within anthropology's jurisdiction, what as yet not pre-empted significations remain in the notion of social process, that justify sociology's special claims upon it? These kinds of questions have, of course, challenged and engaged the attention of every major figure in sociology, but it is perhaps in Simmel's thought that, in principle at least, they are most lucidly resolved. For Simmel it is not the *content* of society (as exemplified in such psychic categories as purpose, motive, impulse and interest, or cultural categories reflecting congealed habits), but rather society as *form*, as function, as "something quantitative and essentially dynamic," that is sociologically relevant. Accordingly, *"forms* of socialization," *"formation* of classes," *"processes* of assocation," "principles of group *formation,"* "network of *relationships,"* in brief, *"relationships* and *interactions* which constitute human *association"* are the essential and critical categories of cognition, that identify and legitimate the distinctive domain of sociology for Simmel.[30]

Armed with Simmel's approach, we are in a better position to address the boundary problem with respect to the psychological, cultural and social meaning patterns ascribed to "assimilation." The difficulty may now be seen as arising from a tendency to treat all three processes, conceptualized under the single term of "assimilation," as though they operated on the same empirical plane. More properly, they might be recognized as representing conceptual organizations of behavior at three different phenomenal levels and, accordingly, the problem of meaning-boundaries would be resolved through a recognition of distinctive analytic hierarchies. Unfortunately, this recognition and the implications it bears for sociological analysis have not been always heeded. In sociology in general, they are treated frequently as occurring at a common empirical level where their analytic treatment is regarded as carried out adequately through apprehending such processes at a common level of conceptual abstraction, and thus in terms of a construct that turns out to be conceptually ambiguous and vague. Consequently, the notions of the social, the cultural and the psychological tend to be blended into one another, as they meet at their peripheries, and the loci of their empirical referents, usefully segregated for analytic purposes into social, cultural and personality "systems," become infelicitously merged.[31]

The range of sociological literature on assimilation stands as testimony to the vague specification of each, and the ambiguous and opaque usage of all the dimensions of meaning, with which the assimilation concept has been freighted. It would be unfortunate, however, if we left the impression that this state of affairs is peculiar to the concept of assimilation. The difficulties that we suggested still attach to the broader conception of "social process," should persuade otherwise.

Some indication of the extent of this conceptual chaos is conveyed by a perhaps benignly neglected remedial effort that was undertaken some thirty-five years ago. The proliferation of unspecified and unsystematized concepts in this area led to the formation, by the *American Sociological Society*, of a Committee on Conceptual Integration, which was charged with the task of introducing some order. A special Sub-Committee on Definition of Definition, after an intensive scrutiny of the literature, offered a "Classification of Social Process Concepts" which is instructive both in terms of the conceptual anarchy it found, as well as the ordered heterogeneity it bequeathed after submitting its report (Hart, 1943). Since our primary interest lies in the process of assimilation, it is worth noting that out of well in excess of a hundred "social process" concepts that were ordered, in the report, under merely one sub-classification (that of "Social Interaction"[32]), the following ones were relegated as properly sub-typical to "Assimilation":[33]

imitation; suggestion; sympathy; education; training; amalgamation; fusion; acculturation; conversion; unification; coordination; consolidation; integration; merging; recruiting; domestication.

By any standard, this constitutes an incredibly heterogeneous collage of concepts. What strikes the contemporary reader of the Sub-Committee's schema as even more remarkable, is the elusive rationale on which the entire taxonomy must have been based. Evidently, there has taken place a considerable shift in the meanings and the usages of some of the terms in the thirty-five years since the report was published. It would seem extravagant, however, to expect a similar effort, undertaken today, to result in a better taxonomy, unless "better" simply means one that is more in tune with the current conceptual conventions.

It is clear, in any case, that the concept of assimilation, then or since, remains a "bothersome concept," indeed. Plagued by an untenable conceptual elasticity, it embraces a range of meaning that includes processes of psychological adjustment, cultural adaptation and social structural integration. To the extent that the concept of assimilation plays a central role in the conduct of race relations theorizing, it is no wonder that van den Berghe (1967: 6) is moved to make the bold assertion that "the field of race relations has come to resemble a theoretical no-man's land between psychology, sociology and anthropology."

V

We have examined, in the preceding sections, some general considerations respecting conceptual terms and their introduction into scientific usage; and we have looked somewhat specifically at the notion of assimilation in its earlier application and its subsequent elaborations as a concept in sociology. A few summary comments are in order.

It is apparent, as might have been anticipated, that the sociological literature on assimilation, taken as a whole, generally subordinates itself in its emphasis to the shifts in orientation that have characterized the growth of the over-all American sociological enterprise. As long as the discipline was heavily indebted to the biological sciences for its vocabulary and conceptual analogues, the notion of assimilation was rarely invoked without pointedly being preceded by the modifying adjective "social." The process thus denoted, however, continued to be described in faithful analogy with biological prototypes. With the growing prominence of psychology, sociology, still groping for its proper identity and jurisdiction, gradually modified its genetic, hereditarian and instinctivistic assumptions. In their place, it began to favor the newer psycho-dynamics that now appeared so much more appropriate to the study of the human condition. Not only had the biological strait-jacket raised difficulties in accounting for certain empirical findings, but is also proved inconveniently resistant to reconciliation with the optimistic faith in social progress that came to distinguish sociology as the "American Science." Psychic factors, mentalistic "givens" and the psychology of learning seemed to offer a much more congenial foundation from which to broach the study of social conduct and social institutions. In accordance with these influences, the concept of assimilation underwent renovation and was refurbished in the direction of the psychological genre.

However, a new shift in sociological orientation, or at least a new dimension of sociological sensitivity, was interjected with the gradual accumulation of a body of reliable knowledge in comparative ethnology. Mounting evidence from this field led to the suspicion that neither biological nor psychic factors served quite as satisfactorily in accounting for diversities in human conduct and institutions, as did ethnic or cultural considerations. This recognition was hardly lost on those, whose professional interests focused on the problems engendered when peoples of diverse behavioral and institutional traditions encountered one another in modern societies. The sociological study of assimilation began to concentrate on, and the concept of assimilation increasingly connoted, the processes by which cultural diversities, through diffusion, underwent transformations in the direction of cultural fusions.

This newer conception of assimilation as *cultural adaptation* did not, however, provoke the formal reconceptualization of the concept that would have purged its already established connotation as a process of *psychological adjustment*. Rather, both meanings came to be subsumed coextensively under the single term of assimilation, thereby compounding its already vague specification with the fault of ambiguity and further compromising its integrity, Lachenmeyer (1971: 34-36) would argue, with the flaw of contradiction. To confuse the issue even more, a sociologically more apt, but never fully explicated notion of assimilation as *social structural integration* insinuated itself throughout the discussions, thus adding further complexity to an already over-burdened and spongy concept.

The accommodation of a single conceptual term to such a multiplicity of meanings and applications (not to mention its dual reference to both a *process* and a *fait accompli*) violates basic strictures respecting scientific concepts, and compromises the term's analytic utility. In scientific, as in conventional languages, as more and more meanings are conferred on a concept, it necessarily comes to mean less and less. To the extent that psychological, cultural and social processes operate empirically as related, or even as functionally interdependent dimensions of some broader societal process, these phenomenal distinctions would appear to necessitate a parallel conceptual repertoire that offers analytic sensitivity commensurate with this empirical complexity. Yet, the wide-spread sociological interest in assimilation processes did not appear to take sufficient account of either the multi-dimensionality or the nature of the inter-relatedness of the phenomena involved.

Furthermore, one would have reason to expect that the *sociological* interest in assimilative processes would center in the kind of patterns that are pre-eminently *social* in their manifestation. Thus it might pertain to matters of status integration, group convergence, consolidation of group structures, recruitment to élite positions, even more basic demographic patterns, and, broadly, to social-structural fusion. Yet, significantly, this focus, which perhaps uniquely legitimates sociology as an independent discipline, does not seem to dominate the sociological research literature on assimilation. Instead, there is a wide-spread concern with social-psychological questions relating to the dynamics and configurations of *attitude* formation toward out-groups; with modifications or crystallization of out-group *stereotypes*, or with persistence and change in reference group *identifications* among out-groupers. Where, on the other hand, the research focus is not essentially social-psychological, out-groupers are conceptualized as *ethnics*, and assimilation analyses are preoccupied with delineating *ethnic traditions*; with assessing the functions and dysfunctions of converging *life-styles*; and with measuring the extent of reciprocal or unilateral cultural adaptation.

To a very large degree, the difficulties that attach to the "bothersome concept" of assimilation arise from the fact that the concept is neither a strictly empirical term, nor a legitimately theoretical term. Thus, ungoverned by either of the sobrieties of rigorous empirical observation or adroit theoretical deduction, the concept of assimilation generally shows the effects of having enjoyed immunity from some of the disciplinary controls that normally and properly order the scientific enterprise.

Notes

1.   We are excluding from consideration here, on the one hand, more properly bio-psychological theories that may have been smuggled into sociology along with the notion of instinct, and on the other hand Social Darwinist Thought to which the notion was some-times attached. Neither of these, then or now, can be permitted to parade as sociological theory.

2.   See Alfred R. Lindesmith and Anselm L. Strauss (1956: 10-11). Interestingly, the authors' most recent edition (1968) tones down their concern over reductionism considerably. In this connection, it is instructive to look at a more recent reassessment of the reductionism problem in the light of the contemporary develop-mental status of sociology. See William R. Catton, Jr. (1966:

302-319). We are not taking issue here with Catton's argument that the long-standing taboo against reductionism in sociology has out-served its usefulness as a protective wall behind which sociology can come into its own. Yet, the point remains that if reductionism means the borrowing of concepts, constructs, or theoretical propositions from "lower" analytic levels for use in "higher" ones *in which they are not, or can not be reconstructed* to attain formal integration into systematic theory, then reductionism is logically and methodologically untenable.

3. Observational terms are also variously known as "descriptive terms," "empirical terms" or, especially in the "hard" sciences, as "experimental variables." They rest on direct inspection and lend themselves to confident verification. See Abraham Kaplan (1964: 54-55). Such terms have also been referred to as "concepts by intuition" or "concepts by induction." Cf. F. S. C. Northrop (1947: 36, 82).

4. See Richard S. Rudner (1966: 12ff). The process referred to here specifically involves the absorption of language elements described above as observational terms. This is of course not always so, since many of such borrowed terms are not purely descriptive in character. The farther they are removed from direct perception of events, the more difficulties do they pose for their scientific incorporation.

5. In accord with their derivation, such terms have been called "theoretical terms" or "explanatory terms" by Kaplan (1964: 56-57). Perhaps even more apposite is Northrop's reference to them as "concepts by postulation" (1947: 60-64, 83, 104).

6. Not only are the alternatives of appropriating lay terms or deduction from theory an oversimplification of the sources of concept recruitment in sociology, but the distinction between observational and theoretical terms is also deceptively categorical. Kaplan speaks, in addition, of "indirect observables" and "constructs," and suggests that all four types of terms occur on an empirical-theoretical continuum, with the distinctions dissolving into a matter of degree. See Kaplan (1964: 57-62).

7. One of the early sociologists to recognize this and to sound warnings against the employment of "these lay terms" by sociologists, was Durkheim. See Emile Durkheim (1938: 22). See also the passage quoted from Durkheim (19-20, *supra*).

8. For specification of some of the important properties that distinguish scientific from conventional languages, see Charles Lachenmeyer (1971: 45-49).

9. In connection with these distinctive characteristics, see Everett Cherrington Hughes and Helen McGill Hughes (1952: 130-144). Their essay addresses the dilemma that results for sociologists, as their concepts, at the juncture of these two languages, tend persistently toward corruption through erosion or distortion.

10.   While lexicographic efforts, as Blumer points out, serve to fix
       meanings and to encourage a common usage of terms by eliminat-
       ing definitional inconsistencies, they neglect the methodological
       necessity of empirical or theoretical linkage. Thus, such efforts
       bear a relatively sterile significance in science. See Blumer (1940:
       712-713).

11.   For the sake of clarity, it may be useful to distinguish here
       between etymological and conceptual inquiries. The former
       pertains to a *lineal* tracing into the root origins of a term or its
       elements. Conceptual analysis, in contrast, implies a *systemic*
       inquiry, one that assesses the position and function of a term
       within the network of a given empirico-theoretical (or intellectual)
       system.

12.   Such contamination is of course not only one-sided. The popular-
       ization of scientific knowledge serves a latent function of
       "rationalizing" popular terms to some extent. With respect
       to poetic enterprises, at least, this may in fact be dysfunctional;
       see Northrop (1947: Chapter IX, especially 175-176). However,
       the contaminating influence of popular meanings on scientific
       terms, particularly sociological ones, is clearly inimical to the
       discipline. This accounts, in part, for the recurring efforts to
       "neutralize" the language of science by mathematicizing it.

13.   Implicit in this, and basic to the problem, is of course the intru-
       sion, along with popular meanings, of the pre-scientific or
       common-sensical presuppositions which sustain those meanings.
       It is the tenuousness of, and even ignorance about such pre-
       suppositions, which complicates the formalization of such terms
       in scientific theory. See Rudner (1966: 49-50).

14.   In fact, this may only aggravate the problem. As Hayakawa has
       emphasized, definitions are not statements about events, but
       statements about linguistic conventions, and the academic nicety
       of "defining one's terms," by itself, merely leads to "chasing
       oneself in verbal circles." For a fuller discussion of this, see S. I.
       Hayakawa (1949: 171-173).

15.   This involves what Hayakawa (1949: 58-60) calls the "exten-
       sional" meaning of a term, as distinct from its "intensional"
       (connotative) meaning. However, the outward extension of a
       term to its empirical anchorage does not guarantee the exclusion
       of these kinds of presuppositions. It is not the empirical referent,
       after all, that is being imported into the discipline, but the term
       symbolizing it; and its empirical specification does not screen out
       its symbolic context.

16.   The counterfeit character of such a system may express itself, as
       the example of "instinct sociology" illustrated, in the form of a
       logically-closed explanatory circle in which the appropriated
       item, being neither a direct observational term nor a theoretical
       term with systemic meaning, is distended into such "theoretical"

proportions, that it comes to be taken as its own explanation.

17. Others who figured prominently in developing the idea of social process were Gumplowicz and Tarde; see House (1936: 178, 189-190).

18. It is not to be expected, of course, that stripping away the convention of biological thoughtways would, or could result in perspectivistic neutrality. Ward's aim, and to a considerable extent, his achievement, was to demonstrate the greater pertinence of the "psychic factor" in the study of social structure and social process, thereby laying a foundation for psychological thoughtways.

19. "I do not hope to add anything to their masterly presentation of this truth, which is without any question the most important contribution thus far made to the science of sociology" (Ward, 1903: 203-204).

20. It is interesting that Lester Ward never once referred to this series of articles in his discussion in *Pure Sociology*.

21. He would have referred to it as a "principle." See Ward (1903: 169-170).

22. See particularly the discussion of "compound assimilation" in Ward (1903: 212-215).

23. See for example James D. Davidson, Jr., and Joseph A. Schlangen (1970). The authors take this second approach. Notably, acknowledging the difficulties encountered with "this bothersome concept" (443), they distinguish carefully between *cultural* and *structural* assimilation. In this regard, this study stands apart from most of the literature on assimilation.

24. See Ralph Ross (1962: 19ff) for a discussion of the difference between ambiguity and vagueness in concepts. See also Charles Lachenmeyer (1971: 30-50), who adds to this distinction the further problems of opacity and contradiction as troublesome characteristics of sociological concepts.

25. Thus, assimilation has been described as the process by which individuals are "conditioned" and learn "roles." See Howard Woolston (1945: 416).

26. In this connection, see the extended discussion of "concepts by intuition" and "concepts by postulation" in Northrop (1947: 59-75).

27. We might note that Warren, himself, recognizes and acknowledges that he has been observing an instance of "role playing"; nevertheless, he persists in considering the matter as one of *assimilation*.

28. In view of the "imperfectly defined" relationship between sociological and cultural categories, one must wonder whether, in sociological terms, this is indeed a distinction — or merely a particularization of one *kind* of cultural concept.

29. See such recent top ranking texts as Brewton Berry (1965: 247-271); Charles F. Marden and Gladys Meyer (1968: 438-439);

George Eaton Simpson and J. Milton Yinger (1965: 230-233); James W. Vander Zanden (1966: 298-307). The notable exception is the aforementioned text by Shibutani and Kwan (1965: 21, 121, 504-515), who frankly favor a social psychological approach to racial and ethnic phenomena, and in whose treatment assimilation retains an unequivocal psychological cast and remains linked closely to matters of personality.

30.   Among the best expositions of Simmel's writings, in English, is that of Spykman, and all the quoted items were taken from his translations. See Nicholas J. Spykman (1965: 34-59).

31.   For a general discussion seeking to clarify some of the dimensions of this problem, see Abraham Edel (1959). For a discussion of how this problem arises in connection with the sociological use of the notion "counterculture," see Bash (1979).

32.   The other two sub-classifications under the "Classification of Social Process Concepts" are "Social Change" and "Personality Adjustment."

33.   See Hart (1943: 339). While "Assimilation" is classified as a sub-category under "Social Interaction," a footnote indicates that it should also appear under "Social Change" but not, it seems, under "Personality Adjustment." Although the sub-classification of "Social Change" is not elaborated in this respect, presumably its listing under "Assimilation" would yield an additional battery of sub-types. Clearly, even the sub-types quoted above are not exhaustive, and do not, for example, include an obvious one like "socialization," or Novicow's "denationalization."

CHAPTER 4

The Concept of Assimilation: Its Multiple Meanings and its Conceptual Status

I

In the preceding chapter, we have traced the assimilation idea from its early pre-sociological sources as a biological concept and a biologically-tinged popular notion, through its absorption and subsequent conceptualizations as a concept in sociology. The analysis has been primarily historical and semantic. While we have had to look at the contexts out of which the assimilation idea was appropriated into sociology, our primary interest centered in its conceptual interior — the kind of meaning intensions and, only by implication, the corresponding meaning extensions, with which the concept was freighted in the course of its sociological career.

The ensuing discussion will assume a somewhat more critical posture, and assess the influence which the assimilation concept has exerted in shaping the tone and molding the perspective of the sociology of race and ethnic relations. More specifically, we want to examine the consequences that have accrued to this field as a result of the particular contents of meanings with which the concept had become furnished; and we wish to explore the role which, given its somewhat amorphous character, assimilation has been permitted to assume as an ostensibly scientific concept within the field's theoretical superstructure. The questions posed, then, are: "does 'assimilation' qualify as a *sociological* concept?" and "does 'assimilation' qualify as a sociological *concept*?"

With respect to the contents of the assimilation concept, we have sought to show how the mutually re-enforcing liabilities of vague specification and ambiguously designated referents have served to so elasticize its conceptual boundaries, as to embrace an untenably opaque, and even contradictory conglomerate of meanings. The resulting homogenizing tendency has proceeded to a degree which transcends, we have suggested, the mere compounding of distinguishable processes that transpire at a single phenomenal level. Rather, it extends to embrace sets of processes that would be fruitfully recognized, for analytic purposes, as occurring at several conceptually distinct levels of social experience. Thus, the useful discrimination between assimilation as psychological adjustment, as cultural adaptation, and as social structural integration tends to be submerged under a blanket conceptualization which is less than conducive to analytic acuity. Furthermore, for reasons that mirror some of the developmental characteristics of American sociology in general, the not entirely conscious focus of actual assimilation research was found to reflect a primary assumption of psychological or cultural definitions of assimilation, leaving the empirical and theoretical aspects of its *social* conception relatively unexplored.

As regards the *status* which assimilation has been accorded as a scientifically legitimate conceptual form, it was noted in the previous chapter that as a concept it qualifies as a strict observational term, not as a proper theoretical term. That the concept of assimilation constitutes a considerable abstraction from the empirically observable is clear; but, as we have suggested in pointing to the dearth of theory in the field of race relations, it would be difficult to claim that it represents a construct deduced logically from some independent theoretical frame. As a result, "assimilation" enjoys relative immunity from the kinds of methodological constraints that are normally exerted upon concepts from either "end" of the scientific endeavor.

In view of the prominence accorded the assimilation idea within the sociology of racial and ethnic relations, it would seem inevitable that this inadequate specification of the notion's content and questionable formalization of its conceptual status would have profound repercussions on this field. We shall therefore proceed first with a critical examination of assimilation's interior furnishings and then assess its conceptual status, and note with special interest the resulting analytic focus and the methodological implications that have accrued to the field.

II

Scientific concepts, as intellectual abstractions, occupy a logical space somewhere between their ostensible empirical referents and the range of theory purporting to constitute the explanatory frame. The role that concepts play in the conduct of scientific inquiry is unavoidably dependent upon the nature and the quality of the linkage that is sustained between the concept and its referent at one end, and the concept and its theoretical frame at the other. It is precisely these linkages, or their respective absences, we would argue, which distinguish sociology, as a science, from its related enterprises of substantively concrete social analysis on the one hand, and logical abstract speculative social theory on the other. These distinctions are important.

Thus, we would reserve the term "*social* theory" as the proper designation for an enterprise in which concepts fail to be grounded, systematically, in the concreta of observable events or where, in any case, their empirical foundations are irrelevant; its focus of inquiry lodges, instead, in the *logical* relationships between propositions at various levels of abstraction. Where, to the contrary, concepts do not admit of a specifiable, logically adequate linkage with assertions at the level of theory, the only feasible kind of research enterprise is one which traffics between the datum and its conceptualization. Its yield is, accordingly, restricted to descriptive statements which assert the discovery of patterns, relationships, correlations, etc.[1] Identification of such *empirical* regularities, or their assertion in the form of empirical generalizations, as Merton (1968: 149) has argued, can not pass for sociological theorizing; and devoid of demonstrable explanatory implications, such studies do not, to our view, constitute sociological inquiry. They involve, more properly, social research or *"social* analysis" in the sense that we have discussed these undertakings above, and in Chapter 1 (see 15-17, *supra*).

In the case of the assimilation concept, especially recalling the generally-conceded absence of theory in the race relations field, it is virtually impossible to demonstrate a chain of logical connections with some prior theoretical framework. As might be anticipated, a deficiency so glaring is not likely to go uncompensated in a discipline that is as self-conscious with respect to its legitimately "scientific" foundations, as is sociology. We shall defer our consideration of how this deficiency was redressed until the following sections.

We are arguing, then, that assimilation studies represent essentially *social*, not sociological, analyses. They typically emanate from *socially* perceived problems, approach their data through *socially* constructed concepts, proceed through analyses geared to *socially* significant conclusions, and culminate in *social* descriptions. Their contributions amount, typically, to a sketching in of the terrain of a social map, as it appears at one or another point in time. In this sense, the results may constitute detailed and systematically obtained *social information*, but they do not cumulate to *sociological knowledge*. Another way of putting this is to say that the concept of assimilation, and the studies which address themselves to the processes so designated, are predicated on a *social construction* of reality — not on its *sociological re-*construction. From the perspective of sociology and of science in general, whose primary commitments are to knowledge, this represents an instance of what Nagel had referred to as the frequently encountered confusion between knowledge (see 8, *supra*).

If we are to account, then, for the content of the assimilation concept, specifically its elaboration in psychological or cultural terms, the explanation is not to be found in the realm of sociological theory, but rather in the world of social events. The content of the assimilation concept is informed by the popular social perception that the strangers in our midst are somehow "different." They are recognized as different in their "mentality" in that they are "inscrutible," or "lethargic," or "lackadaisical," or "conniving," or "criminally minded," or "imbued with alien ideologies," etc., and they are not assimilable until they have undergone a psychological transformation. Thus, common-sense social constructions of reality serve as cues which, *without* further sociological *re*construction, furnish both the content and the focus of the "sociological" concept of assimilation-as-psychological-adjustment. In the same vein, perhaps even more accessible to common-sense observation than the "different mentalities" of alien peoples, is the recognition of their "strange customs." Their worship, their dress, their food, their talking, courting, mating and mourning are "different." The "raw" social perceptions, ethnocentrically filtered, become the basis, in unreconstructed form and through *ideological* extension, for a "sociological" conception of assimilation-as-cultural-adaptation.

By thus by-passing Carl Hempel's caution (1952: 47) that "concept formation in science can not be separated from theoretical considerations," the *socially* generated and formulated concept of assimilation remains just that — a *social* concept — and fails to qualify as a scientific (i.e. sociological) one.[2] Yet, the matter can not be simply left to rest there, for "assimilation" *does* sustain theoretical linkages, albeit not *sociological* ones. We must now examine its curious status as a concept *in*, but not *of*, sociology in terms of these linkages.

To the extent that the concept is employed in its psychological meaning patterns (and we have shown sufficient precedent for this tradition in the previous chapter), it necessarily channels the directional thrust of the research it engenders into an analysis of essentially psychological variables. Thus, the evidential criterion for the extent of assimilation between groups or, in longitudinal studies, for its progress or regress, is based typically in one form or another of *attitude* assessment. Milton Gordon (1964: 70ff) has offered specific designations for this particular " dimension of assimilation." He proposes that "Attitude Receptional Assimilation" refer to the favorable attitudes indicated by the "host" or "core" group toward their reciprocals[3] in the assimilation process, while the latter's feeling of a sense of shared peoplehood with the "host" group be designated "Identification Assimilation."

In either case, the critical variable under consideration turns out to be a psychological factor, or a social-psychological one — the distinction, in this context, is largely immaterial. "Attitude Receptional Assimilation" occurs under conditions, Gordon (1964: 71) states, where there is an absence of prejudice. "Identificational Assimilation," as the term itself indicates, is predicated upon the psychological process of identification, and posits identification groups and reference groups which are both central to the concerns of social-psychology. Consistent with Merton's observation (1968: 143) that "concepts constitute the definitions (or prescriptions) of what is to be observed," the initial assumption of the assimilation concept as formulated in its psychological vein, sets in motion a methodological chain which of necessity ends in casting the entire assimilation issue into a psychological frame. Nor does the process, once begun, readily allow for breaking out of this frame since, as Karl Mannheim (1936: 22) points out: "Every concept represents a sort of taboo against other possible sources of meaning — simplifying and unifying the manifoldness of life for the sake of action" and, we might add, for the purpose of research.

We referred earlier to Shibutani and Kwan, who defined assimilation as a mental process involving a psychological transformation. Given this version of the concept, their treatment of "Assimilation into the Larger Society" (1965: 504-515) comes to be posed, in social-psychological terms, as a "displacement of reference groups," rather than an exchange of membership groups. In its more detailed pursuit, it even comes close to edging across that fuzzy line between social-psychology and psychology, when Shibutani and Kwan assert (505) that "assimilation involves the transformation of one's self-conception." Few, if any, contemporary assimilation studies which proceed from this type of definitional content, direct their analyses to strictly psychological variables — or perhaps we should say, to variables in their strict psychological specification. Most do, however, regard attitudinal factors associated with the respective group members in the assimilative relationship as the crucial datum, and the point at which the social-psychological perspective shades off into that of psychology is difficult to discern.

Given their commitment to assimilation-as-attitudinal-convergence or, as we designated it earlier (and perhaps more appropriately), assimilation-as-psychological-adjustment,[4] these studies make use of a variety of indicators in their common approach to attitudes. Probably the three most extensively employed are stereotypes, prejudice, and the concept of social distance. In accordance with the major psychological processes that investigators generally subsume as constituents of the notion of attitude, these indicators correspond, respectively, to its cognitive, affective, and conative components.[5]

Since Katz and Braly's (1933) pioneering and widely replicated investigation of the characteristic traits ascribed to some ten racial, religious and nationality groups, the cognitive dimension of attitude, conceptualized in terms of the crystallization or dissolution of stereotypes, has commanded major research attention. If assimilation is a condition of the host society's willingness to accept strangers on equal terms, and this in turn depends on an absence of perceived differences (or at least an absence of negatively evaluated differences[6]), then the salience and persistence of stereotypes constitutes a "measure" or indication of the process of assimilation.

Similarly, and in correspondence with the affective component of attitudes, assessments of the assimilative process in its psychological intensions have relied heavily on the prevalence and intensity of prejudices among host-group members.

That the study of prejudice is regarded as a major and integral part of the sociology of racial and ethnic relations, is attested by the prominence of such studies in the sociological literature, and the attention accorded them in the field's major text books. Of particular interest in this regard is a survey by Peter Rose (1968: 144-151), indicating the type of texts and orientational emphases favored by college instructors in their race relations courses. It is therefore hardly surprising that this overwhelmingly social-psychological predilection should be harnessed to the investigation of what Gordon had quite properly designated as "Attitude Receptional Assimilation."

A third and related mode of approach to this version of assimilation accords with the conative, or policy-oriented dimension of the attitude concept, and frequently involves the use of a social distance scale. Originally formulated by Emory Bogardus and published in two articles in sequential issues of the *Journal of Applied Sociology* (1925), "social distance" represented Bogardus' attempt to "operationalize" a metaphor that had been previously employed by Park (1924). Such scales have since been widely implemented in a variety of adaptations. They are generally used to determine how host-group members (think they) would treat individuals of other racial, religious or nationality groups in specified social situations. The implication, of course, is that the "narrower" the social distance, the greater the strangers' assimilability or, at least, the host-group's willingness to tolerate assimilation.

There is no need to extend our brief discussion of the kinds of analytic approaches that attach to, and support the concept of assimilation in its psychological meaning pattern. It is of course intrinsic to this orientation, that the issue of assimilation is confronted in terms of thoughts, feelings and (self-proclaimed) predispositions toward behavior. In other words, these types of analyses constitute a determination of the degree of *attitudinal readiness* for assimilation, rather than an assessment of the extent of its *social attainment*. That (solicited) social attitudes are not necessarily coincident with actual social behavior has been demonstrated empirically by LaPiere (1934) some time ago and, along with many subsequent confirmations,[7] has also been posed prominently by Gunnar Myrdal (1944) in the form of a moral dilemma. That Attitude Receptional Assimilation *must* logically, psychologically, or historically precede assimilation-as-social-integration, is not as evident. Indeed, there is room for argument as to which "dimension" of assimilation in fact facilitates which other, and any unstated general assumption lurking in the literature as to cause and effect, or even mere antecedence or subsequence, is at least an open question. To the extent that such assumptions are indeed entertained, the fault, one must suspect, lies not so much in our sociologies as in our ideologies.

From the foregoing discussion it is clear that the notion of assimilation, conceptualized in terms of these meaning patterns, articulates with the theory language (Lachenmeyer, 1971: 4-5, 60-64) of psychology and social psychology. However vague, ambiguous and, perhaps, opaque the concept may be in its present specification, it does therefore connect with theoretical considerations and it meets Hempel's minimal conditions for a (potentially) scientific concept. But, the question remains, can it be regarded as a *sociological* one?

While the assimilation concept is still widely employed in its psychological meaning pattern, probably its preponderant use in recent years has embraced its *cultural* intensions and extensions. Assimilation-as-cultural-adaptation is frequently used interchangeably, or at least in broad over-lap, with the anthropological concept of "acculturation." To the extent that a distinction is preserved, it probably lies in the association of "acculturation" with a piecemeal, formalistic, behavioral *adoption* of culture traits or items, while "assimilation" is used to indicate a more integral *commitment* to entire culture patterns or complexes.[8] Gordon (1964: 61) is inclined to think that the option for "acculturation" or "assimilation" may be more a function of whether the investigator is a cultural anthropologist or a sociologist, than of any substantial difference in the terms' meanings.

In any case, assimilation in its reference to cultural factors has gained extensive usage in the contemporary (American) sociological literature, and Gordon incorporates it in his assimilation paradigm as "Cultural or Behavioral Assimilation." It involves a change of cultural patterns to those of the host society (1964: 70-71).

The precedent for this variant of the assimilation concept is certainly rooted, as must be said also for its psychological version, in Park and Burgess' basic definition. Yet, as rich and productive of subsequent research as their definition surely was, a careful reading (see 68, *supra*) provokes a number of questions. Purporting to define assimilation as a *social process*, the definition, instead, points to the acquisition of "memories, sentiments, and attitudes" and an incorporation into "a common cultural life." The weight of the definition rests, respectively, on *psychic* and *cultural outcomes* of some as yet unspecified social process. Again the question must be raised: is assimilation to be understood as a process or as a product? In a subsequent passage, Park and Burgess (1921: 736) seem to indicate their answer: "As social contact initiates interaction, assimilation is its final perfect product."

The point is not, we think, trivial, for it attaches to the question which continues to occupy us, as to whether "assimilation," as generally used, can be properly regarded as a *sociological* concept. If assimilation is indeed to designate a social *process*, it ought not to be conceptualized in terms of its resulting products; and if it is to refer to a *social* process, then the fixation of its meaning extensions on essentially psychic and cultural variables raises the kind of logical and conceptual difficulties for sociology, on which we commented earlier (see 74-76, *supra*).

Now let us be very explicit in acknowledging, that no concept is an inherently psychological, anthropological, or sociological concept. Nor, of course, does any concept possess an immanent, intrinsic meaning. Without taking too much liberty with Percy Bridgman's (1927: 7) early, and extreme operationalistic admonition, we must agree that ". . . the true meaning of a term is found by observing what a man does with it . . ." and, we would add that its legitimacy within a discipline must be similarly judged by the frame of reference in which it is employed. If the concept had been invoked by deduction from properly *sociological* theory, then there would hardly be any question about is *sociological* legitimacy. We have argued that with respect to assimilation, this condition did not prevail. On the other hand, if the concept was appropriated from biology, through psychology, into sociology without being integrated formally into the latter's established theoretical system, then despite its occurrence *in* sociology (as a primitive term), it would at best be premature to regard assimilation as a concept *of* sociology.

Of course, a frame of reference need not be defined only by its theoretical parameter. But if, alternatively, psychic or cultural factors form the concept's *empirical* base, then its specifically *social* relevance still needs to be formally explicated, and its peculiarly *sociological* propriety remains in question.

We are led, therefore, to the conclusion, admittedly but not improperly that of a "purist," that the concept of assimilation as used in sociology, is not a *sociological* concept. A similar case might of course be made, especially from a "purist's" position, about many concepts in sociology. Optimistically, this condition will resolve itself, as the development and formalization of sociological theory proceed.

Such developments will, no doubt, occur, and through them a less equivocal repertoire of sociologically adequate concepts will emerge. Meanwhile, however, we can not ignore the fact that the relationship between theory, concepts and the empirical base is not simply undirectional. Theory does inform the concepts which it subsumes, but concepts are not simply passive entities. As selectively abstracted symbolizations of empirical phenomena, they are instrumental in lending shape and tone to theory. Indeed, they arrogate an easily underestimated power which tends, particularly in the social sciences, to trigger troublesome theoretical repercussions.

The psychic and cultural specifications in terms of which the assimilation concept has been elaborated in its most frequent usages, entail some very serious implications for sociology, and for sociological theory. The adoption of any given concept must be recognized as *commitment*. It commits the investigator to only a partial sector and a limited facet of the empirical totality, and it narrows his attention to selected and abstracted properties of objects or events. We refer again to Merton's remark, quoted earlier (see 90, *supra*), and to Abraham Kaplan (1964: 46) when he comments that:

Since Kant, we have come to recognize every concept as a rule of judging or acting, a prescription for organizing the materials of experience so as to be able to go on about our business. Everything depends, of course, on what our business is. A "man," for example, is not just a rational animal or a featherless biped, but many different things, different as conceived not only by the soldier, statesman, and scientist, but different even among scientists — different for the economist and the anthropologist, different even for the physical and the cultural anthropologist, and perhaps different according to whether a prehistoric or a contemporary culture is in question, and so endlessly. A concept as a rule of judging or acting is plainly subject to determination by the context in which the judgment is to be made or action taken.

The commitment, then, goes even further than to a narrowed empirical base. The adoption of a particular concept entails a commitment to an *analytic perspective*. And this commitment becomes categorical, if we recall Mannheim's previously quoted statement that "every concept represents a sort of taboo against other possible sources of meaning . . ."

Within the confines of such an analytic perspective, and in terms of it, the various concepts employed must, and usually do, reflect a certain compatibility which lends the perspective its coherence. Indeed, in our effort, earlier, to stay superficially clear of *all* analytic perspectives, we were led to awkward terms in designating the groups involved in an assimilative relationship. To find a genuinely "neutral" term, one that is untinged with the analytic biases that lurk in all designations, is a futile quest.

Thus, if "assimilation" is invoked in its psychological intensions and extensions, the tendency is to conceptualize the groups concerned in essentially psychological (or social-psychological) terms. They are likely to be viewed as "reference groups," as we have seen above; or, following Sumner (1907: 12-13), in terms of "in-groups," and thus "out-groups," or as "we-groups" and "they-groups."[9] Alternatively, if "assimilation" is employed in its cultural meanings, then "ethnic group" (see E. K. Francis, 1947) becomes the logically consistent label which, with the subjective "logic" that inheres in the "host" group's perspective, comes to be ascribed (peculiarly) to the cultural "strangers." Finally, the conceptualization that appears to us as the most appropriately sociological one, is that of "minority group"[10] and its reciprocal of "dominant group." With their implication for the possession of relative social power or of relative access to it, and of the relative ability to *wield* it, these terms appear to be particularly suited to the uniquely social orientation that provides sociology with its *raison d'être*.

Now, before we close our discussion of the contents of the assimilation concept and some of the ramifications of these particular meanings, a few concluding remarks are in order. We have tried to show that "assimilation" is not a theoretical term, that its occurrence in the sociology of race and ethnic relations can not be accounted for by deduction from a body of systematic sociological theory. We have also indicated that "assimilation" is not an empirical term, that it is not a result of direct observation from the world of events. How, then, might the concept of assimilation be properly characterized in the context of sociology?

Herbert Blumer (1954), in a criticism of theory in sociology, attributes its deficiencies basically to the "distressingly vague" and "ambiguous nature of concepts."(5) He points to what he calls a "definitive concept," which "refers precisely to what is common to a class of objects, by the aid of a clear definition in terms of attributes or fixed bench marks" (7). (This is, of course, commonly referred to as an operationally defined concept.) Because in the social world every empirical instance is unique, he continues, "one moves out from the concept to the concrete distinctiveness of the instance instead of embracing the instance in the abstract framework of the concept" (8). Accordingly, Blumer suggests that concepts in sociology are fundamentally sensitizing instruments, and he therefore calls them "sensitizing concepts." "Whereas definitive concepts provide prescriptions of what to see, sensitizing concepts merely suggest directions along which to look" (7).

In view of much that has been said in the course of the preceding discussion, the characterization of "sensitizing concept" would seem to be eminently apt in the case of the assimilation concept. We would reiterate however, that if assimilation is to serve as a *sociological* concept, then an urgent reassessment and reconstruction of its general meaning content is in order. Failing this, the direction along which it suggests we look may lead the sociologist up a psychological or anthropological alley.

III

In the course of our examination of the meaning *contents* of assimilation, we have raised the question whether, in its typical application, assimilation can in fact be regarded as a *sociological* concept. We want now to look at the question in its other emphasis and consider whether, in the role it has assumed or the function it has performed in the context of race and ethnic relations inquiry, assimilation qualifies for the status of a legitimate sociological *concept*.

"Concepts," Max Weber (1949: 106) had asserted, "are primarily analytic instruments for the intellectual mastery of empirical data." According to Gordon DiRenzo (1966: 9) a "concept" is usually taken to mean "a rational representation of universal application which comprehends the essential attributes of a class or logical species of phenomena." Concepts thus function as symbolic representations of phenomena or events. They constitute the structural elements of the thought process which seeks, quite literally, to "come to terms" with phenomenal realities. Thus, as Karl Mannheim points out, fixed categories "give experience its reliable and coherent character" and, to repeat, "every concept represents a sort of taboo against other sources of meaning — simplifying and unifying the manifoldness of life for the sake of action" (Mannheim, 1936: 103, 22).

Now, consistent with their intellectual functions as abstractions from and symbolizations of phenomena, it is important to note that concepts *per se*, and this applies particularly in the case of scientific concepts, perform neither an inherently descriptive role, nor one that is, in and of itself, explanatory. Their function is characteristically designative or indicative. As we have pointed out earlier, concepts prescribe what is to be observed (Merton, 1968: 143), they suggest directions along which to look (Blumer, 1954: 7), they "mark out the paths by which we may move most freely in logical space" (Kaplan, 1964: 52), they are "a way of construing certain contents of experience" (Blumer, 1931: 518).

If then, as DiRenzo warns, scientific concepts are sterile unless they possess both descriptive and explanatory power (DiRenzo, 1966: 13, 16), it would be misleading to infer from this that concepts possess some *intrinsic* capacity for describing or explaining phenomena. A concept's power is derivative. Its descriptive power follows only in consequence of some precise definitional linkage that must first be established with its intended referent; while its explanatory power is a condition of its logical nexus with some theoretical system.

Scientific concepts, then, are not descriptions of empirical phenomena, nor are they explanations of empirical events. *Their precise location in the topography of scientific research places them at the vital juncture where the empirical quest for descriptive data intersects with the theoretical impulse toward explanation.* If their location, between these mutually dependent requisites for scientific inquiry, confers upon concepts a not-to-be-underestimated strategic significance, it does not, thereby, endow them with an autonomous status. Above all, scientific concepts are *contingencies*; they are conditioned by the sobrieties of those selected aspects of the world of events to which they are definitionally attached; and they are informed by the logical directives of the theoretical frame which lends them meaning and cogency.

These matters need to be stated rather explicitly, because problems connected with strictly conceptual issues have received relatively less systematic attention in sociology than have those associated with considerations of a more empirical or of a primarily theoretical nature. If our assessment of the general role of concepts in science is taken seriously,[11] it points to the indispensable function that theory performs in giving direction and specification to the designative role that concepts play in the conduct of inquiry. Indeed, where there is no systematic theory to exert this kind of guidance, or where concepts have been appropriated from outside the discipline without having been formally and systematically integrated into a body of already established theory, concepts remain inert, sterile, and methodologically awkward to accommodate.

In the case of the assimilation concept, as our foregoing discussions should already have suggested, the difficulties of accommodating the notion empirically, theoretically and, consequently methodologically, come to assume major proportions. They engender some fundamental practical problems of application, and raise some critical questions of legitimacy regarding the concept's participation in the process of sociological inquiry.

In tracing the "natural history" of the assimilation idea, we came to label it, once it was admitted into the language of sociology, as an "appropriated" concept.[12] As such, it became part of the rhetoric of sociology, but not, as yet, an integral element of the discipline's formal repertoire of concepts. As a concept *in*, but not *of* sociology, and not withstanding the vagueness and ambiguity which we have seen as characteristic of its meaning intensions and extensions, its popularity in the literature must be interpreted as reflecting wide-spread consensus that "assimilation" has a particular, and indeed, unique applicability to the substantive field of racial and ethnic relations.[13] We have also, however, indicated the general agreement among scholars, that the race relations field is peculiarly devoid of the kind of theory that would warrant its distinctive treatment as a substantive concern apart from general sociology.

Now let us be very clear on one point. That the race relations field, to repeat van den Berghe's phrase, "has no theoretical leg to stand on," hardly means that race relations *research* need be theoretically disengaged or even impoverished, or that it fails to qualify as *grounds* for proper scientific inquiry. The thrust of van den Berghe's criticism is that the so-called field of racial and ethnic relations has no *scientific* warrant to claims as a relatively autonomous, substantive *specialization* in sociology. The point is that the field's theoretical impetus must derive from, and its theoretical yield must accrue back to general sociological theory; that the field of race relations constitutes merely one of many substantive areas of *social* life in which propositions of general theoretical significance in *sociology* may be put to the test.

Unlike "assimilation," the overwhelming majority of concepts that figure prominently or serve vitally in sociological research in race and ethnic relations, are not circumscribed by a unique applicability to this substantive area alone. Their utilization extends through a wide range of sociological "specializations" covering many facets of social life. Virtually any concept might serve as illustration, but the point is perhaps most effectively made by citing Park and Burgess' companion concepts of "assimilation," the three social-process concepts of "competition," "conflict," and "accommodation." Each of these has found fruitful application across several institutional spheres in society, and in a variety of substantive contexts in sociology. It is very likely that the prominence and vitality of such concepts is due precisely to their extensive applicability, which serves to designate for analysis, in a variety of *particular* social contexts, those common variables that are hypothesized to underlie the patterning of similar phenomena in *any* social context.

In striking contrast, the assimilation concept, with its boundaries of applicability seemingly restricted to the area of racial and ethnic relations, stands devoid of theoretical attachment. In the absence of an indigenous or special theory of race relations in which it might participate, and with its

inability to bridge the substantive gap and thus achieve linkage with general sociological theory, "assimilation" becomes,
from the point of view of science, a sterile concept.

Its sterility, or powerlessness, becomes evident in its
effective methodological isolation. Being devoid of theoretical
linkage, "assimilation" remains theoretically uninformed
as to its designative role, and thus unfocused with respect to
its empirical referents. This accounts, in large part, for its
conceptual "fuzziness," or its extraordinary range of denotative attachments, as well as for its connotative plasticity
which permits its conceptualization in the form of psychological adjustment, cultural adaptation or social structural
integration. To the extent that the assimilation concept lacks
descriptive precision, it also lacks explanatory power. Its
failure to achieve crisp, unitary empirical specification, compounded with its lack of theoretical integration, simply
renders the concept theoretically unproductive.

In the light of these considerations we are led to conclude
that the notion of assimilation can neither be regarded as a
properly *sociological* concept, nor can it be considered
as a legitimate sociological *concept*. Yet, as we have tried to
show, the assimilation idea became firmly ensconced in the
sociology of racial and ethnic relations, and came to figure
prominently in its research agendas over the period under
consideration. Moreover, it did so to the extent of not only
becoming a dominant concept in the field, but of gradually
coming to serve as its central, guiding motif. In view of some
of the points raised in the preceding discussion, this must
appear as rather astonishing in a scientific discipline, and we
shall direct our attention toward accounting for it in the
following chapter.

Notes

1.   If this distinction between *social* theory and *social* analysis is
      granted, then *sociology* proper would characteristically employ
      concepts that attach, in systematic fashion, to both their

relevant theoretic frame and their appropriate empirical referent. Accordingly, *sociological* theory involves explanation on the *basis of empirical evidence*, and *sociological* analysis comprises empirical investigation *in the light of theory*. Both, of course, proceed through the mediating realm of concepts.

2.   It is with this thought in mind, that we made a point all along, of speaking of assimilation as a concept *in* sociology, rather than as a concept *of* sociology — or a sociological concept.

3.   The labels "host," "core," and, especially, "reciprocal" group are indeed awkward terms. But their use here is deliberate, and points up a problem of terminological neutrality or bias, which we shall indicate (see 96-97, *infra*).

4.   Convergence, of course, suggests a mutual rapprochement, while adjustment implies conformity on a unilateral basis. Gordon refers to these, respectively, as the "Melting Pot theory" and the "Anglo-Conformity theory" of assimilation. He suggests that it is quite likely that the latter has been "the most prevalent ideology of assimilation in America throughout the nation's history." See Gordon (1964: 89).

5.   We can only touch upon this very briefly here. For an excellent critical review of this aspect of the social-psychological literature, see John Harding, Bernard Kutner, Harold Proschansky, and Isidor Chein (1954).

6.   If, as we believe, Gordon is correct in regarding the "Anglo-Conformity" assimilation ideology as the more prevalent in America, then this parenthetical qualification becomes redundant. Differences *per se*, ethnocentrically perceived, tend to become negatively evaluated distinctions.

Pierre L. van den Berghe points out that this kind of "cultural assimilation is a proof, not of liberalism, but rather of ethnocentrism and cultural (though *not* of racial) arrogance" on the part of the dominant group. See van den Berghe (1970: 70).

7.   See for example the delightful and comprehensive treatment of the relationship between what we say and what we do by Irwin Deutscher (1973).

8.   An analytically more fruitful distinction, not often made by sociologists, might be maintained if "acculturation" were reserved for the *unilateral* adaptation by only one of the groups involved; while "assimilation" be set aside for a condition of *mutual* cultural rapprochement.

9.   The terms are generally traced to Charles Horton Cooley and his discussion of "we-feelings" in primary groups. See Cooley (1912: 23-24, 29-31). However, they were also used by Sumner, who spoke of "we-groups" and "others-groups."

10.   The introduction of the term is generally traced to Donald Young (1932).

11.   We are consciously ignoring here the many *types* of concepts in

science that might be distinguished, and their several distinctive
functions that might be identified. For example, in the course of
the symposium of which the DiRenzo essay, referred to above, is
a part, at least fourteen types of concepts, distinguished along
several different dimensions, are examined. For our purposes, the
preceding more general treatment appears sufficient.

12. On the problem of conceptual integration of such appropriated
     terms, in addition to Richard S. Rudner's discussion cited in
     Chapter 3 (*supra*), see also the treatment of "borrowed terms" in
     Hans L. Zetterberg (1965: 49ff).

13. The Nisbet and Warren articles, discussed in Chapter 3 (71-72,
     supra), stand as striking exceptions which, as the cliché goes,
     "prove" the rule.

PART III

*Ideology and Theory
in Race and Ethnic Relations*

CHAPTER 5

The Entrenchment of Assimilation and its Normative Nexus

I

However questionable its role as a specifically *sociological* concept, and however untenable its status as even a properly scientific *concept* may be, the fact remains that the notion of assimilation has been the central topical concern in the sociology of racial and ethnic relations since the nineteen-thirties. Except for a very recent, and as yet somewhat hesitant reassertion of a conflict approach to such group relationships, the study of racial and ethnic relations has been overwhelmingly concentrated on matters relating to the description or measurement of assimilation. How is it possible, we must therefore ask, that a scientific discipline can sustain for more than three decades the study of assimilation as a *substantive* concern which, in view of a demonstrable theoretical vacuum, remains disengaged from the kind of facility for focal direction, hypothesis derivation, interpretive orientation, and cumulative growth, which only formal theoretical linkage affords? How can it be, moreover, that assimilation as a *concept* can thrive for so long in such an atheoretical context, especially when its only demonstrable theoretical affinities extend to (social) psychology or to primarily anthropological thoughtways?

One answer might be suggested by pointing to the partially

coinciding developmental period in American sociology, when intensive concentration was lavished on narrow questions of precision in descriptive and quantitative techniques. Issues of theorizing, and broader problems of methodology that probe the roots of a scientific logic of inquiry were, for the most part, set aside. The preoccupation with "securing its scientific methods" and "engaging in abstracted empiricism" has been amply documented by, among others, Hinkle and Hinkle (1954: 18-43), and criticized by none more devastatingly than C. Wright Mills (1955: 50-75). However, this answer quickly fades into implausibility in the light of the imprecision, ambiguity and opacity which, we have tried to document, continued to plague the notion of assimilation throughout even this period of concerted efforts toward setting sociology's empirico-inductive house in order. While general sociology eventually proceeded to develop in the direction of gradual empirico-theoretic integration, the field of race and ethnic relations continued to amass, for the most part, discrete, theoretically impoverished, descriptive accounts of assimilation and the statistically correlated conditions of its enhancement or inhibition.

An alternative explanation, and one that gains support from our analysis of the content of the assimilation concept and the kind of meaning patterns it encompasses, can be advanced with the argument that the concept is not, in fact, theoretically isolated. It derives its meaning pattern, its analytic thrust and its empirical focus not from *sociological* theory, but instead through its logical interdependence with systems of psychological and anthropological theory. Accordingly, its conceptual validity would be in question only insofar as it is challenged in the context of *sociological* inquiry. Since, however, its sociological validity is precisely what we are questioning, and since the concept of assimilation has been typically invoked as an ostensibly sociological concept, this explanation begs the question we have raised.

The answer to the question, we believe, rests in several points that we have developed in the course of this inquiry. Let us first recall a major prerequisite for even the possibility of a science, the capacity of disengagement from a common-sense world view. In sociology, we have suggested, this requires an intellectual disentanglement from those routinized perceptions and conventionalized conceptions of events and their interconnectedness, which give shape and meaning to what has come to be spoken of as "culture." The fact that assessments of these "realities" vary, sometimes radically, from culture to culture, from era to era, and even among some observers who participate in the same culture-time, lends support to the suspicion that "reality" is "read" into, not out of the world of events.[1] Another way of stating this is through the recognition that all "reality" is socially constructed. Such social constructions of reality represent shared symbolic fabrications which make individual and collective social life possible.

However indispensable the social construction of reality is in ordering and conferring meaning upon men's lives, it tends to neutralize a sociology that misapprehends its own relationship to it, and fails to reconstruct it into accordance with its own analytic imperatives. The social construction of reality constitutes part of what sociology seeks to study, part of its data, a facet of its *objects* of knowledge. To the extent, however, that it is permitted to shape sociology's mode of knowing, to determine its cognitive categories, or to define the discipline's *own* perspectives on social events, it compromises sociology's *raison d'être* and negates its promise. In place of the sociological imagination (Mills, 1955: 5-18, 212-217) it substitutes social conventionality, sociological interpretation is reduced to social analysis, and the quest for cumulative scientific knowledge is bartered away for a compendium of discrete information. In short, sociology becomes coopted by, and coterminous with common sense.

The concept of assimilation, we have concluded, does not represent a theoretical term in sociology, since it is not deducible from (nor, it appears, attachable to) a body of systematic sociological theory. It also does not satisfy the criteria of an empirical or observational term in sociology, since it refers to complex processes or outcomes that are the products of considerable intellectual abstraction from primary, directly observable social facts. Very much like perhaps the majority of concepts in sociology, assimilation is in the first instance an appropriated term; but unlike most of these, it has never been effectively specified, properly formalized and theoretically engaged into the apparatus of systematic sociology. Accordingly, assimilation must be recognized in its identity as a *social* concept, part of a *social* construction of reality.

It appears to us as vital for the sociological endeavor, that the distinction between a social and a sociological concept be fully grasped and effectively implemented. As we have indicated in Chapter 1, among laymen the distinction appears to be largely lost, and too often it remains unobserved even among sociologists.

What is at issue, of course, is not some essential, or intrinsic attribute on the basis of which social and sociological concepts might be sorted out, but rather the implications of their *extrinsic* relationships with the respective intellectual frames in which they participate. The significance of these frames becomes readily apparent, if we recall their directive influence on otherwise "powerless" concepts, guiding them in their designative function of illuminating a particular facet of a considerably more intricate and complex reality, and endowing them with potential toward explanation. In recognition of this relationship, we had characterized the adoption of a concept as a kind of commitment, actually a two-directional one. In the direction of greater concreteness, it limits the observational field by focusing on particular properties of only certain select empirical phenomena; and in the direction of higher abstraction, it restricts the potentially available integrating intellectual structures to a minimum number of those relevant ones, that remain conceptually compatible.[2]

In a significant sense, then, concepts are "locked in" as mediating symbols between a "real" world of empirical events and an abstract ideational structure through which that world is apprehended and interpreted. Inasmuch as any one of these ideational structures focuses only on a limited aspect of some total reality, we are justified in referring to them as *perspectives*, as points of view, each of which constitutes only one of a number of possible alternative modes of construing reality.

In distinguishing social from sociological concepts, then, we are discriminating principally between broad orders of symbolic elements that pertain to, and support, two significantly distinct perspectives on reality. Each may, and indeed does, subsume numerous, often competitive reality constructions of its own, but the processes by which each of their respective fabrications are negotiated are sufficiently distinct as to warrant their categorical differentiation into a (popular) social construction of reality, and a (scientific) sociological construction of reality. The latter, moreover, properly represents a *re*construction of the former since, as we endeavored to show in the opening chapter, the emergence of a science occurs typically in conjunction with a conceptual transformation ("putting on a different thinking-cap"), which takes its departure from the prevailing common-sense ordering of events.

In certain respects, this transformation is closely comparable to the "paradigm shifts," which Thomas Kuhn (1962: 110-134) has associated with the advent of revolutions in science.[3] In suggesting this parallel between Kuhn's "paradigms" and our "reality constructions" (and in a limited sense they are perhaps more synonymous than merely analogous), we seek to emphasize the logical and methodological impropriety of naively transposing concepts from one paradigm or reality construction, to another. In the case of either, concepts serve as integral elements of an intellectual structure to which they lend coherence and upon which their meanings are predicated. Their transfer (without respecification and formalization) would render them at best harmlessly irrelevant, and in the more serious instances, disruptive to the coherence of their new context.

There is, however, an additional ground for remaining mindful of preserving the distinction between social and sociological concepts. While differences between competing paradigms in science are, as Kuhn observes, "both necessary and irreconcilable" to the point of rendering the paradigms "incommensurable" (1962: 102, 149), once the scientific

revolution has occurred, by definition the insurgent paradigm will have categorically supplanted its earlier and less
adequate competitor. As the now defunct paradigm recedes
into the annals of the History of Science, its constituent
concepts also become relics that are unlikely, at least in their
original, now often "quaint" conceptualization, to coexist
and compete with those of the ascendant paradigm.[4] In this
respect, the relationship between a social and a sociological
construction of reality departs significantly from that characterizing successive scientific paradigms, at least as reflected
in Kuhn's ideal-typical formulation. A social construction of
reality must remain similarly incommensurable with a sociological reconstruction of reality, but unlike the supersession
among scientific paradigms, they *coexist* as distinct reality
constructions, either in a complementary or a dialectic
relationship.[5] Significantly, they do *not* compete with one
another in terms of such criteria as superior cogency or
better "fit." Very simply, the social construction of reality
and its sociological reconstruction serve the rather distinct
purposes of their respective fabricators, and constitute
differential *interpretive levels* for the apprehension of reality.[6]

In the light of this recognition, it becomes particularly
vital for the integrity of the sociological perspective that, to
the fullest extent possible, an effective segregation be maintained between its constituent concepts and those popular
lay terms that would contaminate it and reduce its analytic
sights to the level of social analysis. Although expressed in
the context of a somewhat different issue, Ronald Dore's
comment (1961: 850-851) appears particularly apt in this
connection: "There is no more reason for the sociologist to
adopt for his thinking *about* society the terms used for
thinking *in* society (to take, in other words, his analytical
tools straight out of his data) than there is for a carpenter
to use nothing but wooden saws."

Armed with these several considerations respecting the
nature of the assimilation concept and the distinctive reality
constructions that support the popular and the sociological
perspectives toward the on-going world of events, we should
now be prepared to respond to the questions that were posed

in the opening paragraph of this chapter.

The sustained and pervasive sociological attention accorded the substantive issue of assimilation becomes explicable, once it is recognized that the failure of the assimilation concept to enter into coherence with systematic sociological theory is compensated by its linkage, instead, with an interpretive perspective attached to an extra-sociological, popular frame of reference. In its role as a *social* concept, part of a *social* construction of reality, the appropriation of "assimilation" into sociology involves not merely the innocuous transfer of a discrete term. Just as the sociological construction of reality is not a simple, mechanical collage of isolated conceptual elements, so the social construction of reality also constitutes a *Gestalt*, an interpretive configuration, that tends toward coherence and internal consistency. The transposition of conceptual elements from one of these constructions to the other, therefore, entails a concomitant transfer of perspectivistic implications that serve to corrupt, or at least to compromise the integrity of the configuration into which they are injected. This problem assumes particularly aggravated proportions when, as we have argued is the case in this instance, the respective reality constructions reflect perspectives that function at disparate interpretive levels.

The tenacious preoccupation with assimilation in sociology is occasioned, we submit, not because assimilation represents a *scientifically* provocative instance of social process, but because it constitutes a *programmatically attractive option for social policy*. It is informed, not through a *logical* connection with an impelling theoretical system, but by an *ideo*logical extension from a compelling sociopolitical commitment.

From the time of its early establishment by Park and Burgess as a fundamental category of social process in sociology, through its more recent intensive reassessment by Milton Gordon, the notion of assimilation has never strayed far from the level of its socially ascribed meanings, or lost much of its programmatic implications.

Park and Burgess had noted that the popular usage of

"assimilation" derives its meaning from the American immigration experience, and refers to the process of Americanization[7] as expressed by "Zangwill's dramatic parable of 'The Melting Pot' " (1921: 734; see also Zangwill, 1909). Their "sociological" notion of assimilation does not appear to depart significantly from its popular, social specification as a "magic crucible," except insofar as, by linking assimilation with the "Social Orders" of "Personality" and "The Cultural Heritage" (see 39, *supra*), they launch the term into a conceptual current which, given the proclivities of its subsequent users, guided "assimilation" into the harbors of predominantly psychological and cultural meanings. It remains to his credit that Park, himself (1950: 204-220), firmly linked assimilation processes, which he was inclined to view as universal and inevitable (see Metzger, 1971: 631-632), to genuinely sociological issues of the transformation of social structures. Moreover, as Everett Hughes points out with regard to Park's broader conception of race relations as a field of sociological inquiry, "Park's definition makes study of race relations a part of the study of society itself, *not a peculiar problem requiring special concepts for its analysis*" (Hughes, 1963: 879-880, italics added). Nevertheless, the foundations Park laid tended to get lost, and the bulk of sociological preoccupation with assimilation served to obscure any direct and peculiarly sociological significance which the concept might sustain.

The unreconstructed transposition of a popular, social conception of assimilation into its analytic role as a conceptual tool in sociology is apparent also in Gordon's otherwise impressive effort to achieve order among the multiple meanings and applications of "assimilation." In the light of our conviction of the need for analytic dissociation of a social construction of reality from its sociological reconstruction, and our insistence that each of these conceptualizations implies a necessarily unique interpretive and explanatory system, Milton Gordon makes a somewhat remarkable statement (1964: 84, italics added):

Although the relatively brief span of American history to date has been in the main a period whose story must be told within the setting of colonization and immigration, and although the 41 million immigrants who have come to America since the founding of the nation constitute the largest population transfer of its kind in the history of the world, remarkably little explicit attention has been given *by the American people to devising or discussing theoretical models which either would formulate the preferred goals of adjustment to which this influx of diverse peoples might be expected to look for guidance, or would describe the processes of adjustment as they empirically have taken place.*

Accordingly, Gordon proceeds to elaborate, what he chooses to call, three "Theories of Assimilation." He states that these distinctive conceptions arise out of ". . . *'philosophies,'* or *goal-systems* of assimilation, [which] have grouped themselves around three main axes . . . [or] central *ideological tendencies* . . ." (85, italics added), specifically "Anglo-Conformity," "Melting Pot," and "Cultural Pluralism."

It is in these passages from Gordon, that the continuity against which we have argued — the unobstructed interchangeability of conceptions between social and sociological perspectives — receives perhaps its most tangible expression in the extensive literature on assimilation.

Granted, that the relationships between knowledge and the objects of knowledge, between the analytic probe and its substantive target, between the solution of scientific problems and the resolution of human problems, between Sociology and Social Life, still await their definitive formulation. Gordon's formulation, however, tends in the direction of confounding, rather than illuminating these relationships. It provokes the question of whether it is really incumbent upon, or even realistic, on any grounds, to expect "the American people" (i.e. laymen) to engage in "devising or discussing theoretical models" — and if so, whether the terms "theoretical" and "model" would retain any resemblance to their technical meanings and strategic functions in the context of science. Do science and sociology, one must ask, or does social life, for that matter, really work like that?

Gordon clearly indicates his recognition that the three "theories" of assimilation rest upon *socially* defined "philosophies," "goal-systems" and "ideological tendencies." His ensuing analysis becomes an assessment, through the seven "assimilation variables" mentioned earlier, of the extent to which the historical record supports each of these "theories." Since, however, the assimilation "theories" embrace philosophies, goal-systems and ideological tendencies, and thus do not rise above the level of *social* conceptions, it appears that the issue in its *sociological* dimensions has not been broached. From the point of view of sociology, they constitute spurious theories, and as such do nothing to dispel the theoretical vacuum that impoverishes this field.

The persistence and the prevalence of concerns with assimilation in the American sociology of racial and ethnic relations, we must conclude, rests on the perception of assimilation as an American Social Problem and its acknowledgment as an American Dilemma. Assimilation research, although conducted under the auspices of sociology, is informed and impelled less by the categorical imperatives lodged in the structure of scientific explanation, than by the normative impulses that animate the quest for social reform.

II

Before proceeding to the next chapter, a few comments are in order, setting forth in summary form our appraisal of the assimilation idea in its conceptual role in the sociology of racial and ethnic relations.

Our analysis has addressed itself to the relatively unexplored realm of concepts in sociology, and we have suggested that this realm occupies a logical space at the juncture of sociological concerns with methods proper, and those that focus on matters of theory. It would be hard to overestimate the strategic importance of the conceptual realm in the conduct of scientific inquiry, since conceptualization flawed by vagueness, by ambiguity, by opacity, or by perspectivistic bias invites repercussions that travel up the inductive chain to effect fallacious explanation, as well as reverberations that transport down deductively to provoke faulty observation.

In sociology, questions of proper scientific conceptualization are particularly beset with difficulties, because the relationship between the social and the sociological, between the objects of knowledge and the knowledge itself, appears especially elusive, tenuous and intellectually challenging. That in sociology this relationship mirrors, *in principle*, its counterpart in the natural sciences, does not seem, today, to be a matter of controversy among sociologists, whether they align with one or another version of *"Verstehen"* schools or with those of the more Positivist persuasion. What *is* a matter of contention, and what indeed spearates these schools, is not their perception of the relationship between sociology and social life *in principle*, but rather their strategies for scientific confrontation of this relationship *in practice*, in short, their respective methodologies.

We have suggested that the difficulty of negotiating between the substance of social life and a sociology purporting to illuminate it, is complicated by the strains experienced by the sociologist who is at once a participant in, and a dispassionate analyst of the objects of sociological knowledge. The implication that inheres in Roy G. Francis' apt observation (1961: 7) that "The scientist is a marginal man; he emerges from a common-sense culture and partakes of a special one," weighs even more heavily upon the sociologist. Psychologically and socially bound to a synthetic common-sense perspective, and intellectually and professionally committed to an analytic scientific perspective, he is obliged to shuttle between two coexisting levels of abstraction[8] through which social reality is, respectively, experienced and interpreted. We have elaborated these alternative perspectives in terms of the social construction of reality, and the sociological reconstruction of socially construed reality.

In order to explore the problems of conceptualization in sociology more tangibly, we have directed our analytic attention to one particular concept, the notion of assimilation. This selection was guided by our belief that, especially in this instance, the failure of a socially defined substantive issue to achieve proper reconstruction into a sociologically appropriate conceptualization, has been instrumental in compromising sociological knowledge about the social patterning and development of race relations phenomena.

Accordingly, the notion of assimilation was traced from its presociological meaning intensions and extensions in the technical languages of biology and psychology, and through its popular usages in the "natural" language, to its adoption as an appropriated term in sociology. Following its establishment, by Park and Burgess, as one of four basic social-process concepts in sociology in general, an analysis of the assimilation literature led to two significant basic recognitions. First, Park and Burgess' early linkage of assimilation with the two "social structures" of Personality and The Cultural Heritage led to its conceptual specification in almost exclusively psychological and cultural terms, and cast the research it inspired into frames of reference that were more legitimately social-psychological and anthropological in their jurisdictions, than strictly sociological. Secondly, among the four social-process concepts, assimilation, unlike competition, conflict or accommodation, had the peculiar limitation of being applicable exclusively to phenomena embraced by the special field of racial and ethnic relations; and furthermore, within that field, it was assimilation, practically to the exclusion of the other three processes, that attracted the overwhelming share of analytic attention for some three to four decades following the publication of Park and Burgess' statement.

Our examination of the assimilation literature led us to conclude that although assimilation served extensively as a concept *in* sociology, there are substantial grounds for questioning its logical legitimacy and its methodological efficacy as a concept *of* sociology. Its most prevalent specification in terms of psychological variables, or in terms of cultural ones, inclines assimilation in the direction of a logically more defensible and analytically more promising conceptual linkage with psychological or with anthropological theory, than toward integration with systematic theory in sociology. Moreover, in view of the generally conceded absence of theory in the sociology of racial and ethnic relations as such, the already mentioned limitation of applicability of the assimilation concept to this field, virtually precludes its attachment to any significant indigenous theoretical frame.

Consequently, "assimilation" is revealed as an essentially unreconstructed social concept, barren of theoretically meaningful, explanatory implications. Assimilation research, conducted nominally within the framework of sociology, tends more realistically to become social analysis, whose contribution lies in historically-specific or longitudinal *demographic* accounts,[9] or in group-comparative *descriptions* of accelerated or attenuated assimilation patterns and their psychological or cultural correlates.

In terms of our more general interest in the problems of conceptualization in sociology, our analysis afforded an insight into the unrelenting strain toward intrusion, that normative factors exert *vis à vis* the conduct of sociological inquiry. The adoption of a concept, we have suggested, necessarily constitutes a commitment, one that not only ascribes boundaries on empirical reality by defining the proper range of relevance, but a commitment also to a particular analytic perspective. Where appropriated concepts fail to be properly formalized into an established theoretical frame, or where there is, in fact, no body of established theory in terms of which an appropriated concept can be sociologically reconstructed and thus scientifically legitimated, such concepts continue to be governed by the extra-sociological considerations in terms of which they were originally defined. Under these circumstances, and this obtains especially in the case of assimilation, the concept's *social* meanings, freighted with value implications, policy commitments and ideological encumbrances, structure the analytic perspective through which research is pursued. While an analytic perspective that is deduced from a legitimate theoretical frame would be logically defensible and methodologically sound, one that intrudes concomitantly with the appropriation of an unreconstructed social concept is at least ideologically suspect and typically normatively compromising.

On these grounds, then, the normative issue must be raised in the sociology of racial and ethnic relations, and we shall undertake a consideration of this problem in the following chapter.

Notes

1.   For a fundamental analysis of the conditions underlying the construction of diverse realities, see the excellent monograph by Burkart Holzner (1968). See also Berger and Luckmann (1966).

2.   Probably few, if any concepts, even in the physical sciences, are so precisely specified and narrow in scope, that only one interpretive or explanatory frame, unchallenged by competing ones, lends itself as applicable.

3.   For a clarification of what he means by "paradigm," see Kuhn, 1962: 10-11, 23-30, and *passim*. See also Robert W. Friedrichs (1970: 1-10).

4.   This paradigmatic succession, as Kuhn describes it (perhaps in somewhat idealized form) in the history of the natural sciences, is not characteristic of sociology. As a discipline marked by sustained theoretical eclecticism, its paradigms, to the extent that they come to prominence as ruling paradigms at all, more typically do so through only temporary neglect of their competitor(s), rather than through their compelling triumph in the face of shattering anomalies. On the applicability of Kuhn's conception to sociology, see Friedrichs (1970: 11-56).

5.   Whether the relationship is complementary or dialectic probably turns on the recency of a science's emergence from prevailing conventional reality constructions. The polemic tone that tended to characterize the emergence of sociology — Durkheim's early adamance on the reality of social facts readily comes to mind — was clearly indicative of the discipline's dialectic relation to conventional wisdom. It is probably the advent of a technology, which marks the shift from dialectics to complementarity. A successful technology, whatever else it may offer, plays a mediating role between the two reality constructions. Although far from interpreting to a lay public the more esoteric concerns that animate a science, technology does represent a link with science to which the conventional culture base can relate *on its own terms*.

When a technology has developed to that stage, it can serve to promote the *social* legitimation of the science that feeds it. At that point, the competitive reality constructions that appeared *antithetical* and stood in a dialectic relation to one another, come to be viewed as *alternative* reality constructions which, while remaining unsynthesized, sustain complementary relations.

6. Karl Mannheim has pointed out (1936: 22) that "in every concept, in every concrete meaning, there is contained a crystallization of the experiences of a certain group." Of course, he was referring specifically to structurally differentiated groups whose respective socio-historical situations impose on them distinctive experiences and commit them to their diverse interests. Each group's conceptual fabrications therefore represent, on the one hand, the crystallizations of their particular collective experiences, and on the other hand, an appropriate vesting of these experiences with shared meanings, thus ". . . simplifying and unifying the manifoldness of life for the sake of action" (*loc. cit.*).

    Mannheim's understanding of the nature and functions of concepts lends itself to our distinction between social and sociological concepts. Accordingly, *social* concepts and their concrete meanings represent the collective fabrications of a community of men in society, who engage the crystallization of their common social experience for the sake of action toward negotiating their social reality; the fabrication of *sociological* concepts must be predicated on a crystallization of the critico-analytic experiences of the community of sociologists, and harnessed to research for the sake of distilling scientific knowledge *about* social life. As distinctly situated communities with different experiences and divergent aims, their conceptualizations, their reality constructions, their concepts and meanings, even their modes of thought, while coexistent, are not coextensive, and do not reduce one to the other.

    The consequent discontinuity between social and sociological conceptions forms the basis for recurring controversies over the claimed "imperatives" of either preserving the vital integrity, or for transcending the false dichotomy, between contemplation and action, between theory and praxis. At the same time, the disjunction between the social and the sociological turns out to be imperfect, since it is in fact transversed by normative considerations which result in part from the common "natural" language in which their distinct conceptualizations tend to be couched, and in part from the sociologists' actual participation in both communities. This less-than-total hiatus, in turn, gives rise to the sustained debates over, first, the very possibility, and then the actual desirability, of value-neutrality in sociology.

7. The authors point out, however, that its "negative" version, that of "denationalization," describes more accurately the typical European pattern of forcible incorporation of minor cultural groups. Park and Burgess (1921: 734).

8. On the notion of distinctive levels at which the formations of

common-sense and scientific thought occur, see the two discussions by Alfred Schutz in (1953: 1-37) and (1954: 269-270).

9.   It is interesting, in this connection, to note that the sociological study of population and research on race have frequently been treated as a combined specialization by departments of sociology and by writers of early textbooks. Floyd House, for example, while recognizing some grounds for their separation, goes on to treat them conjointly in his review of research developments in various specialized areas. See Floyd Nelson House (1936: 345-354). Similarly, based on a survey of nearly 200 sociologists in the United States in 1942, M. C. Elmer was led to classify the *joint* field of "Race Relations and Population" as the second most cited category of "points of emphasis in sociology." See Elmer (1956: 196-204).

CHAPTER 6

Reality Constructions:
Theoretical and Ideological
Perspectives

I

Science is an enterprise that always, and by its nature, assumes a sustained posture of confrontation. This confrontation, as we indicated in the opening chapter, is actually two-pronged and directed toward readily distinguishable targets. On the one side it confronts "nature," the entirety of physical, chemical, biological, psychological, social, or what-have-you "realities" that academic disciplines are disposed to compartmentalize for purposes that include, one may assume, the more effective attainment of knowledge; and in science, as we noted, the *quest* for knowledge becomes coincident with the assumption of power toward transforming the *objects* of knowledge. We seek to know nature in order to "torture" nature, Bacon had said.

In its other confrontations, science maintains something of a contentious stance with respect to commonly accepted *"knowledge"* about nature. To the conventional, common-sense ordering of events, it counterposes an initially novel, often outrageous conception which, even once it is (scientif-ically) institutionalized, persists as a continuingly contra-puntal, *socially* unorthodox conceptual organization. As a scientific discipline, sociology can afford to be and to do nothing less. Its continued existence depends upon its capacity

123

to exercise, what Mills has called, the sociological imagination, and its vitality is fed, as Robert S. Lynd (1964: 202-250) has suggested, by at least occasionally, if not indeed systematically, entertaining some outrageous hypotheses. A sociology that approaches and accepts the social world on social terms, that fails to sociologically reconstruct, and instead takes for granted, the prevailing social construction of reality, abdicates one of its vital professional as well as intellectual obligations: that of confronting the culturally accumulated convictions by sustaining an institutional posture of detached and unremitting skepticism.

In the preceding chapters we have attempted to show that in the field of race and ethnic relations, and specifically to the extent that within this field the notion of assimilation has been accorded primacy as a conceptual tool and as a substantive research focus over several decades, such a confrontational stance has failed to materialize. In proportion to this failure, the field has been described as innocent of sociological theory, and we have characterized assimilation research as more typically descriptively-oriented social analysis, than explanation-prompting sociological inquiry.

In the present chapter, we wish to direct our attention to some important questions pertaining to the relationship between the *reality* of race relations as social events, and the *sociology* of race relations as the discipline professing to illuminate those events. In particular, we want to explore some normative considerations that structure the sociological enterprise and serve to inform the assimilation idea, thus bearing serious ideological consequences for the general orientation of sociology, the more typical commitments of sociologists, and the juncture of both in the sociology of racial and ethnic relations.

II

Our analysis has led to some rather critical judgments about the notion of assimilation in sociology in general, and about the nature of its participation in the structure of race relations research more particularly. We have come to see that, as an appropriated term, its mode of conceptual implementation has made "assimilation" sociologically inappropriate on several grounds and we have characterized it as a concept in, but not of sociology. Two related considerations figured prominently among the factors that led to this determination. One was the essentially psychological and cultural meaning patterns in terms of which assimilation was elaborated, thus virtually excluding its seemingly more appropriate specification, in sociology, in terms of strictly social variables that attach to structural issues and invite historical treatment. The other consideration attached to the concept's profoundly atheoretical character, its failure to support continuity with a guiding frame of legitimately sociological theory.

In view of its substantively restricted application to the theoretically barren area of race and ethnic relations, the assimilative notion's theoretical disengagement has been compensated for by its attachment, instead, to what may aptly be called an *Assimilationist Perspective*. This characterization, and its implication for a sociology of race and ethnic relations, warrants a somewhat closer examination.

We have seen that the implementation of *any* concept represents a kind of restrictive covenant, a tacit agreement to selectively limit and, indeed, prescribe what is to be observed out of the emperical totality, and what, conversely, is to be deemed irrelevant for the purpose at hand. Moreover, to the extent that we can say that concepts impose boundaries of relevance on the world of events (which must be assumed to be of-a-piece), so we can similarly regard theories as staking out intellectual confines upon the presumably continuous fabric of on-going events. Indeed, we imply just that when we speak of conceptual or of theoretical *frames*. In this sense, then, all concepts entail and bring into relief, and all theories project into illuminated focus, a circumscribed substantive and a narrowed analytic perspective. It is on such perspectives that we now concentrate our attention.

Any effort to confront the welter of empirical events, whether it is pursued formally and systematically through science, or casually and more intuitively in social life, proceeds through some sort of orienting cognitive structure. Such structures offer a relatively coherent point of view in terms of which events may be apprehended, and through which reasonably orderly analysis and interpretation become feasible. But the interpretive efficiency, the sharpness of focus which a particular point of view affords by muting the dissonances that would otherwise accrue from the simultaneous assumption of a variety of distinct cognitive vantage points (or of undifferentiated ones), is purchased at the price of an at least provisionally narrowed, parochial, "single-minded" approach to events.[1]

The elements that lend structure to such broad cognitive frames, and serve as their most proximate points of contact with the empirical world are, of course, concepts. Whether, in a given case, it is formally recognized or not, concepts and such broader orienting structures entertain a necessary, and far from arbitrary relation to one another. In science as we suggested earlier, a concept's power, including its logical facility for prompting explanation and its empirical capacity for designating some property of objects or events, is contingent upon the directive guidance exerted by the theoretical frame to which it attaches. Failure to support such linkage would render the concept theoretically sterile, methodologically intractable and empirically arbitrary.

It is, of course, not only in science that concepts support a necessary linkage with some broader orienting structure. This relationship is paralleled in common-sense modes of coming to terms, intellectually, as well as experientially, with the world of events. The meaning and the designative power of popular concepts is similarly a condition of the cognitive frames in which they participate. In the absence of such meaning-conferring structures, popular concepts become, quite literally, nonsense terms. Some such orienting framework, therefore, of either a formally theoretical type as in science, or of a more popular, or common- sense sort which is not legitimately equatable with scientific theory, is indispensable. One or another point of view is invariably invoked, consciously or not, as a concomitant of employing a particular concept (see Mannheim, 1936: 103).

Now, when we speak of such meaning-conferring structures, cognitive frames or, as we have been referring to them in the broadest sense, social constructions of reality, we need to be quite clear as to just how they relate to what we conceive of as sociological theory. Any confrontation of "reality" in a given culture always occurs *in terms* of that culture or, more precisely, *through terms* (concepts) which, as symbolic fabrications, have been collectively negotiated, socially legitimated, and diffused and transmitted as cognitive and valuational syntheses that lie at the core of a particular cultural heritage. As cultural taken-for-granteds, such constructions constitute what Mannheim seems to refer to when he speaks of "total ideologies" (1936: 265-266), and bear close similarity to Alvin Gouldner's notion of "domain assumptions" (Gouldner, 1970: 29-35). The greater the complexity of a society, as reflected through such indicators as an elaborate division of labor, a proliferation of interest groups, wide social differentation and an extensive range of social stratification, a multiplication of so-called sub-cultures, and so forth, the more profuse the variety of group-specific reality constructions that a culture will embrace.

The reality construction we call "science" in general, with its domain assumptions, its synthesis of cognitive and evaluational stipulations, must be regarded as just one such construction which coexists with alternative reality constructions in contemporary society in either complementary or dialectic relations, as we suggested earlier. The same holds, of course, for sociology as a merely more jurisdictionally circumscribed but essentially consonant reality construction within science. All such reality constructions, then, are primarily *perspectives* through which the world of events is viewed and interpreted and, eventually, acted upon. Social and sociological reality constructions are necessarily distinctive perspectives; but as they are encompassed within a common cultural tradition and similarly informed through its fundamental, incontrovertible, collectively shared suppositions, the latter are not, and cannot be culturally alien, lest they appear, literally, as *nonsense*. If sociological reality constructions thus do not consitute cultural *non*-sense, they

also cannot be considered *common*-sense for that is what, in
a given culture, defines the widely shared *social* constructions
of reality. Like any scientific reality constructions, sociological ones must be marked by systematic and calculated
*un*common-sense in the form of, as we have argued all along,
a scientific *re*construction of the prevailing social constructions of reality.

The guiding motif for such a reconstruction must emanate
from sociological theory which, following Gouldner, eventu-
ates in relation to its own subtheoretical beliefs and sentiments, or "infrastructure" (Gouldner, 1970: 46-47). Yet,
interestingly as well as disconcertingly, the role of sociological *theory* in the generation of *sociological* constructions
of reality finds somewhat of a parallel in the role that *ideology* plays in the formation of *social* constructions of reality;
and both theory and ideology represent, each in its own way,
more or less tentative or provisional *interpretations* of the
social world or some dimension of it. In view of the similar
functions sociological theory and ideology perform in sociology and social life, respectively, they sustain a troublesome
affinity, and their functional *comparability* tends to invite
their uncritical misapprehension in terms of functional
equivalence. Accordingly, it is important to clarify their
diverse origins as well as the distinctive impulses that vitalize
them.

The construction of sociological theory, at least in its ideal
compliance with the norms of science, proceeds exclusively
within the frame of reference of sociology,[2] is disciplined by
a rigorous scientific logic of inquiry, and grows in correspondence to systematically adduced empirical evidence. On
the other hand, we view ideologies as flourishing within a
socio-political frame of reference, guided by a complex
psycho-logic that is unabashedly interest-bound and informed
by perspectives from one or another social-structural vantage
point, and with its dynamic impetus generated by the shifting
socio-historical milieu itself. This conception renders ideological perspectives emphatically extraneous to the normal
course of scientific or sociological "business." To the extent
that they come to engage scientific interest at all, they do so

not as part of a scientific *strategy* of inquiry, as is the case with theory proper, but rather as an *object* of inquiry in their own right. Thus, they may typically become the substantive concerns of the history of ideas, the philosophy of science and perhaps even epistemology, or of the sociology of knowledge, the sociology of ideology and, to the extent they are found to have infiltrated the discipline, of a critical sociology of sociology (see Friedrichs, 1970). Strictly from the point of view of methodology (viewed as "strategy of inquiry") then, ideologies are peripheral to the sociological enterprise. Even questions of their implication for theory do not arise as legitimate *scientific* issues,[3] as long as the theoretical system to which they appear to bear an implicit relation, does not come to be construed as *consonant* with them, and thus challenged, itself, as being pseudo-scientific, spurious, or *intrinsically* normative.[4]

The distinction drawn here is thus seen to follow closely our differentiation between a sociological construction of reality as contrasted with its common-sense, social construction, of which ideologies are a part. In contrast to the latter, the quest for sociological knowledge, including sociological theorizing, unfolds itself at an analytically "higher" level of scientifically-detached and yet socially-engaged reflective thought. Thus, theorizing is pursued at the analytic level of a logically self-contained scientific enterprise, is governed by scientific criteria of "truth" or validity, and is engaged toward the illumination of social life from its relatively detached vantage point. On the other hand, ideological perspectives distinguish themselves by emanating from and remaining bound to the level of social experience, as not so much socially-engaged as they are socially-permeated and culture-bound, and as serving as vehicles, not for sociologic-ally reflective analysis but, more typically, for socially reflexive judgments that remain poised to support and justify potential social action. Unlike sociological theory, ideologies arise *in* social life to *inform* social life; they are, as *social* constructions of reality, subject to *socially* defined criteria of truth, and serve to render social reality *socially* (i.e. immediately and experientially) comprehensible. Finally, both sociological theory and ideology are concerned with power. But as the *power of theory* rests in its facility for conceptual organization and the interpretation and explanation of an extensive range of data with maximal parsimony, so the *power of ideology* lies in its ability to organize experience, lend it a persuasive coherence, and mobilize action toward either social conservation or social transformation.

There are, of course, some points of similarity or, as we suggested, some parallels. As orienting structures, sociological theories as well as ideological perspectives serve as ordering principles for the meaningful accommodation of observations and experience drawn from the world of events. Both are particularistic in the sense that, in any given instance, they offer only one of an, in principle, infinite number of points of view for confronting social reality. But their essential dissimilarity may be underscored with the recognition that social ideologies are both pre-scientific and extra-scientific, pre-theoretical and extra-theoretical and, as pertains to sociology specifically, pre-sociological as well as extra-sociological. In terms of their affective relation toward one another, sociological theories that *fail to imply* some ideological position invite the suspicion that they articulate trivialities; but sociological theories that are *governed* by ideology face eventual exposure as being scientifically spurious.

While their distinct roles, in science and in social life respectively, serve to separate sociological theory and ideology at least in principle, in practice there is a persistent inclination of the latter to intrude illegitimately into the structure of sociological explanation. Sociology, as we suggested in the opening chapter, is probably more severely encumbered than any other established scientific discipline, by the affinity between its intrinsic theoretical insights and the extrinsic social perspectives that envelope them. The more empirical aspects of sociological research can hardly be considered immune, but it is especially through matters relating to theorizing, that sociology appears most susceptible to the intrusion of ideologically conditioned social perspectives. This greater vulnerability of the theoretical endeavor is largely attributable to the indisputable and, by now, banal observation that refinements in the techniques for logical exactitude have simply not kept pace with the technical sophistication and ingenuity in data collection and analysis, which have remained the hallmark of, particularly, American sociology. Two points, both conspicuously unfortified by systematic screening procedures and "located" at opposite "ends" of the logical structure through which theory building is carried on, appear as most liable to an inadvertent intrusion of ideology.

The first one we shall touch upon only briefly, since it lies outside the scope of the present inquiry, and has no immediate bearing on our conceptual problem with regard to assimilation. We are referring to the "highest" or most abstract level of staking out *theoretical plausibilities*, one that is often referred to as "grand theorizing." In a period dominated by the more pedestrian labors of sociological technicians, this is a relatively rarely explored frontier of theoretical enterprise which, by its very nature, remains unfettered by established rules or routinized procedures. It is here, no doubt, that systematic science has its closest encounter with creative art.

Without taking issue with Merton's entirely appropriate and now classic statements on the reciprocal, interdependent relationship between theory and empirical research (Merton, 1968: 139-171), science is not, and cannot be, a *closed* empirico-theoretic system. The creative jump, the novel conceptualization, the "paradigm shift," even the outrageous hypothesis, these do not proceed soberly and judiciously through conservative induction from the evidence. They venture an imaginative, even an intuitive and, at times, an entirely irrational step beyond the established, the known, the demonstrable, or the verified. But the untrammeled latitude which such explorations of theoretical plausibilities command, is precisely what renders them anathema to empirical science, for probably in proportion to the extent that they venture beyond the verified, they indict themselves as unverifiable. It is here, and for these reasons, it appears to us, that the discipline is profoundly vulnerable to the intrusion of ideological perspectives, although their intrusion here can serve as a revitalizing and provocative prod to a faltering sociological imagination. At its best, theorizing at this level is indeed a leap of the sociological imagination, subsequently to be either abandoned or, if found warranted, formalized into an established structure of scientific explanation. At its worst, it may only be a stumble into social conventionality or ideological bondage, sooner or later to be recognized for its scientifically sterile platitudes or its normatively compromising biases.

Of greater pertinence to the concerns of this inquiry is the other major point of weakness which affords a relatively unimpeded intrusion of social or ideological perspectives. It is located at the more mundane "end" of the theoretic endeavor, at the level of *concepts*, and thus involves the basic logical elements on which theoretical propositions are structured.

Those concepts that have attained the status of established technical terms in the discipline, that have already been properly formalized and are guided in their meaning intensions and extensions by the theories in which they participate, are not likely to serve as carriers of scientifically contraband social perspectives. With due regard for the critical functions performed by concepts in the conduct of inquiry, where such properly formalized concepts are employed, the focal concern in research lies primarily in the validation of theoretical propositions; the research impulse is not directed toward concepts as such, or to questions respecting their legitimation.[5] However crucial and sensitive their role in the normal course of research, concepts, after all, serve "merely" as heuristic devices for the logical apprehension of those properties of empirical events to which they, *as theoretical terms*, make symbolic reference. Where, in contrast, concepts are appropriated from outside the discipline, have not been formally specified and theoretically integrated, and where *they*, rather than their theoretic contexts, come to constitute the primary point of departure for research, the situation with regard to social perspectives and ideology becomes extremely problematic.

It is through the appropriation of such sociologically unlegitimated *social* concepts, that social perspectives are most apt to insinuate themselves into the sociological enterprise. Systematic procedures for screening them out simply do not exist, and the matter of unmasking them and purging them from the discipline is left largely to the "good sense" or trained sensibilities of the sociologist, or to the (in the long run) "self-correcting tendencies of the Scientific Method."

III

In the case of the notion of assimilation in the sociology of racial and ethnic relations, we have tried to show that the term was appropriated from a variety of difficult-to-disentangle technical and popular sources, resulting in its inordinate vagueness and ambiguity of meaning and, therefore, applicability in sociology. Indeed, the concept of assimilation was shown to exhibit such elasticity that in its research implementation it has been variously, and less than explicitly, specified in the forms of assimilation-as-psychological-adjustment, assimilation-as-cultural-adaptation, and assimilation-as-structural-integration. We noted, furthermore, that its applicability in sociology, unlike other social-process concepts, is virtually restricted to the special field of racial and ethnic relations, a substantive area that is conceded to be notoriously devoid of specifically pertinent sociological theory.

In consequence, the concept of assimilation stands in theoretical isolation, neither responsible to, nor informed by an established frame of legitimately sociological theory. Research that proceeds from such a theory-detached concept, even though it is conducted in the name of sociology, does not emanate from sociological problems, but from social problems; it is not inspired by theoretical, that is to say sociological issues, but rather by practical, politico-social ones. While it may claim the virtue of eminent social relevance, it remains sociologically disengaged and scientifically sterile. It assumes the form of social analysis, amassing socially significant facts to swell the fund of information, but does not, as expected of sociological inquiry, contribute to the cumulative growth of sociological knowledge.

Now, once all these things are said, the fact remains that the bulk of the race and ethnic relations literature in American sociology reflects a preoccupation with the assimilative process; and a research compendium of such magnitude can not be casually dismissed as sociologically irrelevant, nor can it be glibly summed up as discrete dabblings in social research devoid of an underlying coherence. We have tried to show, in the course of this inquiry, that the massive concern with assimilation can not be justified on empirical grounds — as simply reflecting the predominant reality of socio-historical events; nor can it be explained on logical grounds — as deducible from compelling theoretical considerations in the sociology of race and ethnic relations. There is, however, an underlying impulse that does account for the extensive sociological commitment to assimilation research, and that serves also as a unifying principle, lending assimilation studies, if not a cumulative character, then at least a semblance of continuity.

The key, we submit, lies in the recognition that it is not sociological theory, predicated on a sociological construction of reality, that informs and legitimates the concept of assimilation. Rather, as an appropriated term, assimilation sustains an *ideological* linkage with the popular (Zangwillian) metaphor of the "Melting Pot" which, as an acknowledged social construction of reality, performs as an extra-sociological anchorage, through which the concept, and the research it engenders, is informed. Not sociological theory, we are arguing, but an ideologically contingent social perspective appears as the cognitive frame, the semantic filter, the research provocation, in short, the ordering principle, that impels and lends coherence to the predominance of endeavors that are carried on under the auspices of a sociology of racial and ethnic relations. So pervasive and entrenched has this perspective become, that we feel justified in characterizing this field as dominated by a widely diffused *Assimilationist Perspective*.

What has stood, in the work of Park and Burgess, as merely one among several, essentially co-equal, social-process concepts, has emerged within the field of racial and ethnic relations, and over a period of some four decades, as something more than a widely employed concept of extraordinary empirical versatility. Granted, assimilation, unlike the other social-process concepts, seemed to be peculiarly restricted in its applicability to this substantive field. This, in itself, raises the interesting question as to whether Park and Burgess' four social processes were indeed comparable in the sense of representing similar levels of abstraction — but it does not account for the predilection for assimilation among sociologists of race and ethnic relations.

Be that as it may, we are asserting considerably more than simply that concerns with accommodation, competition and, especially, conflict were all but displaced by a burgeoning preoccupation with assimilation. Far from exemplifying the unassuming heuristic device that Blumer had in mind when he spoke of "sensitizing concepts," assimilation has come to assume the dimensions of a *Master Concept*, a pattern-defining principle in its own right. In the absence of genuinely sociological theory in this specialized field, and facilitated, moreover, by a typically vague, ambiguous, and opaque specification of the concept itself, the notion of assimilation has been gradually expanded and transmuted from a modest conceptual tool, to the proportions and to the more elevated level of an imposing and, indeed, ruling interpretive perspective.

While this perspective may perform some pseudo-theoretic functions, it can not be allowed to masquerade as a legitimately sociological frame; it does not either constitute, or mask sociological theory, because it is not the product of a sociological *re*construction of prevailing popular conceptions. It simply represents an uncritical and, apparently, unwitting acceptance of the latter at face-value — *a transposition of a socially persuasive commitment to a sociologically spurious theoretical presumption*. To the extent that the Assimilationist Perspective thus articulates a "social-world-taken-for-granted," it becomes, for the sociologist who fails to transform it into a *scientifically* appropriate "system of relevances and typifications," sociologically inauthentic (see Alfred Schutz, 1964: 243-249).

This state of theoretic indigence, compounded by the osmotic intrusion of a pseudo-theoretic surrogate in the form of ideologically conditioned social perspectives, has not gone unrecognized by students of this field who entertain widely diverse orientations. Thus, Jerzy Wiatr notes the discipline's increasing abandonment of a critically detached stance regarding interracial relations and, a few studies during the thirties and forties notwithstanding, comments that "soon after the First World War Western-European and American sociology stopped criticizing the existing system and began the process of assimilation" (Wiatr, 1969: 24). Michael Banton (1967: 62) poses the issue succinctly: "Race relations studies therefore suffer doubly: from being unrelated to major theoretical lines of inquiry, and from being regarded as an ideologist's stamping ground instead of as an area badly needing detached analysis."

What had begun as a conceptual analysis of a widely employed notion in sociology, one characterized by an inordinate elasticity and discipline-straddling applicability, has led us to the edge of a grave critical challenge of the scientific legitimacy of a whole area of substantive specialization in sociology. If our analysis holds merit, then it projects some fairly profound implications, for it suggests that a major portion of what is ostensibly a sociology of race and ethnic relations is, on several grounds, little more than counterfeit sociology.

Quite specifically, this critical challenge suggests: (1) that what passes for a *sociological* orientation toward racial and ethnic phenomena, reflects more realistically a *psychological* frame of reference or, alternatively, one that is more consistent with the approach of *cultural anthropology* toward such matters; (2) that rather than yielding cumulative theory-relevant *sociological knowledge*, the research literature reflects an aggregate of largely descriptive, social-problem-relevant *social information*; and (3) that the field compensated for the absence of legitimate *sociological theory* with a unifying *normative persuasion* which became ideologically compromising, and rendered it conceptually and analytically insensitive to the *full* range of on-going racial and ethnic relations events.

We have already discussed the first two of these issues extensively, as they arose in the course of the preceding analysis. We want now to pursue their bearing on the third critical point, as we concentrate on it in the following discussion.

IV

In a Memorial Day address, Oliver Wendell Holmes (1913: 3) expressed his belief that "as life is action and passion, it is required of a man that he should share the passion and action of his time at peril of being judged not to have lived." This admonition might apply not only to the measure of a man but, with appropriate modifications, to a measure of sociology. We insisted earlier, that sociological theories that fail to imply some social perspective, invite the suspicion that they articulate the trivial. Mr. Justice Holmes might well have insisted that a sociology that does not join and illuminate the vital issues of contemporary social life risks the judgment of being arid and even irrelevant.

Very few observers, either within or outside the discipline, would maintain that sociology is, or at any time has been truly irrelevant to the concerns of social life. Critics from outside the discipline, as we suggested in the opening chapter, may ridicule sociology for grandiosely documenting the obvious or, alternatively, they may express outrage at the discipline's irreverence toward enculturated myths. If nothing else, then at least these complaints affirm sociology's relevance to prevailing concerns of social life. Critics from within the discipline and notable among them those who follow in the tradition of C. Wright Mills,[6] may express their impatience with, particularly, an American sociology for trivializing or for failing to confront the "real" issues. For these critics, the indictment is, again, not a charge of irrelevance, but a call for abandoning an establishmentarian relevance in favor of relevances as they appear to "underdogs."

What is common to these various disaffections is not just their backhanded acknowledgement of sociology's pertinence to events as they transpire in and appear from the perspective of social life. More significantly, they reflect varying degrees and types of concern over the *nature* of the relationship between sociological knowledge and social affairs. Thus, if some would dismiss sociological knowledge as redundant in the face of common-sense knowledge, others perceive it as a threat to institutionalized values in social life. Still others might, presuming on Marx, view sociological knowledge as institutionalized false-consciousness — or, put less extravagantly, as having been concocted in terms of dominant cultural values. Others yet, do not strain against normative contaminations at all, as long as they are acknowledged, and quarrel only over *whose* normative perspectives sociology is to reflect. As far as it goes, then, sociology's *relevance* to vital concerns of social life is not really the focus of serious debate.

But in the end, the most telling, indeed the most stunning indictment of the sociology of race relations in particular, emerges from that body of inquiry itself, and stands independent of any ideological persuasions of its professional critics or its self-critical professionals. The embarrassing fact remains that, however relevant to on-going race relations events the discipline's research concerns may have been, *it proved to be a relevance gone awry*! Limited by what Hermann Strasser (1976: 4-13) would term the "guiding interests of cognition" that found consolidation in the Assimilationist Perspective, sociologists were neither led to anticipate, nor prepared to accommodate theoretically or conceptually, the early 1960s advent of what came to be called the Civil Rights or Black "Revolution."

In his Presidential Address to the American Sociological Association in 1963, Everett Hughes was one of the first to recognize this and ask: "Why did social scientists — and sociologists in particular — not foresee the explosion of collective action of Negro Americans toward immediate full integration into American society?" (see Hughes, 1963: 879). His general answer was the stultification of our sociological imagination. But more specifically, he pointed to the field's conceptual isolation from the broader structural and processual issues in society of which it ought to be viewed as a part, and as merely reflecting a special instance. Killian and Grigg were also among the early critics to identify the shared myopias of social and sociological perceptions, commenting that "there seems to be the assumption that gradually, almost painlessly, the present alienation of the Negro community from American society will be eroded away until assimilation takes place" (Killian and Grigg, 1964: 106). More recently, William Wilson observed: "Race relations analysts were shackled for several decades by the narrow perspectives of assimilation models and by the heavy preoccupation with theories of prejudice, and therefore found themselves unprepared to predict or explain the violent confrontation of ghetto revolts, the emergence and growth of the Black Power Movement, and the rapid rise of cultural nationalism within the black community" (Wilson, 1973: 4). Lewis Coser (1967: 148-149) points to the almost studied neglect accorded a Marxian type of analysis in this field:

The fact that American sociology was so ruefully unprepared for the civil rights revolution of the last few years is connected with its systematic neglect of social conflict and of the mobilization of power and interests in racial contentions. Being wedded to the belief that only increased understanding between the races and successful mobilization of guilt about the American dilemma among the dominant racial majority would lead to the gradual erosion of prejudice and discrimination, American sociology was by and large unprepared for the emergence of a situation in which a major part of the initiative for change did not come from the white man but rather from the black. American sociology has systematically neglected analysis of the conditions that gradually led to the emergence of a new self-consciousness among younger Negroes and to the development not only of alienative tendencies in the Negro community but of a militant type of alienation as well. Much professional embarrassment might well have been avoided had attention been paid to certain Marxian leads . . .

It is apparent, then, that even demonstrated relevance and

commitment to "the vital issues of contemporary social life" are insufficient, by themselves, to vindicate a discipline such as sociology. Indeed, they tend to compromise the very posture of detachment that must distinguish sociological perspectives from any one of the ideological ones that arise in social life. The insinuation of ideological biases, normative factors and value commitments into sociological theorizing, and their disposition to warp the accumulation of sociological knowledge, tend to be as unobtrusive as they are prevalent, and they can lead, as in this case, to grossly embarrassing consequences. The challenge, therefore, to which sociology as a scientific discipline must rise, is a simultaneous accommodation to demands for relevance and to norms of detachment: how to develop and maintain standards of accountability that, on the one hand, *justify* a sociology in terms of the expectations of the social ambience on which it feeds, empirically and economically; and on the other hand *legitimate* the discipline in terms of the norms of the scientific milieu in which it participates.

V

Concerns with sociology's *justifications* and its *legitimations*, as these terms are used here, have given rise to an extensive, although somewhat scattered literature, which might be distinguished into discussions of the question of values in the scholarly and professional conduct of the sociologist, and analyses that focus on the ideological implications of sociology as a discipline.[7] In some respects, these concerns are of course inseparable. While, in pursuing our assessment of the Assimilationist Perspective, our emphasis is primarily on the latter types of concern, it is perhaps precisely in the intertwining of the socio-political predilections of *sociologists* with an intrinsic and predominant socio-political posture of *sociology*, that the preoccupation with assimilation as a concept, and as an orienting perspective, becomes explicable.

Both genuine sociological theory and, more patently,

transposed social or ideological perspectives in their performance of pseudo-theoretical functions in sociology, bear very real, if not always explicit socio-political implications. By the same token, so does sociology as a whole. But its quest for theoretical integration is still far from attained, and by thus embracing theories that imply less-than-congruent socio-political positions, the discipline suggests an over-all orientation that is of a somewhat amorphous character. There is general agreement, however, that in its dominant motif and from its early development to its contemporary state, the discipline of sociology has struck an essentially conservative posture.

Robert Nisbet has shown that the rise of sociology in France, contrary to the views of most historians of social thought, was not a logical extension of the liberal ideas that had permeated the Enlightenment. He demonstrated that the central concepts involved in early French sociology emerged from the Romantic reaction to the French Revolution, and in fact reflected a critical break with the liberal assumptions of the eighteenth century. The sociology that took shape in the hands of Comte and developed through the Comtean tradition in France, resonated the profound conservatism that was reflected in its central concepts (see Nisbet, 1943). Not only early French sociology, but the discipline in virtually all of its distinguishable "national" elaborations, radiated this conservative aura. Nor is sociology revealed as a conservative response to the disruptive effects of the French Revolution alone. Perhaps even more significantly, it emerges consistently on the more. or less conservative side in its continuing encounters with Karl Marx. As Irving Zeitlin has pointed out, virtually every major sociological theorist has engaged in a "debate with the ghost of Marx," who, with his liberal-radical posture in the nineteenth century, is the true intellectual heir of the Enlightenment. From each of these "debates," sociology has emerged with an accommodation to the "right" of Marx, in the direction of, if not always in a consistently conservative position (Zeitlin, 1968: vii, 111ff).

In a later essay of broader scope, Robert Nisbet again

observes that although contemporary sociologists may regard
the conservative label as a form of damnation, sociology is a
repository of the legacies of conservatism. At the core of
sociological thought is the conservative view of society, and
Nisbet proceeds to trace some ten conservative assumptions
that animate the modern sociological enterprise (Nisbet,
1952). In a more recent major work that builds on his earlier
interests, Nisbet makes a statement which deserves quoting
here, and to which we shall have occasion to return in the
following chapter (1966: 17):

The paradox of sociology — and it is, as I argue in these pages,
a creative paradox — lies in the fact that although it falls, in its objectives and in the political and scientific values of its principal figures, in
the mainstream of modernism, its essential concepts and its implicit
perspectives place it much closer, generally speaking, to philosophical
conservatism.

Now, where American sociology, specifically, is concerned,
assessments of its general orientation arrive consistently at a
similar conclusion of the discipline's essentially conservative
character. Not surprisingly, the more recent and most articulate of these judgments have come from sociologists whose
focus on the discipline has emanated from the "left." Their
treatments carry the tenor of impatient activism, and their
conclusions often suggest the timbre of polemics. Thus, when
their analyses of contemporary American sociology culminate in agreements on the generally conservative orientation
of the discipline, these conclusions assume more nearly the
overtone of a critical verdict of "guilty!", as contrasted with
the seemingly detached (but clearly tacitly approving)
"vindication," which is implied when Nisbet, given his
posture, arrives at a similar determination.

If Nisbet accepts the conservative character of sociology as
largely a matter of fact while the "activist" sociologists view
it as grounds for critical and, indeed, pejorative judgment,
then their distinctive reactions may not reflect merely their
respective political and scientific values. They are ascribing to
sociology related, but not identical varieties of conservatism.
Nisbet, tracing the history of ideas, finds the idea-system of

sociology structured on the unit-ideas (1966: 4-7) of *Philosophical Conservativism*; the more radical critics, concerned with the involvement of sociology in the vital public issues of the time, identify the discipline with a socio-political form of conservatism, one that Andrew Hacker has distinguished as *Status-Quo Conservatism* (Hacker, 1961: 345-349). Thus Ralf Dahrendorf, in a ciritical essay, asserts that the structuring of much of contemporary sociology, like utopian constructions, does not upset the *status quo* but rather affirms and sustains it (Dahrendorf, 1958: 117). He goes on to charge (124): "By turning away from the critical facts of experience, sociologists have both followed and strengthened the trend toward conservatism. . . . [but] it is, rather, a conservatism by implication, the conservatism of complacency." A similar assessment, one which might well be called *conservatism-by-default*, runs through much of the work of C. Wright Mills, who deplores it as a "cultural and political abdication" characteristic of recent American sociology (see Mills, 1959: 22, and *passim*).

More recently, Alvin Gouldner has eloquently criticized Academic Sociology (contrasted with Marxism) for its entrenched conservatism. But Gouldner views the discipline, in its political and ideological character, as an ambivalent structure with both repressive (conservative) and liberative (radical) dimensions. For all its profoundly conservative trends, he perceives in Western sociology a paradoxical capacity for not only recruiting, but for producing radicals; for not merely tolerating, but for generating its own radicalization. Sociology's liberative potential, he argues, must be extricated from the repressive conservatism that inheres in dominant theories, each of which needs to be confronted point by point (Gouldner, 1970: 11-15, 53, 441).

In a not dissimilar analysis which, like Gouldner's goes considerably beyond the studies cited above, Dick Atkinson (1972) explores the essential conservatism that permeates sociology in general, and its American contributions in particular. He is led to discount as deceptive, at the very least, the conventional view of an operant polar opposition between a (conservative) "cohesion school" and a (radically inclined) "conflict school" of theorizing. Both, he argues, proceed in terms of underlying assumptions, thought modes, and strategic concepts that lead their fundamental similarities to outweigh by far their superficial antitheses, and to converge them toward forming the profoundly conservative stance that marks the prevailing sociological enterprise. The entrenched conservatism that Atkinson perceives is thus considerably more encompassing, since it includes some important theoretical strains that Gouldner would, no doubt, associate with the discipline's liberative potential. Not withstanding the dominant theme of structural determinism which culminates in a conservative "sociology of restraint" (Gouldner's "repressive" dimension), Atkinson also traces a submerged theme of voluntaristic individualism, portending a "sociology of choice" (bearing some similarity to Gouldner's "liberative potential").[8]

Finally, a no less thoughtful but perhaps analytically more portentious recent study by Hermann Strasser deserves mention. Strasser, in tracing the historical and philosophical origins of sociology, also documents its conservative tradition and follows it through its American elaboration. But where Gouldner saw a liberative *potential*, and Atkinson recognized a *submerged theme*, Strasser identifies a *concurrent counter-tradition* of a progressive or emancipatory thrust, which has sustained sociology's antinomic character since the fall of the *Ancien Régime*. The evolving sociological enterprise, he argues, was decisively influenced by the dialectic interplay between an emancipatory "science of progress" and a (more predominating) conservative "science of integration," each reflecting the distinctive "guiding interests of cognition" of antagonistic social groupings (Strasser, 1976: 2-13, 118-122, and *passim*).

In substance, then, these analyses, part of a growing body of literature, document the dominance in American sociology of coherence, consensus, equilibrium, order, or functional "models" of society, and the type of "systems" theory that their assumption seems to entail.[9] Whatever other distinctions there may be among the various "models" and "theories"[10] so designated, they all share a common commitment to an orientation that views order either as an analytic given or as a central tendency in society. Stability, social cohesion, value-consensus, functional integration, organic solidarity, shared meaning patterns, etc., these are only part of a rich "order vocabulary" that accrues from these theoretical stances, and is too familiar to require further elaboration (see John Horton, 1966: 703-704; see also Myrdal, 1944: 1055).

The Assimilationist Perspective, the inclination to approach race and ethnic relations phenomena with a predisposition to perceive, document, analyze and explain (if not, indeed, to tacitly prod) assimilative processes to the relative neglect of others, fits squarely into this order-celebrating orientation of the conservative sociological tradition. Assimilation, simply as a concept, is entirely consonant with the vocabulary of this *genre*; and the Assimilationist Perspective, as a conceptual scheme or point of view, is in accord with the consensual and integrative emphases that mark the conservatism, specifically the Philosophical Conservatism, of sociology in general and of its American elaboration.

Particularly in American sociology of the last several decades, the other variant of conservatism mentioned earlier, Status-Quo Conservatism, has also played a significant role, and it is reflected to certainly no lesser degree in the Assimilationist Perspective. The writer has, elsewhere (Bash, 1957: Chapters 2, 4), traced a number of the developmental conditions that led to an American sociology with a distinctive "Social Problems Orientation" as its characteristic theoretic-conceptual motif.[11] This Social Problems Orientation was shown to rest on an implicit assumption of the essential "goodness" of the established social arrangement, and to entail the logically consistent tendency to identify patterns of deviation from the normative order as "social problems," and to define them as "pathological."[12] The specifically Status-Quo Conservative character that inheres in this orientation rests in its implicit affirmation and sustenance of the established order (Dahrendorf) through defining departures from that order as "pathologies," that mobilize ameliorative strategies of adjustment toward conformity with the more normative patterns (Horton); in its intellectual and political abdication, it fails to confront the salient transformations of structural realities in their historical dimensions (Mills). The study of social problems becomes a tacit prelude, not for the transformation of the established social arrangement, but for the reform or amelioration of "problem" conditions, which more often than not means the rehabilitation of "problem" populations.

The Assimilationist Perspective appears as an integral part of this orientation in American sociology, and must be recognized as sharing its Status-Quo Conservative character. In accord with the framework of this orientation, the mere presence of ethnically or racially heterogeneous groups — to the extent that their ethnicities or racial identities are *socially* defined as significant and problematic — constitutes a persistent reminder of their order-compromising potential. Significantly, and in reiteration of our earlier point, it is as characteristic of the Assimilationist Perspective as it is of the Social Problem Orientation, to accept the *social* definition of the situation, without reconceptualization, as a *sociologically* appropriate analytic frame. In thus confounding the distinction between knowledge and the objects of knowledge, the Assimilationist Perspective becomes implicated in matters of political policy — in conservative strategy, to be precise, although the *particular* ideological affinity involved is not here the point. The critical recognition is the normative element that comes into play and , as Bramson (1961: 51) has noted, "the 20th century American sociologists of conservation were concerned with maintaining the American norm and assimilating vast numbers of 'deviants' (both from within and without) to that norm."

Notes

1.   For an interesting discussion of competitive theoretical alternatives and their implications for research, see James T. Duke (1967: 571-582).

2. Constituting no more than a perspective itself, sociology (or science in general) has of course no superior claim as a reality assessment, compared to any alternate construction. To act as though it did leads to sociologism (or, more generally, to scientism). Nevertheless, its theoretics must be developed in accord with *its* conception of reality, rather than in conformity with that of any other. In proportion to the extent that this is heeded, "the sociological perspective" maintains its requisite distinction from extra-scientific (social) perspectives. To the extent that it fails to be heeded, it simply becomes redundant with one or another of them.

3. While we would insist that any implications which ideological perspectives may hold for sociological theory are scientifically irrelevant (except insofar as they enter in the form of data, i.e. as *objects* of study), we would argue as adamantly that sociological theory *must* bear implications toward such ideologies. That is to say, "any sociological theory should impinge upon some ideology or run the risk of irrelevance." See N. J. Demerath, III (1966: 400).

4. For illustrations of this type of critical analysis, see the very different assessments of Talcott Parsons' work in Daniel Foss (1963: 96-126) and Andrew Hacker (1961: 289-310).

5. That is to say, if there are any grounds for suspecting the intrusion of social perspectives, then it is at the level of theory, not on the basis of concepts, that the issue would here be joined.

6. Typical examples of these criticisms are anthologized in Irving Louis Horowitz (1965), and Maurice Stein and Arthur Vidich (1963).

7. See particularly Alvin W. Gouldner (1962: 199-213) as well as his more recent restatement in Gouldner (1968: 103-116); see also the strong polemic challenge to the *American Sociological Association* by Martin Nicolaus (1969: 154-156). For discussions of these value issues and ideological postures, as they relate to major government-sponsored studies in sociology, see Horowitz (1967), and Rainwater and Yancey (1967).

8. See the present writer's review essay on Atkinson's work in Bash (1974).

9. Besides the works of Dahrendorf and Mills, already cited, see also Horowitz (1962); John Horton (1966); and van den Berghe (1963).

10. In any strict sense, these may not qualify as scientific models or theories; and we agree with Robin Williams that what is involved are, more properly, conceptual schemes or points of view, than general scientific theories. This does not, however, affect our argument. See Robin M. Williams, Jr. (1966: 720n).

11. A similar assessment can be found in Leon Bramson (1961: 48-49).

12. Cf. John Horton's analysis (1966: 720ff), in which he associates
     this motif with an anomie theory of societal discontent (as op-
     posed to an alienation theory), and with an adjustment definition
     of social deviation (as distinct from a growth definition). In this
     connection, it is also worth comparing the discussion in C. Wright
     Mills (1942).

CHAPTER 7

Ideology and the Inhibition of Conflict Orientations

I

We have been developing the argument in the preceding chapters that the Assimilationist Perspective constitutes, apart from but hardly unrelated to the normative issue itself, an *analytic* bias. It focuses selective and disproportionate attention on ethnic and racial processes of assimilation, to the at least relative neglect of alternative social processes. Of the four processes that were part of the legacy of Park and Burgess, the one that appears to be most conspicuous in the short shrift accorded it in the context of the racial and ethnic relations field, is the process of conflict.

It is one of the more intriguing aspects of the American ethos, that a nation that continues to celebrate its revolutionary origins and has remained not unjustly notorious ever since for the violence that appears so thoroughly knitted into its institutional fabric, should profess a combination of historical obliviousness to, and a contemporary repugnance for acknowledging its persisting and various intergroup conflicts. In a volume designed to promote the development of effective techniques for "the reduction of intergroup tensions," Robin Williams (1947: 4) observes:

There is a strong tendency in American thought to ignore or minimize the very considerable amount of intranational group conflict which has appeared in various periods of our history. Yet an examination of the record will show that internal hostilities and disorders have been by no means infrequent.

In this context, as of course in many others, American sociology may almost be viewed as a *Doppelgänger* of American society, insofar as its reality constructions are concerned. The Assimilationist Perspective, as we have portrayed it, serves both as a reflection of the American social thought tendency to minimize and all but deny group conflict phenomena, as well as a disciplinary conception for the deflection of such phenomena from concentrated analytic attention.

There is little question that, historically, conflicts specifically involving racial or ethnic factions had been transpiring in American society since its inception. Thus, the eruption of "Long Hot Summers" and of "racial confrontations" or "disturbances," of "Black Militancy," or "White Backlash" in the early 1960s must be viewed in terms of a continuity with nearly three centuries of inter-group contentions that reflect a heterogeneity of peoples engaged in exploring, by fits and starts, a uniquely American basis for a viable sense of nation, of common peoplehood. Such struggles did not, in each particular case, pit one racial or ethnic grouping against another in open, undisguised *physical* violence. However, one need not be inordinately astute, politically, to recognize that innumerable such conflicts occurred in forms and in forums, in contexts and in controversies that only thinly veiled the ethnic or racial issues at their core.

For better or worse, history books incline to record past events under precisely those popular designations, which the headline pitch of the contemporary press saw fit to confer on them when they were "news." To the extent that they do so, they enshrine in the historical record particular social constructions of reality through conceptualizations that obscure significant commonalities and an underlying relatedness. Many of the events that are of interest to us here and were thus recorded, highlight their conflict character, but their historical labels tend to mask their racial or ethnic agendas from almost any but the penetrating scrutiny of historical scholarship.

One might cite such nominally disparate events as the "Draft Riots" of the 1860s, the frequently explosive unionization struggles and "Labor Strife" of the early decades of the century, the intermittent "Gang Wars" between syndicated adults as well as among pugnacious cadres of juveniles, the "Zoot-Suit Riots" of the 1940s, or more contemporary confrontations over "Forced Busing" which would ostensibly compromise "the neighborhood school principle."[1] These share, in common with innumerable others that could be added, significant root elements of racial or ethnic dimensions. To simply recognize as their common denominator a "breakdown in law and order" would appear as descriptively correct as it would prove analytically obtuse. The advantages of a sociological imagination, we should recall, include a facility for reading newspapers, as well as history, intelligently.

That there exists a protracted American tradition of racial and ethnic conflict is undeniable, and it would be irresponsible indeed, to represent American sociology as having ignored such matters entirely. But if they weren't ignored, then under the influence of the Assimilationist Perspective the discipline did not confront them, conceptually, as conflict phenomena in the tradition of some of its nineteenth century European progenitors. Instead, and consistent with the Social Problem Orientation described earlier, these matters tended to be defined as deviant behavior, and accommodated analytically within the social problem areas of deviance or crime; or within the context of competition for social prestige (rather than in terms of a Gumplowiczian *Rassenkampf* or a Marxian *Klassenkampf*); or, these problems were approached not in their conflict *manifestations*, but rather in terms of their idealized *resolution*: resocialization, or *assimilation*.

Thus, Coser (1956: 20), speaking of the majority of sociologists who dominate American sociology at mid-century says:

They center attention predominantly upon problems of adjustment rather than upon conflict; upon social statics rather than upon dynamics . . . Where the older generation discussed the need for structural change the new generation deals with adjustment of individuals to given structures. In the dominant trend of contemporary American sociology, the psychological subsumes the structural and hence individual malfunctioning subsumes social conflict.

II

The disposition to avoid conflict phenomena *qua* conflict phenomena, and the failure to elaborate and to engage theories of conflict were characteristic of American sociology in general, as we suggested in Chapter 2, until late into the 1950s. In the sociology of race and ethnic relations, however, conflict was never altogether ignored, nor was it simply defined out of existence. Instead, as historical fact or as persistent social possibility, intergroup conflict provided a stimulus for, and a justification of, a very special sociology of intergroup relations within which conflict could be accommodated, once it was rendered conceptually compatible with the developing Assimilationist Perspective. The attractiveness of the Assimilationist Perspective, both as a social commitment and as a sociological orientation, may well be seen as a programmatic response to the reality, or to the ever-present potential, of intergroup conflict in American society. Accordingly, conflict *was* acknowledged as part of the empirical reality (Williams, 1947: 1-6) but, consistent with the Status-Quo Conservative character of the Assimilationist Perspective, it was rendered "harmless" through disengaging it from immediate and critical social structural implications.

This inclination toward detaching the analysis of intergroup conflict from its social structural roots can be shown perhaps most authoritatively, as well as in its indication of the general tenor of the field at the time, by referring briefly to the stimulus that led to Robin Williams' report. In 1945 the prestigious *Social Science Research Council* established a Committee on Techniques for Reducing Group Hostility, which, in turn, sponsored and directed Williams' study. Among the Committee's objectives (as stated in the volume's Foreword) is one which conveys clearly its view that social psychological, attitudinal factors are to be regarded as the basis on which intergroup "hostility" and "conflict" are structured (Williams, 1947: ix, italics added):

To consider social psychological theory and research bearing on the problem of group conflict with a view to deriving from any promising theory not now practically applied an action technique which might be tested for its effectiveness in reducing hostility and resolving conflict.

While Williams' resulting work appears, on the whole, to be guided by the Committee's prescriptive social psychological frame of reference, it must be noted that he does, here and there, allude to historical, structural and cultural considerations (5, 48, 55ff), that might serve to pattern the incidence and the types of conflict, psychologically and social psychologically defined, which he addresses. As intended by the Committee that comissioned it, Williams' report stimulated and gave direction to a considerable amount of valuable research; but it also, inevitably, helped to set the bounds on its universe of discourse and to shape its conceptualizations. Characteristically then, in the sociology of racial and ethnic relations, rather than being conceptualized in sociological terms and linked with social structural variables, conflict was typically psychologized, treated in its manifestation as ethnic or racial "hostility" (Williams, 1947: 42) or, more generally, as *prejudice* and tied to personality variables or aspects of collective behavior.[2]

Thus Bernard (1951: 244), arguing against the sociological tendency, in general, to psychologize intergroup relations, wrote that:

Sociologically speaking, conflict exists between groups when there is a fundamental incompatibility in their values, goals, interests, etc., so that if one group gets what it wants, the other group cannot get what it wants. Conflict so conceived can exist independently of the subjective reaction of members of the group . . . In contrast to this concept is that of the psychologist according to which conflict appears to exist in the minds of group members.

Despite a recently rekindled interest in conflict theory and in a sociology of conflict, the tendency to treat conflict phenomena in psychological or, perhaps more properly, social-psychological terms remains in conspicuous evidence. In a more recent article, Bernard (1965: 442) states: "Current thinking in the field of conflict is psychologically oriented rather than, as in the nineteenth century, sociologically oriented," and she quotes Kathleen Archibald's comment that "a sociology of conflict is being constructed without benefit of sociologists."

Thus, the Assimilationist Perspective has flourished, in the context of American sociology, in the virtual absence of an effective contra-conception, such as an established "Conflict Perspective."[3] Moreover, within the confines of its own domination of the sociology of race and ethnic relations, it has tended to sociologically emasculate conflict phenomena, as we have tried to show, by psychologizing them to the level of subjective or collective attitudinal reactions of group members. As a result, the Assimilationist Perspective has not only sustained an *analytic* bias that precludes a sociologically adequate analysis of the full range of social-process phenomena, but it has also supported a *normative* bias, one that attaches to an essentially conservative world-view. Such a conservative world-view is neither unknown, nor entirely incompatible with the outlooks prevalent among many who view themselves, or are regarded as Liberals, of whom Killian (1975: 115) observes:

In addition, to face squarely the reality and significance of both black power and the white backlash would be to accept the fact of the polarization of race relations and their applicability to a conflict model interpretation. This does great violence to liberal optimism, which assumes that the integrative effects of consensus about the American Creed as well as the cohesive qualities of the American social system will limit the destructiveness of the explosion triggered by the collision of white and Negro interests.

The point at issue is hardly that sociological knowledge turns out to be relevant to normative issues in social life. That is, broad consensus has it, as it should be. Rather, the point is that, in the particular case of the Assimilationist Perspective, at least, normative persuasions inform and shape sociological "theory." It may be inescapable, as John Horton (1966: 701) suggests, that "Whatever the possibilities of developing empirical theory in the social sciences, only normative theory is appropriate in the sociology of social problems." The distinction has been well stated by

Martindale (1959: 341-342):

The ultimate materials of empirical theory are facts; the ultimate materials of normative theory are value-*imperatives* . . . empirical theory is formed out of a system of laws. Normative theory converts facts and laws into requisite means and conditions and is unique in being addressed to a system of objectives desired by the formulator or by those in whose service he stands.

But if normative theory is indeed an appropriate, or even an unavoidable attribute of the sociology of social problems, then for the sociologist, as Horton (1966: 701) asserts, the problem "is not that normative theories contain values, but that these values may go unnoticed so that normative theories pass for empirical theories."

But, one must ask, is the sociology of racial and ethnic relations part of a "sociology of social problems"; and if it is, is it unilaterally, inevitably or unalterably so? Is its subject matter broached by sociology only because at this *time*, and in this *place*, and in the *minds* of influentials who have the power to make *their* conceptions count, it is deemed *socially* problematic and *of interest to social life*? Or is its subject matter of legitimate *interest to sociology* because it is intrinsically social, because as such it holds a key toward understanding the structure and dynamics of society, because, in brief, it is *sociologically* problematic?

These questions, and the distinctions, are important because, as we have seen, what is regarded *socially* problematic is *time-, place-,* and *interest-bound*, and to that extent compromises the autonomous pursuit of what is *sociologically* problematic. We have identified sociology's failure to anticipate the overt racial confrontations that became evident since the early 1960s; its recognition of, but inadequacy in accommodating theoretically the at best selective and relative assimilation of ethnics; and its only belated acknowledgement of recent aggressively dissimilative trends toward pluralistic reassertions of racial and ethnic "identities and self-determinations." These constitute serious academic fumbles, and they attest sociology's erosion of its scientific autonomy over its own "business," its perspectivistic cooption by those *social* constructions of reality which serve to define a "social problems" approach to the substance of sociological inquiry.

It is hard, therefore, to avoid the conclusion that the sociology of racial and ethnic relations has failed doubly. Within the boundaries of our inquiry, at least, its failure to predict underscores its theoretical inadequacy as an academic, scientific discipline questing for knowledge; at the same time, as an applied discipline committed to the mediation or resolution of social problem concerns, its contributions to social life must be judged as largely unremarkable, inconspicuous, and inconsequential. If this assessment is acknowledged, then the solution does not automatically turn on the abandonment of either one of sociology's legitimate promises. It does require, initially, the recognition that the sociology of racial and ethnic relations has sought to serve two masters and, in doing so, has availed neither. Accordingly, the solution would seem to point to an appropriate and self-conscious bifurcation of sociological endeavors which, on the one hand, employs explicitly *normative theory* toward addressing a system of social objectives, and on the other hand, promotes the development of ostensibly *empirical theory* toward locating the historical and societal significances of racial and ethnic phenomena in the context of scientific explanation.

Our own analysis supports, but goes beyond the contention that the value-imperatives imbedded in the social constructions of reality have, consistent with Horton's point, intruded unnoticed into the Assimilationist Perspective. It is not merely a question of normative theory passing for empirical theory, but whether, indeed, the Assimilationist Perspective supports theory of *any* sort. We have tried to show that the Assimilationist Perspective is less, if at all, derived from analytic sociological theory, than it is from a programmatic social commitment. In this sense, we have insisted that it constitutes a theoretical presumption, an interpretive inclination which, as an unreconstructed social perspective, is logically prior to the actual conduct of empirico-theoretical inquiry. In the absence of an established theoretical frame in relation to which it might take the form of some hypothetical construction inviting confirmation, it has expanded to fill the theoretic void in the form of an axiomatic given which is more likely to generate self-confirming social research, than critical tests of its assimilation assumptions. Moreover, within this theoretical vacuum, the Assimilationist Perspective has enjoyed a protective immunity from the kind of critical challenge and from a corrective influence overs its perspectivistic insularity, which a contra-conception such as an effective "conflict model" might have exerted.

Van den Berghe (1967: 8) has observed: "In the race relations field, more than in any other, social science theory is little more than a weathercock shifting with ideological winds." Our analysis of what we have called the Assimilationist Perspective, lends strong support to this assessment, with the qualification that, in this case, the metaphor of a three-decade-long ideological "stagnant air mass" seems more apt. Beyond that, however, we would assert what is only implicit in van den Berghe's statement: that in a strict sense, there is no legitimate theory involved at all. The Assimilationist Perspective masks a theoretical void, and in its affinity with a social construction of reality, it remains scientifically spurious and projects no more than a counterfeit theoretical persuasion.

III

Our analysis has traced the notion of assimilation through a major part of the development of American sociology. We have concentrated particularly on a period of roughly forty-five years, that began with Park and Burgess' formulation in 1921 and extends to Milton Gordon's major re-examination. Of the four social-process concepts that Park and Burgess had emphasized, assimilation appears to possess the peculiar attribute of being applicable exclusively within the special sociological concern with race and ethnic relations, an area which has also been of special historical and contemporary significance in American *social* life.

From the time that Benjamin Franklin expressed his concern over "a colony of Aliens, who will shortly be so numerous as to Germanize us instead of our Anglifying them,"[4] through a history of shifting U.S. immigration policy, to contemporary Black impulses toward racial separatism and white ethnic advocacies for cultural pluralism, the American experiment can be read as a protracted, and as yet unresolved, search for a structurally workable and yet morally acceptable sense of American peoplehood. The goal has, at times, appeared hopelessly elusive, at other times tantalizingly imminent. Throughout, however, with probably no major voluntarily or coercively admitted group excepted, the American experience has reflected continuing patterns of racial, ethnic or religious contention, as the foundations for a genuinely American nationality were explored and put to the test. That some of these contentions may not have had the *appearance* of conflicts *manifestly* structured along racial or ethnic lines, does not preclude those recognitions once sociological analysis penetrates beyond common-sense social facades. On the whole, we have been led to conclude, this has not happened in the American sociology of racial and ethnic relations. In any case, racial or ethnic conflict phenomena in America can be no more interpreted out of existence by the "historians of consensus,"[5] than they could be denied by the sociologists of racial and ethnic relations, had their conceptual models and theoretical orientations not desensitized them to these realities.

But American sociologists were, in general, desensitized to these realities or, more accurately, led to misapprehend them, guided as they were by reigning functional and consensual models and by their habituation to a "social problems" orientation. Until the 1960s they still found it possible, aided by a blithe ahistoricity that inheres in these conceptual dispositions, to view seemingly sporadic instances of racial or ethnic "disturbances" as rather discrete happenstances. They appeared as idiosyncratic surface flaws on an otherwise rather nicely assimilating social order, and its ultimate "integration" attended only a diminution of prejudices in the direction of (Judeo-) Christian "tolerance," the dissolution of stereotypes through education and enlightened intergroup contact, and the narrowing of social distances toward a properly democratic minimum. Within this tradition, the preoccupation with the concept of assimilation and the proportionate neglect of other social-process concepts in this substantively circumscribed area, laid the groundwork for what became, in effect, a trained incapacity for dealing sociologically, that is structurally and historically, with racial and ethnic conflict phenomena. The legitimate *study* of assimilation became an implicit *commitment* to assimilation; and the vaguely and ambiguously specified concept of assimilation, given the poverty of theory in this *socially*-defined field, expanded in the direction of an assimilation model of society and ascended to the explanatory level of a counterfeit theoretical persuasion.

The scientifically spurious character of the resulting assimilation "theory" is clearly evident in the three "theories of assimilation" that Gordon presented in his effort to bring order to what he, himself, recognized as a welter of poorly articulated (*social*) "philosophies," "goal-systems," or "ideological tendencies" (see 115-116, *supra*). "Anglo-Conformity," "The Melting Pot" and "Cultural Pluralism" simply do not constitute legitimate sociological theories, but represent, at best, coherently articulated "models" of alternative programmatic options that remain sociologically unreconstructed.

In seeking to account for the dominance and persistence of what we have designated the Assimilationist Perspective in the sociology of racial and ethnic relations, it is useful to refer back to the paradox of sociology that Robert Nisbet had posed (see 142, *supra*). He had suggested, it will be recalled, that sociology sustains a fruitful tension between the discipline's philosophic conservatism and its principal figures' modernism.[6] But what Nisbet perceived as "a creative paradox"[7] seems in this case to lack that vital cutting-edge. In its ideological affinities, the Assimilationist Perspective offers a creativity-blunting accommodation of these opposing tenets, for it appears to be as compatible with the intrinsically conservative orientation of the sociological tradition, as it is congenial to the generally liberal persuasions of American sociologists.

The Assimilationist Perspective represents the conservative Order, Coherence, or Consensus model of society in its special pertinence to the race and ethnic relations field. In terms of this orientation, the (eventual) homogenization of ethnically or racially diverse groups is assumed as an analytic given (thus, assimilation as *product*), or as part of a "natural" tendency of (American) society in the direction of stability and consensus (i.e. assimilation as *process*). The concept of assimilation, itself, appears as the most conspicuous term in a commodious "vocabulary of Order" that lends expression to the conservative ideal of Community, and diverts attention from possible structural strains that might impede its realization. The concept's made-to-order (a phrase that can be read in its double-meaning) conservatism is especially magnified through its predominant meaning-specifications as "psychological adjustment" or as "cultural adaptation." Accordingly, impediments to the attainment of Community tend to be perceived primarily in discordant attitudes and prejudices, or in the disorderly patchwork of folkways and mores associated with ethnic diversity. Significantly, what might have been seen, from a radical perspective, as merely *symptoms* that accrue from alterations among broader social structural realities, become instead the primary substantive materials of an essentially conservative sociology. In this sense, speaking more generally of the developmental trend of American sociology, Bramson (1961: 95) points out that "what I have referred to as the conservative character of many sociological concepts prevented many sociologists from dealing with the changes which were taking place in American society before their very eyes."

The other factor in Nisbet's paradox is the characteristic value-orientation of American sociologists themselves. It is necessary, here, to maintain a clear distinction between the underlying *philosophic* orientation of the *discipline*, and the *ideological* commitments or sympathies of its *practitioners*. By virtually any standard, American sociologists have typically inclined toward what Nisbet called "modernism," toward "progressivism" or, more specifically, toward some ideological mix of what in his Political Theory text Hacker (1961: 237-244) has defined respectively as "Reformist Liberalism" and "Democratic Liberalism." Their undisguised Reformist Liberal zeal animated much of American sociology in the first two decades of this century (Hinkle and Hinkle, 1954: 12-14). Since then, their individual Reformist Liberalism has become institutionalized although, as Mills (1942: 171-172) has argued, cloaked in the mantle of scientific objectivity, as part of the "professional ideology" in terms of which they defined and studied "social problem" conditions.

If sociologists of racial and ethnic relations became preoccupied with the notion of assimilation to the neglect of that of conflict, it was not, as we have tried to show, due to any empirically-based sense of proportions between the prevalence of assimilation relative to the incidence of conflict among the groups in question. *As a social policy option*, assimilation has surely represented the Reformist Liberal solution for the "immigrant problem" in America and, until very recent years at least, for the "racial problem" as well.[8] Not the dispassionate imperatives of scientific inquiry, but the Liberal implications of the American Melting-Pot ideal seem to have captured the professional energies of these sociologists. Thus, what came to take shape as the Assimilationist Perspective in the sociology of racial and ethnic relations must be regarded as the product of sociologists who, consciously or not, transmuted their more-or-less liberal *social* persuasions into a *sociological* perspective.

Whatever implicitly liberal values may have guided the professional conduct of sociologists, the (perhaps unintended) result, expressed in the form of the "Assimilationist Perspective" appears, over the period of its ascendance and dominance, to have been equally in harmony with the intrinsically conservative tradition of sociology, and with what came to constitute a liberal posture in social life. This mutually accommodating coincidence of world-views, we believe, accounts for the prolonged and virtually unchallenged dominance of the Assimilationist Perspective in this field. It also served to mute the productive potential of what Nisbet had described as the creative paradox of sociology, and it thus helped render the sociology of racial and ethnic relations, as a substantively specialized field, relatively stagnant.

Armed with the Assimilationist Perspective, the sociologists of racial and ethnic relations were conceptually distracted from the occurrence of conflict events. Like the "Social Pathologists" in general, their "professional ideology" led them to conceive order-compromising phenomena as Social Problems, to be approached analytically in terms of one or more of the "social disorganization," "personal deviation" or "conflict of values" frameworks.[9] This last approach is particularly interesting, because it appears as a revealing intellectual expression of the conjoined Liberal Rationality and Conservative Idealism that inheres in the Assimilationist Perspective. Where, from a Radical posture, or from the (not necessarily coincident) point of view of a sociology of conflict, the focus of attention is likely to be directed to "real" conflicts between "real" groups acting out immediate, social-structurally conditioned imperatives, in the intellectual style of the Liberal-Conservative consciousness, these struggles tend to be projected to the level of ideas and anchored in the minds of men.

Just as Nisbet was disposed to see (logical) "paradoxes" where others might see (structural) contradictions, so the Assimilationist Perspective promotes the conceptualization of "real" conflicts in the form of "moral dilemmas" which, in Myrdal's classic analysis (1944), pose the discontinuity between expressed attitudes (the American Creed) and divergent behavior (American deeds). Defined as a dilemma, the solution is appropriately envisioned through the reintegration of attitudes and behavior. Within the parameters set by the attitudinal element of prejudice and the behavioral component of discrimination, the problem becomes detached from its historical dimensions and dissociated from its structural moorings, inviting a neat, mechanistic cause-and-effect formulation. Consistent with the conclusive *convictions* that vitalize ideologies, as distinct from the probing, provisional *hypotheses* that must guide scientific inquiries, there is little hesitation as to what constitutes "cause," and what "effect." It appears attractively self-evident that attitude antecedes and generates behavior, that prejudice determines discrimination; and within the limits of such a *socially* constructed problem-formulation, perhaps quite sensibly so.[10]

The solution to the social problem which the moral dilemma epitomizes, follows as logically as it appears to have been ineffective. Liberal-Conservative strategies of resolving intergroup tensions, social-psychologically defined, have not led *significantly, unidirectionally*, or *universally* toward the goal of "tolerance" with regard to various racial or ethnic minorities. Assimilation continues to occur *intermittently*, and to proceed *selectively* both among and within certain minorities; conflict remains endemic, varying over time only in terms of *frequency, intensity, type* or *style*, and *protagonist* or *target*; and so with competition, accommodation, or cooperation as social processes that are frequently associated with patterns of racial or ethnic relations.

Clearly, the key to understanding and explaining such variations and fluctuations has eluded the overwhelming proportion of sociologists who, during the period under consideration, sought to come to analytic grips with racial and ethnic pattern through the conceptual framework of the Assimilationist Perspective. That this perspective has predominated for so long, bears witness to the triumph of ideology in its intertwined relationship with sociological theory. Their disentanglement becomes highly problematic for, as we have tried to show, in sociology perhaps to a greater extent than in any other discipline, theory and ideology bear a subtle affinity for one another. Their inevitable coexistence has provoked insufficient scholarly attention, to effect their unambiguous distinction, achieve their effective segregation, and re-establish their appropriate relationship.

IV

We have tried, in our analysis, to raise and elaborate a number of points of criticism that attach to a long-prevailing dominant orientation in the American sociology of racial and ethnic relations — an orientation which we traced from its inception at the modest level of a concept to its emergence as an explanatory principle, and which we have designated the Assimilationist Perspective. At the root of the various difficulties that have been discussed, we believe, is the failure of this orientation to achieve intellectual and scientific emancipation from a merely social construction of reality. Our identification and criticism of this failure is emphatically not an argument for the disengagement of sociology from the significant issues of social life; it is, however, a recognition of the analytic and interpretive necessity, in sociology, for maintaining a profound detachment from any and all *socially* generated definitions of these issues.

The scientific *re*construction of common-sense conceptions appears as the most elementary prerequisite for a viable discipline of sociology, one that is capable of reflecting its insights back to the social world in the form of relevant knowledge. Failing such a reconstruction, its knowledge is compromised, its insights become pedestrian and its *raison d'être* is subject to challenge. The all-too-frequently confounded distinction between sociological problems and social problems is a vital one for sociology, and cannot be overstressed. The words of Alfred Schutz (1964: 248) in this regard bear noting:

The problems of the theoretician originate in his theoretical interest, and many elements of the social world that are scientifically relevant are irrelevant from the viewpoint of the actor on the social scene, and *vice versa*. Moreover, the typical constructs formulated by the social scientist for the solution of his problems are, so to speak, constructs of the second degree, namely, constructs of the common-sense constructs, in terms of which everyday thinking interprets the world.

The Assimilationist Perspective, we have tried to show, represents the forsaking of this most elementary prerequisite of science in that it fails to constitute a "construct of the second degree." Its role in the sociology of racial and ethnic relations is therefore revealed as scientifically spurious, and its unreconstructed transposition from a particularistic social interpretation of the world marks it as a counterfeit theoretical persuasion.

Notes

1. The intellectual style of seeing such journalistically defined events only in their immediate configuration as a discrete newsworthy "happening" bears close parallels with the "Social Problems Orientation" discussed in the preceding chapter, and presents comparable challenges to the historian and the sociological theorist. Georg Lukács, for example, points to the "unhistorical and antihistorical character of bourgeois thought" in terms of which historians remain imprisoned by the immediacy of events, totally unable to break out toward interpreting "the problem of the present as a historical problem." This complete failure, he argues, "has reduced otherwise meritorious historians and subtle thinkers to the pitiable or contemptible mental level of the worst kind of provincial journalism" (Lukács, 1971: 157).

    For sociologists, the failure to penetrate the superficialities of various popular designations of social events and to grasp their historical genesis, their structural foundations and their underlying linkages, leads to their atomization as "social problem" issues, and results in what C. Wright Mills has criticized as "abstracted empiricism" and "The Professional Ideology of Social Pathologists" (Mills, 1959; 1942).

    Thus, the journalistic cast of the conflict events cited above deflects attention from their common denominator of ethnic and racial antagonisms. The so-called "Draft Riots" only thinly veiled Irish-Negro and, to some extent, Catholic-Protestant dissentions behind the orgies of mob-violence that Herbert Asbury (1927: 118-147) portrayed as convulsing much of New York City. The conduct of urban political machines, labor struggles, crime in general and organized crime in particular, must similarly be recognized as masking powerful aggressive or defensive ethnic and racial strategies (Bell, 1953). The more recent "Forced Busing" and "Forced Housing" contentions differ only, in that their designations constitute conscious obfuscations of their manifest racial agendas, seeking instead to pose the issues in terms of such Liberal-Conservative democratic homilies as "freedom of choice" and "non-interference by government" (see Bash, 1978).

2. This is, of course, just one instance of a wide-spread pattern that lent American sociology its distinctive character. For example, John Horton (1964) has shown how ideological factors served to deflect classical sociological concepts from their social structural references and to psychologize them into attitudinal variables.

3. For a discussion of the *usefulness* of paired dichotomous constructs, see Reinhard Bendix and Bennett Berger (1959: 97f, 110-112). for a discussion of the *history* and various *types* of paired contra-conceptions, particularly in their dialectic relations, see Robert Friedrichs (1970: 51-55, 296-297); for an argument for the *need* for contra-conceptions, particularly "order" and "conflict" models, in order to afford mutual comparison and the possibility of correcting respective interpretive biases, see Hermann Strasser (1976: 16); for a counter-argument, challenging as a "myth" the "schism" reflected by the "order" and "conflict" dichotomy, see Anthony Giddens (1976: 714-715, 716-718).

Giddens holds that the dichotomy is misleading and inadequate as a conception for the development of theory, as well as crude and unsatisfactory as a device for distinguishing the theoretical traditions they were ostensibly designed to epitomize. Accordingly, he favors abandoning the schizmatic conception, or overcoming the dichotomy by "combining" or "integrating" it.

Our own view adheres closer to that of Bendix and Berger, and of Strasser. Any conceptual or theoretical position articulates a particular perspective and is therefore narrowly exclusive of other perspectives. Therein lie the potentials for its analytic insight and power, and the inevitability of its commensurate bias and distortion. The development and distillation of theory, we would argue, depend on and, indeed, are vitalized through the possibility of contrary, and the potentiality for contradictory interpretations of research findings. It is precisely the appearance of anomalies, frequently generated through competing theories and models as Kuhn (1962) and Friedrichs (1970) have traced them in science and sociology, that lead to revolutionary "paradigmatic" reconstructions.

When we speak of "society" we generally have reference to a social complexity which, at one and the same time, appears as a sustained normative order, as well as its incessant discombobulation, frequently through the mechanism of conflict. This makes our problem loosely analogous to that of subatomic physicists who, in terms of Heisenberg's Uncertainty Principle, experience measurement difficulties that result from their inability to deal simultaneously with both position *and* momentum of a particle.

Sociologists face the conceptual and operational problem of being able to focus either on order *or* on change, on society as structure *or* on society as process, but not on both at one and the same time. The present state of theory does not appear ready to embrace this seeming antimony, and its more immediate task would best lie in the refining of adequate partial theories relating to the dimensions of order and conflict.

To that end, "order" and "conflict" models retain their distinct heuristic properties, which are probably far from analytically exhausted. Any effort toward merging, combining or integrating them as Giddens urges, or even effecting their synthesis (in the technical, dialectic sense) as van den Berghe (1963) has attempted and Gerhard Lenski (1966: 17-20) regards as well on the way, would seem premature and unappreciative of the insights which their alternative perspectives afford. The absence of such an alternative perspective or contra-conception, as we have tried to show, has helped to entrench the Assimilationist Perspective to the distortion and detriment of race and ethnic relations theory in sociology.

4. Quoted in Brewton Berry (1965: 329).

5. It is worth noting that criticisms of "Consensus" and "Order" assumptions are not peculiar to sociology. These types of assumptions appeared to find wide-spread favor among post-World War Two historians, and were the subject of severe criticism in John Higham (1959). For a broader and more recent critical overview of orientations among historians, see Irwin Unger (1967).

6. This tension between sociology's conservatism and its practitioners' typical liberalism is also discussed in Bendix and Berger (1959: 112).

7. It is noteworthy, in passing, that Nisbet's own conservative disposition leads him to couch this tension in the form of a "paradox" — a *logical* opposition, an *intellectual* incongruity, an antimony of *principles* — where a critic of more radical inclination is disposed to point to contradictions, oppositions or dialectic antagonisms that are *structurally* generated and merely *reflected* at the ideational or superstructural level.

8. "THE racial problem" subsumes, of course, a wide variety of definitions both as to *what* "the racial PROBLEM" is, and *who* constitutes "the RACIAL problem." However, during the time under consideration in this inquiry, and phenotypic distinctions aside, in the North its salient features did not appear significantly different from those of the "immigrant problem" in that Blacks, as (im)migrants from the rural South, "simply" constituted an additional category of competitors in the urban industrial opportunity structure.

In the South, where former slaves had been transformed into a rural proletariat of increasing irrelevance under conditions of rapid agricultural mechanization, "the racial problem" was differently conceived. If assimilation appeared as a liberal policy option in the North, in the South it was viewed as untenably radical. But solutions that appeared more realistic in terms of the Southern conception of "the racial problem" made strange bed-fellows indeed! On the one hand, some white Southern leaders, along with the Ku Klux Klan, supported resettlement proposals that would remove Blacks "back" to the Republic of Liberia, a plan that paralleled the goals of the Marcus Garvey Movement; on the other hand, some of the most notoriously racist Southern Senators urged the establishment of a separate region in the U.S. for the exclusive settlement of Blacks, and with the promise of cultural, economic, and at least internal political autonomy, a proposal that was essentially congruent with the then official policy of the Communist Party, U.S.A. in its agenda on behalf of American Negroes. For a discussion of such "a strange concourse of social logic," see Oliver C. Cox (1965).

Contemporary Black arguments for racial separatism, due to their recency and their less-than-concerted articulation, may be difficult to assess with sufficient perspective. However, despite their "radical" (more properly "militant") rhetoric, and even considered as short-range strategies, this writer is less inclined to view them as radical or liberal options, than as "romantic" retreats or reactionary responses, leading to an historical dead-end.

9.   For a fuller statement of each of these approaches, see Paul B. Horton and Gerald R. Leslie (1965: 31-41).

10. But again, what appears as socially sensible must be treated as sociologically problematic, as Robert Merton (1949) showed some time ago when he posed the various hypothetically possible relationships between prejudice and discrimination.

PART IV

*Transcending the
Assimilationist Perspective*

CHAPTER 8

Toward a Sociological Reintegration of Racial and Ethnic Relations

I

Our assessment of a period of more than four decades of very lively and intense sociological interest in the field of American racial and ethnic relations has thus led to a severely critical view of the discipline's dominant preoccupations and contributions in this area. Without retreating from such a critical assessment of this period's predominant course of development, we need now to pause, shift attention, and pick up some more or less latent and subordinated strands of sociological engagement with racial and ethnic concerns, as a departure for exploring constructive directions for the field's future course. Specifically, it appears vital to indicate necessary conceptual reorientations which would permit its reintegration with general sociology, and would redress the kind of theoretical impoverishment and insularity to which we had attributed much of the field's slanted social relevance and questionable, if not spurious, sociological posture.

Whatever may be said in criticism of the distinctive traits and leading motifs that have been ascribed as the mark of American sociology in general or of its various specialized fields of inquiry, the discipline has never been entirely monolithic in its conceptual and theoretical perspectives. That there have typically been undisputably dominant and,

171

indeed imposingly dominating theoretical perspectives (or, as it has become the fashion to say, "paradigms") which have guided the direction and modulated the inflection of the bulk of American sociological efforts, should not be allowed to obscure a tradition of alternative conceptual-theoretical orientations. It should go without saying that the existence of such an alternative tradition, however obscure, is implied by the very ascription of "dominance." Critics such as Gouldner, Atkinson and Strasser who have pointed to that tradition (see 143-145, *supra*), may not agree precisely on its character, its salience or its role vis à vis the dominant theoretical motif, but there is no question that alternative perspectives, quiescent or on occasion stridently contrapuntal, have been a sustaining feature of the American sociological enterprise.

Needless to say, in the special field of racial and ethnic relations, too, there were during the period under consideration a relatively few sociologists whose perspectives rendered them peripheral to the vastly predominant orientation we have called the Assimilationist Perspective, and whose work is less, or not at all, vulnerable to the kind of criticisms we have developed. Also, there were, of course, a handful who approached racial and ethnic concerns through Marxian orientations which committed them to postures that were antithetic to Concensus models of society in general, and to the Assimilationist Perspective in particular. The impact of their contributions, as a potential corrective, for example, to the perspectivistic excesses of the dominant orientation, was regrettably muted, since the temper of the times (even in academia) relegated their work decidedly to the periphery of mainstream sociological exposure and recognition. A prime example of such largely disregarded rather than critically discredited contributions would be the major work of Oliver Cromwell Cox (1948). In consequence, the Assimilationist Perspective remained, virtually unchallenged by an effective contra-conception, as the governing orientation that structured the preponderance of research in the field over the decades we have subjected to consideration.

It was not until the early 1960s that a growing social

unrest effectively forced upon sociologists a recognition that
the confrontations were of a systematic, rather than a merely
sporadic and idiosyncratic character, and that their liberal-
conservative assumptions had to be regarded as demonstrably
irrelevant and recognized as increasingly untenable. The
growing demands and escalating militancy among Blacks
towards "Freedom, Now!" could not but, first, confront
white intransigence, and then collide with white counter-
organization and aggressive resistance strategies that reached
their epitome in the reviving Klan's recalcitrant slogan of
"Never!". Intergroup conflict, seemingly structured along
racial lines, with a not-fully-understood but clearly significant white ethnic group dimension involved, proliferated
to the point of polarizing communities, and threatened to
eventuate in a polarized society.

The effect, predictably, was a period of conceptual and
theoretical disarray in sociological concerns with ethnic and,
particularly, racial relations. The extensive "racial unrest,"
manifested through "sit-ins," boycotts, marches, "lynchings,"
bombings, assassinations, confrontations centering about
voter-registration and the desegregation of schools, neigh-
borhoods and public accommodations, etc., to say nothing
of annual "Long Hot Summers," provoked profound
uncertainties about sociological conceptualization and its
theoretical frames.

As regards conceptualization, the turn of events virtually
halted assimilation in its "psychological adjustment" sense
as an operant social process, and all but transformed the
notion, at least as it pertained to Blacks, into a conceptual
anachronism: Blacks who already had been thus "assimilated"
(Gordon, it will be recalled, had termed it "Identificational
Assimilation") demanded their full and long-past-due citizen-
ship perquisites; other Blacks, if anything, "dissimilated" in
the attitudinal or identificational sense of the term, preferring
to shift their identification away from "Americanization" to a
probing "re-Africanization" — while insisting, socially, on their
full civil rights just the same. Persuaded that convenants had
been broken and dreams deferred too long, the racial cleavage
deepened and many Black Americans opted for varieties

of Black Nationalism (Essien-Udom, 1962). "Assimilation-as-psychological-adjustment" as well as "assimilation-as-cultural-adaptation," both subsumed under Novicow's concept of "denationalization," threatened to come to a grinding halt and shift into reverse toward Black "renationalization." Notably, and clearly not unrelated to such developing patterns among Black Americans, white ethnics and American Jews[1] showed evidence in the course of the 1970s of retrieving and reasserting their cultural identities toward a proliferation of ethnic nationalisms. The general mood clearly shifted away from assimilation and the "Melting Pot" ideal, in the direction of a society characterized by an uncertain Cultural Pluralism.

Conceptually then, assimilation as a social process had lost much of its empirical base, and as a reigning concept it had shed its imperial clothes and stood revealed in all its hollow form and its normative inflection. As a "theory," no matter how spurious, it could no longer function in its role as a guiding motif for sociological inquiry, especially in proportion to the extent that it articulated with psychological or social psychological theoretical frames. As social unrest and "racial" confrontations proliferated across the "conservative" South as well as through the "liberal" North, among "culturally disadvantaged" rural and "cosmopolitan" urban areas, they could but expose the explanatory poverty bequeathed sociology by asking essentially psychological, attitudinal questions about "prejudice" and "hostility" in regard to events that begged to be understood in historical and social structural terms. Social psychological approaches, particularly collective behavior and social movement theories, have an obvious bearing on and explanatory potential for the study of some of these events, but they tend toward the organizational rather than the historical in scope, and toward social rather than societal dimensions in range. Such theories offer little toward identifying or accounting for the common structural provocation for these phenomena, or why, *as a class*, they precipitated in American society in this manner, and at the time, that they did.

Quite apparently, as a guiding motif toward sociological

interpretation and explanation of the structure and processes of racial and ethnic relations in the United States, the Assimilationist Perspective had been relegated to swift and professionally embarrassing obsolescence. But perhaps more fundamentally — resorting again to Gouldner's terms — the kind of "domain assumptions" on which it was predicated and the theoretical "infrastructure" in which it had been immersed, were called severely into question. The sharpened ideological debate over racial issues in society spilled openly into critical controversies over their sociological apprehension, and where the polemic heat did not preclude entirely the generation of light, a path was cleared for the possibility of a theoretical reorientation. As might have been anticipated, the initial reactive tendency was toward a complete swing of the pendulum: from Consensus, Coherence or Order Models, and Functional and Value-Integration Theory or, in our case, from Assimilation Models and "Theory," to Conflict Models and Conflict Theory. In our view, as we had developed it earlier (Chapter 7, note 3), this kind of either-or approach appears fundamentally fallacious, and the unilateral and uncritical assumption of a "Conflict Perspective" commits the discipline to the equal, if opposite, distortions engendered by the "Assimilationist Perspective."

What is called for, it appears, is a judicious reconceptualization, of a fundamental sort, of the sociological approach to the field of racial and ethnic relations, one which would serve to reintegrate this conceptually and theoretically detached area with general sociology. Throughout our analysis, we have pointed to a basic and wide-spread failure to transcend the common-sense, social constructions of reality toward their scientifically requisite sociological reconstruction. In the proceeding discussion we shall attempt to contribute toward redressing this failure, to suggest how racial and ethnic phenomena might more appropriately be conceptualized in sociology, and to indicate the kind of theoretical frame with which this field may fruitfully be linked. Throughout, our abiding concern remains the deflection of ideological instrusions, that tend to infuse the conceptual and theoretical apparatus of sociological endeavors.

II

Our inquiry had begun with an examination of the special problem of concepts in sociology. It is in this, the broadly conceptual realm, it was argued, that the discipline appears most vulnerable to the intrusion of distortive and biasing contingencies. However impeccable and systematic a design for the collection of data may be, and however judiciously the gathering of data and their statistical analysis may be carried out, even the initial determination of what shall constitute data in a given inquiry inescapably filters through semantic elements in the form of concepts. Such abstracted and generalized semantic filters consign for apprehension certain properties, and conceal from attention other characteristics of the phenomena which constitute their empirical referents. For better or for worse, this relationship *between* concept and referent is beyond our control, once the concept has been objectified in the sense of having congealed in its consensual meaning. The only matter that appears open to negotiation thus turns on the prior, frequently unreasoned, and broader process of conceptualization, which Robert Friedrichs (1970: 142-148) refers to as "the crystallization of bias." It poses the Humpty-Dumptean question of whether our concepts are to control us, or whether we shall be their masters. The very possibility of a sociology, as we understand it, hinges on the answer.

In order to pursue this problem further, with the view of approaching a more sociologically appropriate conceptualization of racial and ethnic relations, it is necessary that we take a somewhat circuitous route. Heretofore we have done little more than make reference to the notion of "reality constructions," and indicated (mostly by assertion) their distinctive bearings on social life and on the sociological enterprise. We need now to take an excursion into a more analytic and systematic consideration of this notion, and trace its specific significance for our concerns.

The point of departure for such an excursion, as well as its ultimate termination, fixes attention on concepts. In the narrow sense, concepts appear as the basic designative terms that give empirical focus to a *particular manner of conceptualizing*, which includes not only an interpretation of a category of events but, even more fundamentally, their *categorization* in the first place. Such a conceptualization stipulates what phenomena are deemed of-a-kind and therefore to be sorted into a common cognitive bin, as well as what bins they are logically related to and in what manner, including to which ones they are properly superposed, juxtaposed or counterposed. As concepts are the terminological elements of a conceptualization — and indeed, as a language code they serve as primary *evidential* features of the much more tacit conceptualizations from which they emanate — so conceptualizations constitute cognitive patterns within a broader perspective.[2] The latter, along with the even more general and substantially less explicit frames in which they participate, reflect and lend coherence to each of the multitude of possible social constructions to which whatever "reality" is "out there" is subject, and through which that "reality" becomes knowable by virtue of the meanings that are imputed into it.

These kinds of concerns are not only of epistemological interest, but also pertain significantly to the foundations of a sociology, and form a frame, specifically, for the subject matter of the sociology of knowledge. This has been shown particularly by Berger and Luckmann who, through their "redefinition of the scope of the sociology of knowledge" toward concerning itself "with the social construction of reality" (1966: 15), have shifted this field from its in-many-regards tangential, German philosophic moorings, into the central locus of American sociology. Part of the consequences that their effort accrued to sociology in general was not only a renewed sensitivity, built on Mannheim's legacy, to the perspectivistic character of both "reality" and "knowledge," and their relationships, but also the significant possibility, through their reformulation, of rendering these concerns more empirically amenable.

Consonant with such a sociology of knowledge perspective, it appears most useful for our purposes, to conceive of multiplicities of reality constructions sustained by diverse groupings in society; as well as (and carefully distinguished from the former) a variety of reality constructions entertained within the discipline of sociology, and issuing into alternative theoretical orientation or "schools." Each of such constructions, social ones and sociological ones, stipulates and lends meaning to what is to be regarded as properly "real" and what is to constitute appropriate "knowledge," and it conditions just how such "knowledge" of such "reality" is to be distilled, validated and institutionalized or, to use Berger and Luckmann's term, "objectivated" (1966: 35-36, 60-61).

The role of language is a crucial one in both the social construction and the social maintenance of such reality complexes. Berger and Luckmann (1966) point out that the "common objectifications of everyday life are maintained primarily by linguistic signification" (37); that "[l]anguage provides the fundamental superimposition of logic on the objectivated social world" (64); and that "[l]anguage builds up semantic fields or zones of meaning that are linguistically circumscribed" (41). It appears then that language is of major significance for the *maintenance*, the *coherence* and, importantly, the *integrity* of any given social construction of reality. In other words language, apart from *articulating* it, *sustains* a social construction of reality, and through the extent or scope of its utilization, *stakes out the province* within which a particular reality construction prevails and enjoys validity. It is this last function of language, its role in marking the boundaries to the domain within which a social construction of reality is held meaningful and perceived to carry validity, that interests us here in particular.

It is generally recognized that the complexity of, particularly, industrial societies, provides the basis for multitudes for social constructions of realities, traceable to various stratificational, occupational, ideological, ethnic, religious, etc. subgroupings. Within a given society (and so-called "counter-cultures" perhaps excepted), each of such operant reality constructions is likely to constitute little other than a variation on the dominant cultural givens, with little likelihood of abrupt discontinuities from one such social construction to another. The prevailing "canopy of legitimations" (Berger and Luckmann, 1966: 62, 102ff) and, significantly, the processes of "primary socialization" (129-137), are strong cognitive and normative control devices that ensure the essential compatibilies of most of such alternative constructions of reality, and lend a basic coherence to everyday life.

Yet, their general compatibility must not be allowed to obscure the genuine distinctions which such reality constructions do engender, distinctions which uphold their integrities and inhibit their fusion. To the extent that alternative constructions of reality represent cognitive responses to the historically-relative and situationally-specific shared experiences of their respective carriers, they constitute meaning-conferring structures that are, to some degree, discrepant with one another. This recognition is indicated by Berger and Luckmann in their frequent use of such terms as "reality enclaves" and "province of meaning" (26), or "semantic fields" and "zones of meaning" (41). Notably, such terms also underscore again the important role that language plays in sustaining and circumscribing the interpretive mode of a given social construction of reality, and protecting its integrity with regard to alternative constructions.

While Berger and Luckmann restrict their discussion primarily to reality constructions in everyday life, our concerns push us to a consideration of reality constructions that transcend the common-sense knowledge of everyday life, into what Berger and Luckmann refer to as "finite provinces of meaning" (25).[3] Specifically, we are interested in the special type of reality constructions and their existential social base, which Burkart Holzner (1968: 69-71) associates with "epistemic communities." Such "communities" are predicated on a "meshing of highly similar role orientations" and they become evident where the "at least partially interlinked roles . . . are unified by a common epistemology and frame of reference," and when a requisite value congruency is sustained among the participants. "All members of such a community, in their capacity as members agree on 'the' proper perspective for the construction of reality" (69), a construction that is typically *not* shared on a society-wide basis. Among other examples of epistemic communities, and only alluded to in Berger and Luckmann's discussion of "finite provinces of meaning," Holzner points to "the scientific community" as representing a social organization of specialized knowledge.

What sets this "community" part from most, if not all, others is that its thematic reality constructions serve ostensibly one and only one overriding purpose: the fabrication of objective, valid and reliable knowledge. As such, it "constitutes a departure of some kind from the 'natural reality' of everyday life" (Holzner, 1968: 122) or, in Berger and Luckmann's terms (1966: 25), the "turning away of attention from the reality of everyday life" that is characteristic of all "finite provinces of meaning." The reason for this rests squarely in just how, given their distinctive purposes, "reality" and "knowledge," along with their modes of relatedness, are construed in science as opposed to social life.

Scientific knowledge must be regarded, in the end, as theoretical knowledge, whereas knowledge in social life embodies, and pertains to the immediately practical. Accordingly, while scientific and common-sense knowledge may both have soundly empirical foundations for what they respectively construe as "real," their reality constructions turn out to be not coincident at all. They are incongruent even to the extent that the scientifically "real" appears as "abstract," "*im*practical" or "merely theory" from the perspective of the layman, while the "realities" of common-sense social constructions may be deemed superficial, or "merely appearance" from the point of view of science.[4] Where, along a controversial social problem issue for example, scientific and common-sense perspectives find themselves in confrontation, time and again their respective spokesmen discover themselves talking past one another, and in the end each concludes that the other simply "misses the point." The recently fashionable social attribution of "irrelevance" (aimed not only at the social sciences) seems quite apropos here since, in a genuine sense, they *are* talking about different "things" — different "realities" — and their respective pertinences appear, indeed, as not relevant to each other's "realities."

In everyday life, the "real" tends to be defined by the *situationally* relevant, the *experientially* significant and the *intuitively* cogent, with its validity heavily influenced by the criterion of what appears *plausible*. It is thus typically conditioned by the culture-bound, historically-myopic, ideologically-constrained, and biographically-idiosyncratic factors that structure such plausibility judgments. In contrast, scientific knowledge (or theory) makes claims to *universality* (Willer, 1971: 6), and what is considered "real" transcends the limits of the scientist's direct biographical and familiar cultural "natural" experience. Accordingly, it necessitates the conscious "fabrication" of a research "design," the "concoction" of conceptual and statistical "devices," the "artifice" of experimentation or the empirical "contrivance" of systematic data gathering — in other words, the synthetic strategem of "methodology." In brief then, generally in everyday social life "reality" is accepted as a *given* ("received"), and knowledge of it is largely derived *experientially* ("naturally") and treated as *conclusive*; in "good" science, at least, "reality" is construed as *problematic* (to be "discovered") and thus approached *hypothetically*, and knowledge of it is approximated *experimentally* ("artificially") and entertained as *tentative*.

It appears then, that the various reality constructions are characterized by an epistemological and cognitive distance that may reflect discrepancies which are only mildly discontinuous, as in the case of most of the alternative *social* constructions that prevail in the everyday life of a given society at a particular point in historical time. On the other hand, they may indeed be virtually incommensurate, as we are claiming is the case between social and properly *scientific* reality constructions. As such, they appear to confront one another, separated by a gulf not unlike that observed by C. P. Snow between "The Two Cultures," and must be regarded as incommensurable as Ruth Benedict found it necessary to view distinct cultures in the more traditional anthropological sense. Indeed, as participants in a "social organization of specialized

knowledge" (Holzner, 1968: 122ff), scientists share a camarad-
erie much like that von Clausewitz had noted with respect to
military generals, regardless in what nations' services they
practiced their profession. By virtue of similar training,
perspective and professional commitment, scientists (and this
holds even more demonstrably *within* disciplines) share
membership in and identification with an "epistemic
community" that cuts across conventional socio-cultural,
political and national demarcations, such that they, as
scientists at least, have more in common with one another
than with their respective lay communities.

As noted earlier, the semantic cement that not only maintains the internal, logical coherence but also protects the
integrity of a reality construction over against the incursion
of others, is language. It would be difficult to overestimate
the importance of language for the social construction of
realities, and its role in their institutionalization. Without
language, there would only be individual sensations, and only
through it can "raw" perception be processed and fabricated
into conceptualizations or meaning-infused constructions of
reality that admit of collective sharing and transmission in
the form of a collective (social) heritage. However, the
unique capacity that language provides for the codification
of an epistemic system, and its very facility as a vehicle for
its communication within such a sub-universe constitute, by
their nature, serious impediments to meaningful communication *across* such sub-universes. So-called sub-cultures provide
a good example.

It is one of the notable and typical characteristics of a
sub-culture that it generates a specialized and shared "sub-
language" — a patois, argot, slang, a technical language or, as
it is viewed pejoratively from the outside: jargon or cant —
or, as it is perhaps most appropriately termed, an *idiom*. It is
clear that an idiom serves, among other functions, to enhance
the cohesion and solidarity among the participants in a sub-
culture, and is therefore also a measure of their relative
dissociation from other reference or identification groups.
Such an idiom is more than a concomitant but is, indeed, an
integral element of any reality construction, and where the

vernacular of everyday life codifies and sustains common-sense, social constructions of reality, the technical languages of "epistemic communities" articulate and lend coherence to such "finite provinces of meaning" as exemplified by scientific constructions of reality. In this regard, an idiom is not unlike a more conventional "foreign" language which, on the one hand, encapsulates, but also serves to express a unique cultural heritage. Accordingly, the vernacular of common-sense everyday life and the technical language of a scientific discipline should, like "foreign" languages, admit of translation into one another.

This matter of translation, however, constitutes a serious problem, for just as one social construction of reality is, by its "nature," irreducible to another, so the respective languages in which they are couched may be "bridged" into approximation with each other through translation, but they can not be reduced into one another through direct corre-spondence. The problem of translation from the vernacular to a scientific language is even more acute than comparable renditions from one "foreign" or national language into another. The latter, representing more-or-less nation-specific vernaculars, may be assumed to give expression to common experiences of everyday life that are in large part shared, in the Western world at least, across political boundaries which are, in this regard, essentially arbitrary. Subtleties of meaning do, of course, remain highly problematic, as anyone who has had the experience of translating literature can attest, or as is recognized in the conduct of diplomatic affairs and demon-strated periodically in the politically sensitive United Nations, where an "international incident" can materialize merely through a translator's innocent or careless misconstrual of a delicate nuance. Such subtleties aside, however, common-alities that may prevail across national languages can not be assumed so readily when it comes to everyday life and scientific constructions.

Berger and Luckmann note a tendency toward "hermetic sealing," which characterizes finite provinces of meaning and creates autonomous "esoteric enclaves" inaccessible "to all but those who have been properly initiated into their

mysteries" (1966: 87-88). Nevertheless, they observe, the
dreamers, scientists, artists or mystics who inhabit such
enclaves "*also* live in the reality of everyday life. Indeed, one
of their important problems is to interpret the coexistence of
this reality with the reality enclaves into which they ven-
tured" (26). Holzner, too, observes that "no matter how
specialized a mode of reality construction may become, no
matter how 'abstruse' its products may look to lay man,
somewhere and sometime it must be referred to this sphere
of common sense" (1968: 122). The scientist's "esoteric
work (which he may be quite unable to explain to his children or even his wife) must connect, if only by means of
lengthy social 'bridges,' to the reality of common sense" (123).

The difficulty of extending such bridges *meaningfully*
varies, of course, relative to the remoteness and autonomy
of a scientific reality construction from those of everyday
life. The problem would be minimal, for example, if the
translation need merely span two distinguishable reality
constructions *within* everyday life, where it would be accomplished through relatively minor "shifts of attention." When,
in contrast, it becomes a matter of bridging seemingly incommensurate reality constructions such as those characterizing
common-sense everyday life and some more esoteric
"epistemic community" or "finite province of meaning," the
challenge can become formidable indeed. Rather than being
enabled by a moderate cognitive "shift of attention," it may
demand a major epistemological "leap" and, in the absence
of some transcending meta-language, the problem is exacerbated by the limitations of either of the very languages
available for its accomplishment. As Berger and Luckmann
(1966: 26) observe:

The common language available to me for the objectification of my
experiences is grounded in everyday life and keeps pointing back to it
even as I employ it to interpret experiences in finite provinces of
meaning. Typically, therefore, I "distort" the reality of the latter as
soon as I begin to use the common language in interpreting them, that
is, I "translate" the non-everyday experiences back into the paramount
reality of everyday life. This may be readily seen in terms of dreams,
but is also typical of those trying to report about theoretical, aesthetic

or religious worlds of meaning. The theoretical physicist tells us that his concept of space cannot be conveyed linguistically, just as the artist does with regard to the meaning of his creations and the mystic with regard to his encounters with the divine.

What appears needed here, then, is not simply the service of a translator but that of an *interpreter*, a distinction that is rarely drawn in common parlance. The "leap" from common-sense constructions to scientific ones involves not as much of a translation in order to correlate corresponding meanings, as it does a *transmutation* that somehow manages to connect rather disjunct epistemologies across the distinct languages in which they are couched. It becomes crucial, therefore, to recognize language not simply conventionally as a facility for communication but, significantly, also for its obverse role as a system-specific guardian of meanings, and therefore as an inhibition to the synthesis or fusion of systems, and a serious impediment to the ready translation of system-bound meanings and significances into one another.

We are now ready to turn our attention back to concepts. What has been observed about languages in their specific pertinence to and reflection of particular modes of conceptualization or, more broadly, systemic constructions of reality, applies equally to concepts as the terminological nodal points on which a language is structured. But there is a difference that leaves concepts even more circumscribed than the language in which they participate. As suggested in the opening paragraph of this section, conceptualizations constitute alternatives, in the sense that there is some degree of freedom, some room for negotiation, as to which construction is to be entertained for a particular purpose or in a given context. As alternative constructions, they sustain the option, within some limits no doubt, of shifting from one conceptualization to another as occasion demands and ingenuity affords. Not so with concepts. In effect, pick your conceptualization, and you "buy" along with it a parcel of the concepts that are meaningfully imbedded in it. Probably more frequently, it works in the other direction: one chooses to employ a particular concept, and inexorably one has "bought into" an entire conceptualization — too often without conscious awareness or due appreciation for either its theoretical or its empirical implications. As Karl Mannheim (1953: 19) has noted: "However isolated it may seem, a concept still has systematic presuppositions."

Not only are concepts lodged *meaningfully* in a particular conceptualization, but their arbitrary extrication and interpolation into a different conceptualization entails semantic hazards that are directly proportional to the respective epistemological autonomies, and the remoteness of the two constructions. This is emphasized by Mannheim (23) as he elaborates on the previous point:

It cannot be doubted, however, that concepts only occur in series, and that consequently there is no such thing as an isolated concept; this is demonstrated beyond doubt by the fact that even the most "inexact" concept has a place where it properly belongs, and that it will show at once if it is "transferred" into an alien sphere, where it can only be applied "metaphorically."

This same point has also been made more recently as the central thrust of John Horton's (1966) article on the (ideologically competitive) vocabularies that lie imbedded in Consensus and Conflict theoretical approaches to the (normative) sociology of social problems. Building on C. Wright Mills' arguments about the perspectivistic character of the "vocabulary of motives" reflected in (at least then) current American sociological modes of explanation (702), Horton points to the "not very accurate sociology" that results when the "situated actions" of one group are interpreted "theoretically" (by sociologists) *through* the perspectivistic and ideologically contaminated vocabularies of another. Horton concludes that "[o]nce the sociologist is involved in the study of anything that matters, he has the unavoidable obligation of at least distinguishing his vocabulary from that of the group he is supposedly observing . . ." (713). In an earlier discussion, Horton addressed a similar issue, and implied strongly that the sociologist should "accept the premise that a social fact is behaviour *seen from a perspective*," lest he become imprisoned in the role of ideologist: "The ideologist represents socially determined knowledge as not socially determined, claims that *his perspectives have nothing to do with his concepts*" (Horton, 1964: 298, italics added).

For our purposes, the implications of Mannheim's and Horton's thought are clear: a sociological "vocabulary" must, in that sense, constitute a "meta-language," one that transcends the "vocabularies of motives" of *any* of the groups that are to be sociologically apprehended. If the language of any group-specific common-sense construction of reality also becomes the language of its scientific construction, if the conceptual constituents of a *social* construction of reality become the semantic "coin of the realm" of a *sociological* construction, then the "epistemic community" of science becomes coincident with the reality constructions of everyday life; the perspective of sociology is reduced, through common coinage, into equivalence with common-sense, or any of its variants. In other words, it virtually guarantees a blurring of the distinction between knowledge and the objects of knowledge, against which Ernest Nagel had warned, and it underscores the recognition that a sociology, *including its conceptual tools*, must be predicated on a sociological *re*construction of prevailing social constructions of reality.

There is one more point of clarification that must be made, before we move to the next section. From what has been developed over the last several pages, it is apparent that as *meaningfully* integrated constituents of a particular conceptualization, construction of reality or perspective, concepts must be viewed as rooted rather integrally in a specific congitive system. Accordingly, and mindful of Mannheim's comment that however seemingly isolated, "a concept still has systematic presuppositions," we have argued that concepts that are intruded into a different conceptualization, function in their new context as *metaphors* at best, as innocuous *malapropisms* at least, or with a capacity for considerable systemic *distortion*, at worst. It is worth reiterating that it would be erroneous, to infer from this that concepts sustain an immanent meaning of their own. Rather, concepts have no intrinsic meaning (Willer, 1971: 23-24), but function as *carriers*, freighted with the meanings conferred on them through the cognitive structure in which they participate. Judith Willer shows this quite clearly in the context of science, when she observes (32, italics added):

The elements of scientific systems are concepts and their referents. Concepts are symbols, not observables. Conceptual meaning cannot be reduced to a set of empirical observations. *Instead concepts gain meaning by their relation to other concepts at the theoretic level.* They are not identified with their empirical referents but are connected to them through abstraction ... *Empirical objects, regardless of how "real" they are thought to be from a viewpoint outside the scientific system of knowledge, can only enter into the system if means exist for their measurement.*

Willer's last point will be picked up again in the following section. Here, finally, we want only to note that as concepts are inherently meaningless, the "same" concept may indeed be encountered in different conceptual settings. Importantly, however, in properly integrated and logically coherent conceptual constructions, such concepts will turn out not to be the same concepts at all, their *nominal* synonymity or identity not withstanding. Specifically, their empirical referents may turn out to be rather different "things" (even to the point of participating as constituents of alternative reality constructions); or, perhaps more typically, such concepts will focus attention on distinct properties of similar "things." To the extent that this is found to be so, it is a consequence of the concepts having been formally specified and logically connected in "their relation to the other concepts at the theoretical level" in each of the conceptual systems, resulting in some degree of conceptual closure,[5] and in distinctive crystallizations of conferred meanings. The imperative for such system-specific meaning bestowals should be appreciated especially (in the light of the preceding discussion), when the "same" concept occurs in both an everyday life construction of reality and a scientific one or, as happens so frequently in sociology, when it is "conveniently" transferred from the former into the latter.

III

Our excursion into matters of reality constructions, their affinities with specific languages or idioms along with their integral concepts, and the semantic problems of "bridging" across the idiomatic integrities and even epistemological gulfs that insulate one such construction from another, should serve as a logical foundation for our sociological concerns with concepts. It is our intention then, specifically, to address the issue of inadvertent intrusions of biases, particularly ideological ones, into sociological conceptualizations; we want also to examine the problem of "cause-and-effect" attributions and the related one of distinguishing mere "symptoms" from "substance," as such determinations are conditioned by the assumptions that diffuse through alternative reality constructions; and finally, we want to suggest the direction of a rapprochement between what we have characterized as the theoretically isolated, if not downright atheoretical "sociology of racial and ethnic relations," and the general structure of sociological theory.

In order to "come to terms," then, with concepts, probably the place to begin is head-on with the amorphous notion of "race" and its inviting but insidious accessibility for the conceptualization of certain group interaction patterns as "race relations." To begin with, so-called "race relations" have of course little, if anything, to do with race in that term's technical scientific — and that would mean most specifically genetic — sense of meaning. On the assumption of their monogenetic origin, the prevailing distinguishability of races among mankind may be attributable to some early geographic isolation of groups to form discrete breeding populations under distinctive environmental conditions, and possible introductions and gradual diffusion of genetic mutations. To the extent that this is valid, it attests rather precisely to an absence of "race relations."

Today, neither such geographic isolation of groups, nor an

effective containment of such populations' gene-pools can be said to prevail. It is apparent that in the modern world, if not perhaps all along, variations *within* a so-called race are greater than genetic differences *between* races. At best then, the notion of "race" becomes a statistical concept, bespeaking the absence of abrupt discontinuities between "races," and expressing the probability that certain discrete, genetically transmittable characteristics may be expected to appear in one population only in greater preponderance than in another. This recognition was evident already in the work of Johan Friedrich Blumenbach as early as 1775, and led to the transition from typological thinking to "populationist thinking, from the search for pure forms to the statistical analysis of variety" (Banton and Harwood, 1975: 24-25, 47). The inevitable decline of geographic isolation to the point of its effective absence, as in the United States, has made possible — while ineffective containment and even massive breaches of the integrity of such populations' gene-pools stand as testimony to — not wide-spread "race" relations, but extensive and (if one may say) intensive *social* relations.

Now, this distinction is crucial and needs to be firmly grasped and established, lest words get the better of us. First of all, the distinction does not rest in "race relations" being merely a subtype of a more generic "social relations." Nor is the distinction "merely semantic" for, as we have tried to show, words are knit integrally into more or less specific cognitive structures, and to invoke a term is to mobilize a way of looking, to trigger a depiction — to engage a construction of reality. The propensity *to view* certain social phenomena *as* (though they were) "race relations," *to regard* certain types of group encounters *as* "racial confrontations," or *to look upon* certain collective behavior incidents *and see* "race riots," fails to give due regard to the significant process of *interpretation* that intervenes. It leads us either to be dishonest with ourselves, or to encounter "reality," without conscious awareness, through *metaphors*.

This failure, to treat with due care the interpretive processing to which perception is subjected, has become an unfortunate but widely practiced journalistic custom and is complemented by unwary habits of apprehension by a reading public. In conjunction, they constitute a popular pattern that is *magical* in effect (see Willer, 1971: 25-28, 39ff), for it invites us to "see" what, on several levels of "fact," is not there to be seen; or, to state it in the less dogmatic form that applies in many instances, it guides us unwittingly to a conceptualization of events that, in fact, lend themselves as well to numerous alternative conceptualizations.[6] The magical effect is, however, insidious in consequence, for as public definitions are congealed, as they are objectivated as social constructions of reality, they acquire a "reality" of their own (something of a self-fulfilling fatalism, Merton would say), and thus carry implications for public policy. If "racially" defined problems engender "racially" based solutions, and the implementation of such solutions turns out to have no impact on the problems, might not the problems have been *misconceived* as "racial" in the first place?[7]

The propensity to "see" race relations where there are none to be *seen* occurs, as we had put it, on several levels of "factual" observation, and it entails fallacies that carry insidious consequences for reality constructions in both everyday social life and in sociology. In everyday life, the fallacies assume something on the order of a combination of Bacon's Idols of the Market Place and those of the Theatre. What appears to be involved is an elementary level of "factual" observation where, by a blithe and popular inferential alchemy, a social event is magically transmuted into a spurious *racial* "observation." For example, violence, committed by persons who happen to be "white" or who happen to be "Black," is transmuted into violence *by* "whites" or "Blacks," and thus into *racial* violence.

While such observational transmutations must also constitute a matter of logico-empirical concern for sociology, there is another "level" at which observation does not just undergo transmutation horizontally, as it were, but is compounded by an inclination ("diagonally") toward *mystification*, and thus becomes particularly problematic, methodologically, for empirical sociology. This inclination is as disconcerting to those who assume a posture of *methodological* individualism in sociology, as it is distressing to those who take a stance of *ideological* individualism in social life, and it no doubt constitutes the foundation of what provoked W. H. Auden's aspersion: "Thou shalt not commit a social science." Here, "factual" observation is conjugated, conceptually, into the abstraction of an aggregate term, a "universal," or a collective concept, thus inviting the fallacy of misplaced concreteness. For example, violence committed by groups construed as "Blacks" or "whites" is not merely transmuted into "racial violence," but is conjugated into violence viewed *as a function of race* or, more crudely, as violence "caused by race." Abraham Kaplan observes (1964: 81):

From a methodological point of view, the most serious shortcoming of collective terms is the continuous temptation they hold out to commit the sin of reification. Though they are constructs or theoretical terms, they invite treatment as indirect observables, as if they designated individuals of a larger and more elusive kind than those ordinarily encountered in experience. This notion is reinforced by a mystique of "wholes," according to which these are "more than the sum of their parts," the parts being individuals and the whole the entity presumed to be labelled by the collective term.

The *"sin"* of reification lies in that it tends to "let the world get away from us." To reify a (merely heuristic) conception is to assign to it an ontological status, thereby placing it beyond our control, only to have it turn back upon us, as it were, and turn man into a creature alienated from his own creation. It is ironic, although this was very clear to Marx, that the very objectivation of the institutional order, the externalization of subjective processes and meanings whereby they became *inter*subjectively shared, objective constructions of reality that make social life *social* and, more fundamentally, *possible*, contains the potential for its own contradiction. Having "realized" the essentially *social* basis of human existence, it opens the possibility for apprehending that social basis as non-human facticity (see Berger and Luckmann, 1966: 20, 34ff, 88-89). Thus, the objectivation of social life through human activity that is indispensably facilitated through language, presents the "paradox that man is capable of producing a world that he then experiences as something other than a human product" (61).

This is of course precisely at the root of John Horton's previously quoted point, that the ideologist represents socially determined knowledge as not socially determined. In social life, where the ideologist (rightly) resides, the notion of "race" becomes hypostatized into a facticity that is apprehended as social only in its consequences, not in its origins. What an earlier science had formulated into the now discredited (?) postulate of racial determinism, is alive and well in contemporary social life in the form of the ideological posture of racism.

From the perspective of this ideological stance the notion of "race" is interpolated into observed events, thus goading their conceptualization as "race" relations, "racial" confrontations or "race" riots, etc., and turning the imputed "racial" dimension into an explanatory principle, rather than a (hypothetical) factor that needs to be explained. At minimum, "race" comes to assume the role of an independent variable (*explanans*) that presumptively accounts for what was observed, rather than that of a dependent variable (*explanandum*) which, itself, must be accounted for. Thus, to be told that a "high crime" area coincides with a neighborhood that had recently undergone a "racial" transition, is to be offered not merely a set of observations, but an account that contains, tacitly, its own "explanation": it tells us "all we need to know." Our ideologically-structured sense of cause-and-effect will conceive the coincidence as a correlation, and sort out where the "proper" causal attribution is to be assigned. In social life, therefore, "racial" assertions function as question-begging "explanations," predicated on something that, empirically, simply is not there — on a mystification of "reality" that assumes the proportions of a social and, potentially, sociological myth. As a reality construction with deep historic roots and wide ideological appeal, the "racialization" of social phenomena has not only permeated the common-sense constructions of everyday life, but diffused into the perspectives of sociology where it prevails as an amorphous presence. It therefore does not appear extravagant for Ashley Montagu to observe that "Race is the phlogiston of our time" (quoted in Banton and Harwood, 1975: 59).

The problem as it intrudes on sociology is, that what "begins by modestly assigning to its constructs merely heuristic status . . . all too frequently ends by confusing its own conceptualizations with the laws of the universe" (Berger and Luckmann, 1966: 186-187). Perhaps no notion illustrates this tendency toward reification better in sociology, than that of "race." Much like the concept of assimilation that we had traced through its domination of the sociology of "racial and ethnic relations" for a period of several decades, "race" slipped into the discipline from its popular and ideologically-condtioned use in everyday life, as well as through adoption from another scientific discipline, in this case from population genetics in particular, and human biology in general. From both sources, it imported the presuppositions, the domain assumptions, with which it was enmeshed in the respective prior contexts and, while thus adopted, it was never formally adapted through proper specification and conceptual integration into the "epistemic community" of sociology. The notion of "race" continued to be freighted with all the connotative baggage it carried in popular discourse, and some of the denotative meanings it sustained in population genetics. The former could not but ideologize sociology; the latter had to become increasingly irrelevant, as concerns with race were gradually dissociated from their pertinence to population studies in the hands of demographers (see Chapter 5, note 9), to become the special locus of "race relations" addressed by sociologists and, importantly, social psychologists. Patently, what race means to population geneticists and demographers is one thing; what "race" means to sociologists and social psychologists is quite another.

Just what "race" means to those who study "race relations" sociologically or social psychologically, actually remains surprisingly unclear. It can be argued that the notion is employed as a "construct" with "merely heuristic status," but it would be quite unjustified to claim that in its conceptualization in sociology, it was actually confused with a "law of the universe." Thus, to say that the notion was subjected to widespread reification in sociology, would be an unfair misrepresentation of the literature. More accurately, and consistent with Mannheim's caution, it tended to be "applied metaphorically," but as a *guiding* metaphor nevertheless, as an idiomatic expression in terms of which sociology "racialized" certain types of *social* relations in close accord with their popular conception in everyday life. In terms of our discussion in the preceding section, its transfer into sociology turned "race" into a malapropism which none but the unwary or naive took particularly seriously. Still, the notion's intrusion can not be considered harmless for, as an idiomatic expression, its sociological fit is uneasy and awkward, and constitutes a persistent strain toward the distortion of an appropriately sociological perspective.

In line with our earlier argument that for the sociologist, at least, "race relations" have nothing to do with *race*, we must now ask the rather pointed but obvious question: how did a non-social concept such as race get so deeply entangled in sociology as to become a substantive specialization in the first place? The answer is perhaps no less obvious, and parallels our previous accounting for the popularity of the notion of assimilation in the sociology of "race and ethnic relations." While assimilation, either as process or as product, had at least the saving virtue of offering a linkage with *social* (or psychological or cultural) referents, both notions intruded into sociological constructions because they were vital *ideological* elements of a *social* construction of reality and its concomitant "social problems" orientation. However "real" the notion of "race" may appear in social life, and whatever compelling plausibility it may hold there as an "explanatory key" to the experienced social disruptions associated with certain group encounters, in sociology the notion of "race" is empirically spurious and, to quote van den Berghe (1967: 6) again, "has no theoretical leg to stand on."

One of the scientifically insidious effects of adopting social constructions of reality *as* sociological ones, is the fallacious ascription of "cause" to what may, indeed, be "effect." It was noted earlier that laymen and scientists tend to "talk past one another" as a result of being led to regard the "realities" of each other's constructions as, respectively, "abstractions" and "mere theory," and "superficiality" and "deceptive appearance." The failure to sociologically reconstruct popular social constructions of reality, even where there is no serious question of actual reification of constructs such as "race," nevertheless tends to endow the notion with the substantial reality that is imputed to it so readily in social life. The resulting risks for sociology are that "effect" tends to go disguised as "cause," that *explanandum* may be confounded with *explanans*, that symptom is easily confused with substance or that, to borrow from genetics, the "phenotypical" might be taken for the "genotypical."

Now, metaphors make an enriching contribution to humanistic discourse, and idiomatic expressions can add a certain charm and elasticity to an otherwise overly-conventional language. In scientific discourse, however, their attractions exact a costly price in diminished semantic and conceptual precision. The notion of "race" in sociology can only be seen as functioning metaphorically, and in the form of a "foreign" idiom that has no empirically fixable *social* foundation. An empirical sociology preoccupied with "race relations" would be difficult to view as other than a sociology engaged in the pursuit of myth. To a considerable extent, as we have tried to show, sociology did address this field from the perspective of a *social* construction in everyday life, and to the extent it did, the field has stood in the kind of isolation from general sociological theory, that we had pointed out earlier with regard to the sociologically detached "theory" of assimilation.

However, as noted in the beginning of this chapter, the discipline has never been entirely monolithic in its conceptual and theoretical perspectives. There have been those who, particularly (but not only) in recent years, have avoided predicating their inquiries on "racial" presuppositions (metaphorical or otherwise), and several who have urged a conceptual shift that would direct the field toward a reintegration with sociological theory — and not incidentally, away from its ideological affinities. Thus, van den Berghe (1967: 6) has urged that "the sociologist might regard racial distinction as a special case of invidious status differentiation." Similarly, Reece McGee (1962) sought to knife through the socially and often sociologically disconcerting metaphor, when he wrote:

Contrary to first impressions, there is no objection in this country to a close association between white and Negro people. There has never been any particular objection (on the part of the white) to even the most intimate association with the Negro so long as he is clearly labeled as the inferior partner in the interaction. Status is the variable that structures the interaction between the white and the Negro and it is the only such variable. [33]

And again:

When whites object to sitting on the bus with the same Negroes who care for their children, cook their food, and clean their homes, it is clearly nothing about the Negro *individuals* that is feared. There is something else in operation, and when behaviors with regard to race are analyzed . . . it is plain that the "something else" is social status. Status is the scarce value and the Negro is an *identifiable competitor* for that value. [34]

This not yet fully accepted or systematically implemented shift from a conceptualization of certain types of intergroup relations in terms of "race" to one that builds on the basic sociological concept of social *status*, entails a number of constructive consequences for the field. It emancipates the sociological consideration of intergroup relations of this type from their fluctuating, racially-defined, and ideologically-permeated contexts in everyday life; it moves this field of inquiry out of isolation and into a position that permits its conceptual articulation with other substantively specialized areas in sociology; it leads, logically, to the accommodation of spurious "racial" groups under such general *group-status* concepts as "dominant group" and its reciprocal "minority group," with their logically implied and analytically potent concept of *power*; on the basis of an extensive adoption of these last concepts, it virtually guarantees that *conflict*, as a social process, will neither be obscured nor go ignored in sociological analysis; and finally, the shift promotes a fruitful nexus with a considerable range of broader sociological theory.

In the concluding chapter we shall explore rather briefly some of the directions of the theoretical rapprochements that are afforded through such a reconceptualization of this field from its common-sense social constructions to its sociological reconstruction.

Notes

1.   In regard to this reviving "nationalism," Jews present a special problem, as do Catholic Americans who should of course be mentioned also in this connection. The latter, particularly, point up a conceptual matter which we can indicate here, but to which we shall have to return, later in this chapter, as a more general concern.

     As a religious category, American Catholics lend themselves to subdivision, broadly, into Catholics of Irish, Italian, East-European and Hispanic ethnicity. It is by no means clear to what extent their stigmatization in American society on the one hand, or their resurgent nationalism on the other, are based on religion or ethnicity. In the case of Hispanic-American Catholics such as Puerto Ricans and Chicanos, the issue is further complicated by an additional ascription of "race." One might anticipate that in the American rank-order of stigmatization, racial identity is the most salient, followed probably by ethnicity and then religion — related, no doubt, to the facility with which a stigmatized identity can be renegotiated toward a more prestigious one (for a discussion of "passing," see Goffman, 1963: 73-91).

     Such "nationalist" strategies may be assumed to serve either or both of at least two functions: they can be defensive organizational devices for combatting, collectively, the stigma and its social consequences imposed by the larger society; and they can serve as a means for nothing more ominous than the preservation of a valued cultural heritage that stands in jeopardy of being assimilated into extinction.

     The point is that astute analysis of such social developments turns in large part on just how such groups are to be conceptualized. Their racial, ethnic or religious dimensions get lost in the generally used term "minority group," yet they sustain historically and culturally (and, yes, psychologically) important distinctions that impinge on an adequate understanding, and explanation, of the structural and processual significances of the groups' actions.

2. While it would go beyond our needs for the purposes at hand, a fuller consideration of such a "structure of contexts" within which cognition is guided, would profit from a number of discussions in the sociological literature. Among them would certainly be those of Mannheim on "total" and "particular" ideology (1936: 55-70); Gouldner on "background assumptions," ranging from the narrower "domain assumptions" to over-arching "world hypotheses" (1970: 29-35); Strasser on "guiding interests of cognition" (1976: 4-19); and the carefully crafted formulation by Judith Willer (1971) of the socio-cultural and historical contexts within which such knowledge systems as Magic, Mysticism, Religion and Science are "socially determined" (see especially chapters 1 and 3).

3. Within the "paramount reality" of the "common world of everyday life," there are "enclaves . . . marked by circumscribed meanings and modes of experience." These provinces of meaning are "finite," since they encompass only segmental aspects, rather than the totality, of social life. Examples would include professional, aesthetic, religious, or scientific "subworlds of meaning," entrance to, and participation in which would be afforded typically through processes of "secondary socialization" (Berger and Luckmann, 1966: 25-26, 138-147).

4. This becomes evident through a few illustrations. The desk-top on which I am writing and which, common-sense would appropriately have it, is experienced as a hard, solid, flat and stable surface, appears to the micro-physicist as a loose, tenuous, uneven and potentially unstable coherence of far-from-solid atoms, vibrating at a determinable rate. Or, the yellow paper in front of me "is," in scientific "fact," every other "color" (frequency on the spectrum) than "yellow," which alone it reflects back to my eye. It still jolts my son's common-sense experience to be told that the sun neither "rises" nor "sets"; and it jars mine to "realize" (meaning: "I am prepared to entertain a novel construction of reality") that the "space-age" has made non-sense (!) of the notion "down" — that "down" is no longer a universal direction, but at best a loose gravitational indicator. Illustrations abound, but we might cite the die-hard pragmatism of the still extant and far from facetious "Flat Earth Society," in the face of the long-term scientific recognition of the earth's spherical shape.

Closer to home, we need only note that from a sociological perspective, at minimum that of Durkheimian sociological realism, the "unique" and indisputably "real" individual of, particularly, American culture, becomes a conceptual abstraction, if acknowledged at all, while such a common-sense abstraction as "society" is vested with a reality *sui generis*.

We can't resist one more illustration of the absurdity that attends the interpretation of the language of one reality construction through the meanings that inhere in another. In the common-sense language of social life, and from the perspective of "whites" in particular, "Blacks" are considered part of the "colored races"; yet, viewed from an understanding of optical physics, it is evident that black is precisely the *absence* of color!

5. It is worth noting that even with the most exacting efforts toward refined definition, concepts, and theoretical terms even more than observational ones, sustain a logically and empirically inevitable, but also scientifically salutary "openness of meaning." For a discussion of this combination of frustrating problem and enriching prospect for science, see Abraham Kaplan (1964: 62-71).

6. That a given event lends itself to multiple version of reporting, each no doubt equally "faithful to the facts," is familiar in the context of the popular press. Newspaper examples abound and we could select at random. However, the following will serve as an illustration of our point. In as "neutral" a language as possible, this is what transpired:

> At a late evening hour, in an otherwise deserted metropolitan subway station, six male adolescents assaulted a female student who had just attended an adult evening class in a nearby Catholic high-school.

The event had occurred in August, toward the end of an escalating so-called "Long Hot Summer" of "racial" discontent, characteristic of many U.S. cities during the 1960s. While in June, the press reported such events as "fillers" on the back page, by August they had exploded into front-page headlines.

In this case, the headline read: *BLACKS GANG-RAPE WHITE GIRL*. In another time or another place, it might have read no less "correctly": *PROTESTANTS GANG-RAPE IRISH-CATHOLIC GIRL* (for that is what she was); or, perhaps in a world other than ours, it might have read merely: *BOYS ATTACK LONE GIRL*. (We need not explore here the more subtle question of whether, in this case at least, the term "rape" with its connotation of *sexual passion* is properly employed, or whether "assault," suggesting perhaps a working-class male modality of aggression against females, might be more appropriate. This is clearly a more elusive dimension of the issue of conceptual "neutrality.")

The point is that the headline used was not just a case of "selective perception," but functioned as an explanatory inference. It contained sufficient code-words to offer the reader a fully-wrapped package which included a self-contained explanation that fitted meaningfully into the broader popular belief structure about the summer's sequence of events: it proffered an instant reality construction. But *was* that, *in fact*, what *happened*?

7. Needless to say, critical questions might initially focus on whether there was enough time to effect the solution; whether the solution was a poor one from a strictly technical point of view; whether its implementation was administratively, or otherwise, bungled, etc. One hesitates, in the face of a rampant pragmatic faith, to voice a final critical suspicion: whether *all* problems are necessarily soluble.

CHAPTER 9

Conceptual Shifts and Theoretical Contours: A Concluding Note

I

The conceptual shift from "race" to *status* appears to be gradually restructuring sociological approaches in this field. Increasingly, it is serving to inform the discipline's attempt to understand a variety of *social consequences* that attend various *social definitions* of American population heterogeneity and its relationship to social structural complexity. From a broader developmental perspective, however, it becomes apparent that this shift represents merely a more recent conceptual transformation, having been preceded by one that shifted such issues from an essentially demographic conception to its, in our view, unfortunate embroilment with the racial metaphor.

As we had noted in previous discussions, prior to the earlier shift professional interest had centered on both the Black and the (non-White-Anglo-Saxon-Protestant) immigrant presence in the American population, and thus conceptualized, their study was typically associated with population analysis. Under then-prevailing *social* constructions of reality, the *social problem* tended to be conceived not so much as "racial" *per se*, as it was in terms of "race" generalized to an immigration issue and, more significantly, as the problem of the urban slums, particularly in Northern cities. It thus stimulated the concerns of humanitarians through philanthropic social work, as well as provoking the alarms of a flourishing Eugenics Movement. As a *sociological problem*, primarily defined demographically, attention tended to be focused on matters of population composition, population "quality," population distribution, and patterns of migration and immigration, pursued by demographers whose professional interests in the social consequences of such matters were at best ancillary. With the exception of the South where "the Negro question" was *the* consuming problem, neither "race" as such, nor ethnicity, appeared to be the primary conceptual "handles" in terms of which these issues were defined, either socially or in their social scientific apprehension. In terms of theory, issues so conceived resonated more with population theory than with sociological theory, although they prodded the formulation of the kind of normative theory associated in the discipline with "social problems."

Probably the single most significant piece of scholarship which appears, in retrospect (and paradoxically) at once pivotal, as well as ahead of its time with respect to the actual transition away from this demographic approach, was W. E. B. DuBois' *The Philadelphia Negro*, published in 1899. Written from an ameliorative impulse to serve as a knowledge base for philanthropic intervention, the study must also be seen in its significant conjunction of a demographic and ecological analytic base on the one hand, and a sociological concern with its social implications on the other. Thus, it was pivotal in that it focused on the situation of the urban Negro as a distinctive *social* problem, thereby edging this issue away from its primarily demographic conception toward a potentially central sociological locus of attention. And it was ahead of its time in the sense that a nascent American sociology, at the turn of the century, did not appear prepared to accommodate such a reconceptualization. Indeed, it is worth noting that after *The Philadelphia Negro* had been out of print for several decades, it was not until 1967 that time and, it appears, sociology caught up with it, as the independent decisions of the two New York publishers who, simultaneously, saw reason to republish the volume that year suggest.

II

The *first* conceptual shift, then, was one that appropriated "the Negro," conceived as a population segment with notable demographic characteristics, from the professional jurisdiction of demographers, to be transplanted in reconceptualized form as a "racial" group into a sociology of "race relations." Again, in terms of the fluid and historically fluctuating *social* constructions of reality, the "urban slum problem" in the North, altered by patterns of selective upward mobility among the descendants of European immigrants and their replacement through heavy in-migration of Southern Blacks, became little more than a euphemism for "the Negro problem" and, gradually, "the race problem." Thus, as the *social* definition of the immigrant "slum problem" gradually "racialized" the issue, so did sociology.

As rapidly as sociological attention was withdrawn from analysis of "the social problem of the slum," it was returned, albeit, reconceptualized as "the social problem of race." Slum residents, Blacks as well as those immigrants who, for whatever reasons (see Wiley, 1967), failed to move up and out, became in large measure the focus of analytic attention for the gradually crystallizing sociological specialization of "racial and ethnic relations." Significantly, the conceptual substitution of "the race problem" for "the slum problem" did not, at first, result in comparable shifts at the level of theoretical interpretation. Varieties of social disorganization theory continued to be brought to bear on the reconceptualized problem, until the ideological implications imbedded in this theoretical perspective finally became so evident and transparent as to effectively discredit it. This particular turning point must be associated with the publication of the so-called *Moynihan Report* in 1965 (see Rainwater and Yancey, 1967: 41-124), and the furor it raised over the linkage of certain indices of "social disorganization" and a "tangle of pathology" in the Negro "community," with a "structural breakdown" and "disintegration" of the Negro family.

The conceptual shift from demographic studies of population groups to sociological study of "racial" and ethnic relations eventually did attain linkage within the contours of a special theoretical frame. But again, the irrepressible ideological impulse had its guiding effect. Sociologists, then as now, seem to show affinities for Liberal social ideology, as we suggested in Chapter 7 in accounting for the popularity of the Assimilationist Perspective, and some of the tenets of that ideology tended to intrude upon sociological theorizing. For example, that there may be significant inherited racial differences between whites and Blacks is ideologically acceptable to archetypical Liberals, at least, only insofar as such differences appear to be *socially* irrelevant; and if they do turn out to be socially significant, their prominence must be ascribable to, and thus remediable through, *environmental* influences. As discussed previously, unlike the Radicals' imperative for sweeping societal reconstruction, adherents of both Democratic and Reformist Liberalism tend to view social problem conditions as amenable to piecemeal amelioration. Thus, in closer kinship with a Conservative stance, they regard reforms as properly implemented not through structural change in the first instance, but through superstructural modifications: through a stimulated outbreak of tolerance, through a better informed public that diminishes its reliance on stereotypic thought, through concerted efforts of persuasion, through altered attitudes and reduction of prejudice, through socialization, through general enlightenment.

It should hardly appear astonishing, therefore, that the kind of theoretical contours that sustained ideological congeniality turned out to be those of social psychology. Over the ensuing years, the sociology of "racial and ethnic relations" became, to a large extent, social psychologized and, on occasion, literally reduced to its sub-social psychological elements. In connection with our earlier analysis of the Assimilationist Perspective, it was noted that the predominant use of the concept of assimilation was in terms of its attitudinal significance of "assimilation-as-psychological-adjustment." Moreover, and in logical coherence with that meaning intension of assimilation, the central concepts brought to bear on the analysis of assimilation processes and in the sociology of "racial" and ethnic relations in general, were those of prejudice, stereotype, and social distance. These concepts, of course, reflect the affective, cognitive and conative categories that structure much of the social psychological literature. Social psychological theory, then, and not incidentally a theoretically compatible collective behavior approach, served as the dominant explanatory frames that informed sociological engagements with "racial" and ethnic relations.

Not surprisingly, this affinity with social psychological theory and, indeed, attachments to the theoretics of psychology, left the field vulnerable to the gradual recognition that conceptually, as we had argued, and theoretically as well (see 47-48, *supra*), the sociology of "racial and ethnic relations" retreated into isolation from general sociology. And no less surprisingly, the field had rendered itself concomitantly susceptible to a growing critical consensus (see Chapter 2, note 22) that, under the auspices of sociology at least, it "had no theoretical leg to stand on."

III

Throughout this period, as had been noted at the beginning of Chapter 8, there remained in evidence a modest but persistent maverick tradition of scholarship that contended with dominant patterns of sociological conceptualization and theorizing. It stood in contradiction, partly through assuming conflict orientations, to the established Functionalist motif and Consensus perspectives that had been characteristic of American sociology in general; and, as in the work of Oliver Cox (1948), against the no less ahistoric, largely social psychological, and assimilationist orientation that prevailed in the "race" and ethnic relations field in particular. Much as W. E. B. DuBois' scholarship on *The Philadelphia Negro* had been ahead of its time, so some of these opposed and often neglected perspectives anticipated the *second cognitive shift*, which reconceptualized intergroup relations viewed in "racial" and ethnic terms, to intergroup relations based on invidious status differentiation.

It is quite likely that the *second shift* was provoked more by the turmoil of events in American society in the 1960s, than by judicious conceptual reassessments and refinements, or by recognitions of theoretical inadequacy within sociology itself. Again it would appear, that academic sociology was more effectively informed *by* the events of social life, than it was able to anticipate those events and provide a timely illumination and interpretation of them *for* social life. The conceptual shift from "racial" (or ethnic) relations as pressed by the exigencies of social events must, in large part, have come through the unavoidable recognition that in too many confrontations, members of *different* races stood shoulder-to-shoulder on the *same* side of "the barricades"; in too many riots, neither rioters nor victims, nor intervening police or National Guard were racially homogeneous; in too many jails, particularly in the North, it wasn't race that distinguished the jailed from the jailers. When one can no longer tell demonstrators from counter-demonstrators by their race, it becomes increasingly difficult to continue to believe that one is observing racial demonstrations, even metaphorically, or to designate the resulting patterns of interaction as "race relations."

Nevertheless, the second conceptual shift was slow and halting in its realization, and depended on numerous contributing fragments for its not yet fully achieved consolidation. For example, in the context of a variety of published lectures and books, as well as in a widely reprinted essay addressed to this point, Ashley Montagu (1974: 435-444) had for years deplored the use of the term "race" in social as well as in social scientific discourse. As "man's most dangerous myth," he urged its abandonment just as chemistry had found itself, ultimately, having to relinquish the notion of "phlogiston," and as psychology had, finally, to give up its preoccupation with "instinct." In place of "race" Montagu proposed the adoption of "ethnic group," arguing that its focus on culture relates it to differences that are socially real, where "racial" distinctions, at the *social* level, are spurious. In sociology, at least, and despite its persuasive rationale, the impact of Montagu's argument or, perhaps more accurately, the attraction of his proposed substitution, appeared minimal. The reason is probably two-fold. First, the *historical* situation of Black Americans was distinctive and appears of sufficient salience, sociologically, as to constitute the loss of a significant explanatory dimension, in the event of a conceptual fusion of Blacks with *white immigrant ethnics* in the notion of "ethnic group." The second reason pertains to the empirical difficulty of demonstrating *categorical* cultural differences between American Blacks and *"non-ethnic" white* Americans, a fact that appears to distinguish rather significantly the current American situation from that of South Africa (and, perhaps to a lesser degree, the contemporary situation in England).

There were other contributing pieces that promoted the shift. In a development of his earlier conceptualization of "ethnic stratification" (1963: 20), Milton Gordon (1964: 51-54, 162) proposed the concept of "ethclass" by which he referred "to the subsociety created by the intersection of the vertical stratifications of ethnicity with the horizontal stratifications of social class" (51). So conceived, "the ethnic group is the locus of a sense of *historical identification*, while the ethclass is the locus of a sense of *participational identification*" (53). Accordingly, the concept of ethclass symbolizes a network of subcommunities, partially linked by class and partially by ethnicity (subsuming "race"). Having no ecological basis, this network constitutes a "social space" that affords the "transferability" of social status by any member of a given ethclass from one lateral subcommunity to another (162).

In a recent book, Ransford (1977) presses Gordon's conception further, addressing what appears as an "increasing need for reconceptualizing social organization as a race-class perspective" which he rightly considers as "a remarkably understudied conceptual area" (31). Recognizing that "with the ethnic identity movements of the last decade . . . the acculturation-assimilation assumption seems totally unjustified," Ransford points out that "Sociologists simply have not developed an explanatory model to handle the simultaneous trends of upward mobility and increased ethnic identification among America's conquered racial minorities" (1). In efforts to redress this failure, he generates three complementary models ("Open Marketplace of Status Interaction," "Minority Subcommunity," and "Ethclass") for exploring the interactive effects between the hierarchy of racial-ethnic qualities and the hierarchy of socio-economic characteristics (31-64). Ransford's work constitutes a major step toward the consolidation of the second conceptual shift.

Most recently,[1] William Wilson (1978) has given further impetus to this line of argument, anchoring it historically in the effects of successive relationships between changing systems of production and altering arrangements of the polity, and fortifying it with demographic data, employment statistics, and income and occupational distributions. Wilson maintains that the modern industrial era in the United States is generating a "progressive transition from racial inequalities to class inequalities" (3), and thus a "declining significance of race as a factor in determining the position of blacks in the labor market" (121).

The racial barriers that had been erected through deliberate and overt racial oppression for nearly a century since the Civil War have, for all practical purposes, crumbled under the impact of political, social and economic changes. In response to basic structural shifts in the economy, they are being replaced in the latter half of the twentieth century by obstacles affecting primarily a single segment of the Black population, a Black underclass which, in terms of life chances, does not distinguish itself significantly from its white counterpart. As these emerging barriers to mobility congeal, argues Wilson, they constitute a shift from pervasive racial oppression to enduring class subordination, and are thus racial neither in origin nor in calculated intent but, at

best, have racial significance in certain of their consequences
(2).

To the extent that "economic and political changes have
gradually shaped a black class structure, making it increasingly
difficult to speak of a single or uniform black experience"
(144), they are effectively "decreasing the importance of race
in determining the extent to which individual blacks have
access to or are able to develop resources deemed important
for life chances and survival" (88). Thus, concludes Wilson,
"class has become more important than race in determining
black life-chances in the modern industrial period" (150).

Wilson's analysis is primarily an empirically grounded
assessment of the Black *experience* in America. It is not
intended, in the first instance, as a theoretical thrust toward
a critical reconceptualization within an American sociology
that seeks to interpret that experience. Put another way, his
analysis shows that changing economic and political forces
are promoting subtle but significant alterations in American
social constructions of reality as they pertain to intergroup
relations: i.e., *social* definitions of Black Americans are
undergoing transmutations through which their once pre-
eminent racial identifications are becoming incidental to their
class affiliations. In short, Wilson is demonstrating that
certain social statuses are being historically redefined in
American *society*.

It has been our contention, as developed earlier, that
"race" as a social construction of reality never has constituted
a legitimate theoretical concept in terms of which a sociology of so-called "race relations" can be scientifically
elaborated. When the elastic and popular notion of "race" is
generalized and sociologically reconstructed in terms of the
concept of status as a positional element in society, it sustains a
flexibility for accommodating various specifications that may
be compelled by the fluidity of social constructions. Perhaps
more importantly, such a sociological reconstruction deters
sociology from ideological susceptibility to (and precludes its
complicity in) the shifting constructions of reality that
abound in social life and solidify under socio-historical
change. While the impact of Wilson's work is not primarily

theoretical, it contributes nevertheless to the second conceptual shift. Significantly, it underscores the historical specificity and consequent limitation of the popular notion of "race" as a "sensitizing concept" in the sociological analysis of intergroup relations, and argues implicitly for its conceptual reconstruction in the form of the more neutral and generalizing analytic concept of status.

Of a somewhat different order, but no less a contribution to the shift from "race" to status, is the direction taken by Joseph Scott (1976). Scott argues the thesis:

The "race problem" in the United States has not been nor is it today *at its base* an economic problem. At base the race problem has been a legal-political problem in which blacks and whites have been assigned to separate legal "estates," i.e., legal categories wherein racists have passed laws which guarantee to whites every conceivable economic advantage over blacks. [ix]

In sociological terminology, "estate" denotes a set of legalized social statuses or ranks. In this study the term refers to a set of legal-political and socioeconomic groupings of persons to whom are ascribed superior and inferior statuses or ranks by law. Its [sic] usually imposed on the powerless by those with a monopoly of power. [1]

What distinguishes Scott's conception from those cited above, is that the status dimension into which "race" is recast is *politico-legal* in the first instance, rather than *socioeconomic* in its dimensions as was the case in Gordon's, Ransford's and Wilson's conceptions, or essentially *cultural* as in Montagu's.

These brief examples are presented as representative of a number of relatively unconcerted efforts that are serving to shift the center of conceptual gravity in sociological inquiry from the distortive flirtation with the mystique of "race" toward an empirically sounder and a more ideologically defused sociological engagement with varieties of structured group differentiations. In a broader sense, such reconceptualizations function as genuine sociological reconstructions of the popular, common-sense social constructions of "race," and thus, finally, as social scientific penetrations of what Jacques Barzun had characterized as a modern superstition.

IV

It remains now to identify the kind of theoretical contours within which these gradually consolidating reconceptualizations find a logical nexus with sociological explanatory frames. First, however, we should note that the conceptual shift from the specificities of "race" and ethnicity to the general and more abstract concept of *status* had the effect of de-parochializing the discussion and introducing generalizability. It converted the analytic base from what inclined to be an idiographic consideration of a group's *peculiar* "racial" or cultural properties, toward a nomothetic treatment of the common or distinctive *categorical situations* of such groups in a given society. It made possible (a) the formal conceptualization of "racial" and ethnic groups in terms of their societal status as *minority groups*, (b) a specification of the "relations" associated with such groups as reciprocally linked with *dominant groups*, and (c) the identification of the critical dimensions that structure their interactive relations as varieties of *power relations*.

Once this conceptual foundation has been constructed, this field of inquiry is shifted from the periphery forthrightly into the central purview of sociology. Its now more generalized concepts serve as bridges to other substantive specializations in the discipline, and they sustain logical linkages with established bodies of sociological theory. The concepts of dominant and minority group, for example, literally invite a renewed theoretical rapprochement with Simmel's sociology of conflict, especially through his treatments of dominance and submission, and superordinate and subordinate relationships. The field's articulation with Marxian sociological theory which, prior to the second conceptual shift, was virtually beyond conceptual reach, has now become feasible and is being explored in varieties of ways. The vital concept which structures dominant and minority group statuses, that of power, attaches profoundly to the Weberian theoretical tradition which had been only minimally tapped for its potential, when this field was conceptualized in terms of "racial and ethnic relations."

In order, however, to bring the discussion down to more narrowly focused theoretical engagements which the study of intergroup relations affords as a result of its reconceptualization, we want to identify two theoretical alliances of a more specialized sort that were heretofore, for all practical purposes, conceptually precluded. One of these connections capitalizes on structural and processual matters and links the field to theories of *social movements*; the other is primarily structural in emphasis and attaches to theories of *social stratification*.

While the study of social movements has long been an established sociological tradition in Europe, it had never taken serious hold in American sociology. Even to the extent that it did, it was primarily through the work of the European-trained Rudolf Heberle. Consistent with American Consensus theorizing in general, with the aforementioned Social Problems Orientation of American sociology, and with extensively social psychological approaches in the "race and ethnic relations" field in particular, the American sociological inclination had been toward the study of "collective behavior" defined social psychologically, rather than toward social movements approached structurally and socio-historically. This distinction in conceptual-theoretical emphasis is developed skilfully in Leon Bramson's (1961) analysis in which he showed with regard to "theories of mass society" how their American elaboration in terms of "collective behavior" and "mass communication" gave their European formulation an ideologically conditioned "decisive theoretical twist." For a long time, while an American social psychology of collective behavior thrived, an American sociology of social movements languished.

Gradually, however, as *social* definitions began to refocus in response to the convulsive social events of the 1960s, as they, for example, became less focused on "problem *populations*" in their identification of social problems and more "issue oriented" in their conceptualization of such events, the stage was prepared. A cognitive shift was now possible toward viewing at least some of these issues in terms of social movements. In sociology, there appeared a concurrent reassertion of a social movement conception which did not address "the race problem" and its patterns of prejudice and discrimination, nor even "The Negro Movement" in particular, but a "Civil Rights Movement" and, even more generally, "Liberation" movements, as they began to proliferate.

The conceptual shift from a relatively static analysis of "racial" and ethnic particularities to generalized issues of dynamic societal transformation, is reflected in Roberta Ash's definition: "A social movement is a set of attitudes and self-conscious action on the part of a group of people directed toward change in the social structure and/or ideology of a society and carried on outside of ideologically legitimated channels or which uses these channels in innovative ways" (1972: 1). The definition is then brought to bear not on "race" problems in collective behavior terms, but on (among many others) the "Civil Rights Movement" in organizational and socio-historical terms (233ff). Another contribution to the reawakened interest in social movements is that of Anthony Oberschall. In distinction from Ash's approach, however, Oberschall's is characterized less legitimately by a (theoretical) Social Movement Orientation. More properly, his is a political sociology approach that conjoins aspects of conflict theory with a "mobilization theory" of the management, allocation and mobilization of resources (1973: 28-29), to be brought to bear on social conflict and social movements as *objects* of study. As such, Oberschall also examines, but more intensively and analytically than Ash, the "Civil Rights Movement" (204-241), along with a variety of other movements that have as a common element the goal of societal changes "that result in major shifts of resources from positively privileged to negatively privileged groups" (28).

The reconceptualization of "racial" and ethnic groups in terms of "negatively privileged groups" or, more generally, minority groups (strictly speaking, the terms are not properly synonymous), had the effect of generalizing the *societal situation* of groups that had appeared *intrinsically distinctive* under their previous conceptualization, and promoted a linkage with social movement theory. One of the gratuitous by-products of that linkage may well be that, along with several previously mentioned observers, Pease *et al.* (1970: 127) will not again have to admit: "The Negro movement was as unexpected by most sociologists as it was by other middle-class people who thought that things were getting better."

The other theoretical nexus that had been mentioned as now possible, is with *social stratification* theory. Where social movements appear primarily as collective *political* expressions, although rarely without their economic base, social stratification represents, in modern society, at base an *economic* structure through which varieties of significant social inequalities are selectively allocated across a population.

It needs to be noted that much like the somewhat belated American sociological interest in social movements, and for similar ideologically conditioned reasons, the study of social stratification, a field that one might have considered to be the tacit, if not explicit structural backbone of virtually *any* sociological investigation, was slow in catching hold in American sociology. Until the 1930s, as Pease *et al.* (1970: 128-129) point out, "[s]tratification did not appear to be worth studying," while in the following decade, despite some sociological attention occasioned by the great depression, "the inclination to look hard at the structural sources of institutionalized inequality didn't last long" (129). In the early 1940s, interestingly, it was the "Warner school" of social stratification, otherwise flawed on many grounds, which virtually alone and never fully exploited since, as Pease *et al.* point out, addressed ethnicity in a stratificational context and engaged in the "analysis of the place of Negroes in the community stratification systems of the North and South" (130). Characteristic of the ideologically attuned conceptual-theoretic twist that American sociology, in contrast to much of its European counter-part, gave to stratification analysis well into the 1950s, is Pease *et al.*'s critical summary of the "Warner school's" approach:

Stratification was viewed not so much as a matter of economic and political inequality, as a matter of differences in values and style of life. The emphasis was on status, prestige and esteem. [129-130]

In order to show specifically how the second conceptual shift articulates with stratification theory, it is useful to go back to the examples cited earlier as having contributed to that shift. Montagu's proposed replacement of the notion of "race" with that of ethnic group, it will be recalled, is of course likely to have its closest bearing on cultural anthropology and may serve perhaps particularly as a conceptual refinement in the work currently being done by urban anthropologists. However, with only a little "translation" or conceptual elaboration, the concept of ethnic group also affords a significant theoretical linkage with a sociology of social stratification. The *cultural* differences that constitute the distinctions between various ethnic groups, after all, represent diversities in shared *life-styles*. As such, they may be regarded as being of the same conceptual order as the life-style variations between subcultures other than those associated with ethnic groups in a given society. This would include such life-styles as characterize occupational subcultures, generally categorized as blue-collar, white-collar and managerial, as well as those life-styles associated with social classes. Values and life-styles, which Pease *et al.* quite properly critized for constituting *the* basis on which the "Warner school," among others, predicated a sociology of social stratification, are nevertheless a *crucial dimension* of social stratification. Through invidious comparison, styles of life, vested with relatively stigmatic or prestigious import, become implicated in the differential allocation of social status or prestige through what Weber had conceived as the "status community."

Gordon's and Ransford's efforts to move away from the more structurally-detached, social psychological, and largely ahistorical considerations of "racial" differences and "race relations," as well as from the primarily cultural analysis of ethnic group distinctions, led the former to the concept of ethclass, and the latter to its elaboration as a formalized analytic model. As a consequence of their work, and that of others it exemplifies, the analytic focus was shifted squarely into the context of stratification. What Gordon had visualized as a subsociety, "created by the intersection of vertical stratifications of ethnicity with the horizontal stratifications of social class," becomes the basis for differentially located *classes* in the social structure. Their situation depends not only on the unequal allocation of prestige arising from their ethnic dimension but, significantly, on the differential distribution of *life chances* that Weber had associated with "class situation" and which William Wilson (1978) had pointed to in his analysis.

Finally, one may indeed take some issue with Scott's *specific* reconceptualization of "race" to status in the form of his *legal estates*, a conception that appears critically vulnerable not so much historically, as in terms of its contemporary validity in the United States. Nevertheless, in its more essential conceptual thrust, Scott's contribution is reflective of a burgeoning literature on social *power* that lends itself to both of the types of theoretical linkage that have been discussed. On the one hand, the concept of power, in a variety of specifications, becomes crucial in structuring social movement theory. On the other hand, it serves in its more specific formulation as *political power* as the conceptual focus for the third important dimension of stratification, one that was least clearly elaborated in this aspect of Weber's work, and offered with a measure of German parochialism as "political party."

Writing as recently as 1970, Pease *et al.* had sound grounds for castigating surely the majority of sociologists "who fail to see 'race relations,' minority status, and poverty in the context of stratification," as well as for remarking that in terms of the American stratification literature: "The contributions of Marx and Weber still wait beyond the American ken" (1970: 134). By 1977, it appears, these observations warrant rather considerable modification.

V

Now, the issue that has been argued implicitly in the course of this chapter, is that as a result of relatively recent conceptual shifts that have occurred in the sociological apprehension of so-called "racial" (and ethnic) phenomena, this field has, for all practical purposes, worked itself out of business as a substantive or insight-producing sociological specialization. The question must be raised as to whether its subsumption under the theoretical aegis of a sociology of social stratification, or that of a sociology of social movements can be considered both *viable* and *adequate*. This question requires distinct answers.

The kind of work exemplified by our discussion of the contributions of Montagu, Gordon, Ransford, Wilson and Scott, poses very persuasive evidence that the *viability* of replacing "racial" and ethnic categories with stratificational ones, is not seriously in question. This issue was addressed thoughtfully by David Lockwood in the context of his recognition that the concept of "race" and the study of "race relations" have been relatively isolated from the mainstream of sociological analysis and the development of modern social theory (1970: 57). His critical analysis of the pertinent literature with respect to "the thesis that no special sociological categories are necessary to explain the structure and dynamics of race relations" (62), especially when considered in combination with the more recent stratification literature, leaves little doubt that the field's absorption under stratificational theory is eminently *viable*.

However, whether the theoretical framework of the sociology of social stratification, is *adequate* to the incorporation of all the significant dimensions of the "race and ethnic relations" field, is somewhat more problematic. In contention with the aforementioned thesis that Lockwood examines, he poses a provocative line of critique that has emerged through the introduction of the concept of "plural society" as a theoretical contra-conception to the concept of "class society" (Lockwood, 1970: 62-68). At issue is the question of whether such factors as, impatience, frustration, alienation, exploitation or oppression affecting minority groups, might stimulate a form of group action that is *not* class-based, and does *not* cut across "racial" or ethnic lines, as for example a working-class movement, predicated on a common class-consciousness, might. Certainly, recent events have shown that collective group action can, alternatively, organize *precisely* around a solidarity rooted in "racial" or ethnic consciousness, and effect the mobilization of latent nationalisms that inhere in "plural society." What is the *adequacy* of stratification theory for accommodating these types of phenomena? The answer is very simply that, while the sociology of social stratification can certainly be considered theoretically attractive and *viable* in its accommodation of the "racial and ethnic relations" field, it is neither equipped conceptually nor theoretically, for its *adequate* subsumption.

The answer to the question of the *viability* and *adequacy* of *social movement theory* for subsuming the "race and ethnic relations" field, would have to be the same: *viable*, yes; *adequate*, no. Thus, we are led to argue that stratification theories and social movement theories serve as complementary sets of options for a theoretic linkage of the erstwhile field of "racial and ethnic relations" which, from a *sociological* perspective has, itself, been revealed as devoid of both theoretical viability *and* theoretical adequacy.

However, in the light of our discussion (in Chapter 8) of the close logical relationship that concepts bear to the rather specific theories in which they are implicated, it must be clear that these two theoretical options are decidedly not arbitrary. Stratification theory and social movement theory, each, link with a particular conceptual repertoire, and many of the concepts participating in the one simply do not resonate with the theoretics of the other. This becomes apparent through only a brief look at the conceptual-theoretic integrities that pertain, respectively, to the "class society" and the "plural society" conceptualizations.

Thus, modern stratification theory, deductively bound to a "master" conceptualization of "class society," relates primarily to the economic *structure* of hierarchically connected *classes*, whatever analytically separable social status or political power dimensions may also be involved. In terms of its model assumptions, these latter dimensions, in their *structural* significance, bespeak the probability that class occupancy is consolidated, and entails a more or less commensurate command over economic, prestige, and political resources. The model assumptions of course also include the possibility of status incongruity, of class occupancy that is fractured, entailing incommensurate access to economic, prestige or political resources. This poses a potential for *dynamic* significance, at minimum, for individual attempts at consolidation of status inconsistencies through appropriate mobility adjustments, devoid of serious structural consequences; but more fundamentally, it also raises the potential for revolutionary structural change. It is through the collective, and thus essentially political, *actualization* of this potential, that the balance of *conceptual interpretation* of such collective action is tipped — either in the direction where it must be conceived as reflecting "class politics," or into one where some other type of political modality is conceptually appropriate. If the former, then it falls clearly within the locus of explanation of stratification theory. If the latter, then the most pertinent or powerful theoretical frame will have to be sought elsewhere.

Social movement theory, in its macro-theoretical dimensions, lends itself to logical linkage with either the "master" conceptualization of "class society" or that of "plural society." The type of collective action that is conceptualized as a "social movement" may be recognized either as class-rooted and class-specific, or as class-transcending and grounded in some other kind of identificational, organizational or symbolically circumscribing social principle. For that reason, the theoretical options that follow from the two "master" conceptualizations must remain equally accessible as explanatory frames.

For example, a particular movement may be an essentially class-based, interracial and interethnic political expression that is fortified ideologically through class-consciousness, in terms of which any latent "racial" or ethnic identifications are overridden and stigmatized as "false-consciousness." Such movements exemplify clearly the kind of "class politics" designed to restructure the prevailing hierarchy of the economic order and would, conceptually and logically, articulate with stratification theory.

On the other hand, a particular movement may arise from

the status frustrations of a minority group. As such, it would constitute the political expression of a "racial" or ethnic (or religious) minority, and be organized exclusively around "racial" or ethnic identity, and mobilized through an ideology of "race-consciousness" or ethnic nationalism that defines any surviving sentiment for class affiliation as "false consciousness," and in violation of movement orthodoxy. Minority movements of this type represent a form of "status politics," a conception frequently used to describe the political expressions of élites, but which finds its appropriate application also in the context of minority group movements. Unlike those engaged in "class politics," movements of this type lend themselves to linkage with explanatory frames associated with the "plural society" model, and articulate with theories of political sociology.

The notions of "race" and ethnicity, in other words, have been conceptually transcended and generalized. They have been transmuted and absorbed into one or the other of two constructs, those of *class* and *minority group*, terms that can be empirically grounded without inordinate difficulty and which articulate with either social movement theory or wih stratification theory. Which of these types of theory becomes relevant depends on the substance of the particular sociological inquiry, and specifically on a discernment of the *nature* of the "racial" or ethnic engagement in the phenomena under investigation. If, for example, it becomes apparent that "race is an epiphenomenon devoid of intrinsic significance and that present conflicts and problems transcend race" (van den Berghe, 1967: 94), then it is likely that matters of *class* override matters of "race" (or ethnicity) and become the operant dimension with its theoretical implications structured by a "class society" model. On the other hand, it is important to remain sensitive to Oliver Cox's (1948: 320) caution: "To call that which a group has been pleased to designate a race by some other name, does not affect the nature of the social problem to be investigated." Thus, where it *is* "racial" or ethnic status that becomes the essential impulse for collective action, then the phenomenon under investigation must be sociologically apprehended in terms of *minority group*, with all its conceptual, theoretical and "plural society" model implications.

A final comment on the concept of minority group. It should now be quite clear that *class* and *minority group*, while converging (without loss of their conceptual integrities) toward symbolizing distinctive social dimensions addressed by social movement theory, nevertheless represent discrete conceptual elements. They participate in divergent and mutually exclusive lines of theorizing which attach, respectively, to "class society" and "plural society" models. In no sense does the concept of minority group sustain any conceptual warrant in stratification theory or logical connection with the "class society" conceptualization.

It was noted earlier (214, *supra*) that the terms "negatively privileged groups" and "minority groups" can not be considered synonymous. "Negatively privileged group" is a *stratificational* term designating a group with relatively lesser access to economic, prestige or political resources. In itself, it carries no implications whatever toward prejudice, discrimination or injustice visited upon occupants of lower strata, when viewed in terms of the normative structure of the society at issue — regardless of the value judgments that can of course be imposed from *another* normative perspective. Class distinctions, in "class society," are institutionally legitimated and ideologically rationalized. Thus, it is as much a part of Liberal ideology in such societies to insist on *equal opportunity* for upward mobility while eschewing *equality of condition*, as it is part of Conservative ideology in such societies to regard lack of mobility as a "natural" and legitimate *consequence* of individual inadequacy in motivation, skills or social contribution. The existence of class inequalities in "class society" is not, in terms of its standards of legitimation, ground for a charge of *class discrimination*.

The concept of minority group, articulating with sociopolitical theory and implicated in the "plural society" conceptualization, carries considerably different significances. A *democratic* society, with or without normatively legitimated class distinctions, may include various "racial," ethnic, religious, linguistic, or otherwise identifiable subcommunities or populations. To the extent that, in *democratic* societies, their identifiability along such dimensions becomes the *basis* for categorically distinctive and inferior treatment,[2] such groups warrant the designation of "minority group." Unlike the stratificational concept of "negatively privileged group," minority group status is *not* legitimated through the normative structure of democratic society and constitutes, *by that society's normative standards*, an objective and incontrovertible case of injustice and anti-democratic tendency.

The confounding of this distinction leads to as many fuzzy and ideologically entangled controversies in social life as it engenders conceptual ambiguity, as well as methodological and theoretical derailments in the conduct of sociological inquiry. An awareness of their distinctive theoretical and model attachments should, however, underscore the discrete conceptual significances of the terms. Moreover, it should enhance their role as sensitizing concepts in the *sociological* analysis of key variables that tend to get lost in the *social* constructions of reality in everyday life.

We are ready, at this point, to conclude. What had appeared in American sociology as part of the demographic analysis of populations, and was first conceptually shifted under the impact of *social* constructions of reality into a "sociology of racial and ethnic relations," appears finally to have been reconceptualized out of existence as a sociological specialization. No doubt this was inevitable for a field of sociological concern that was conceptually isolated from the mainstream of sociological inquiry and thus detached from the general contours of sociological theorizing. As such, as we had attempted to show, the field had constituted for several decades little more than a scientifically spurious direct translation into sociology of a popular social construction of reality, complete with its idiomatics and ideological accoutrements which served to sustain a counterfeit theory such as the Assimilationist Perspective.

There is some measure of irony associated with the second conceptual shift from "racial" definitions to status conceptions. While it finally led to a scientifically tenable

sociological reconstruction of common-sense social constructions of reality, it did so in response to *socially*, rather than
scientifically provoked recognitions among sociologists that
"race relations" have nothing to do with race — and thereby
culminated in the nullification of the field as a sociological
specialization. Nevertheless, its proper sociological reconstruction, as we have suggested, has led to conceptual linkages
with structural theories of stratification and dynamic social
movement theory, which appear both viable and adequate as
complementary theoretical options, for subsuming the substantive sociological issues of intergroup relations.

Notes

1. William Wilson's book appeared just as this manuscript was going
   to press. I am indebted to Professor Melvin L. Oliver for bringing
   it to my attention.
2. The conceptualization developed here leads to the interesting
   recognition that the concept of "minority group" has validity
   only in *democratic* societies. Probably every society is characterized by one version or another of superordinate and subordinate
   groupings, and every society represents some system of (intern-
   ally) legitimated and institutionalized inequality. Superordinance
   or subordinance are, however, based merely on the manner in
   which authority and access to economic, prestige or political
   resources are unequally allocated. In a vitally important sense,
   structurally "subordinate" groups are not synonymous with
   "minority groups" and, significantly paralleling that distinction,
   differential treatment is *not* identical with *discriminatory treatment*.
   Something has to occur, before the notions of minority group
   and discrimination become applicable with any validity. What has
   to happen first is that the *justifications* for the structured inequality have to be drawn into questions — not just by a disadvantaged group, but more broadly through general consensus in
   society. Secondly, as a result of such general consensus (or, of
   course, through a successful revolution), *legitimacy* has to be
   withdrawn from the established structure of institutionalized
   inequality. Then, and only then, can a structurally subordinate
   group be redefined as a minority group whose status is incompatible with the principles of democratic society; and then, and

only then, can indisputably unequal and *differential* treatment be recognized to constitute non-normative *discriminatory* treatment.

In democratic "class societies" where achieved rather than ascribed statuses predominate, lower strata are demonstrably subordinate to those higher in the stratification structure, and their unequal access to economic, prestige and political resources marks them clearly as recipients of unequal treatment. They do not, in such societies, constitute minority groups however, and their differential treatment can not be deemed discriminatory. When, in democratic societies, such groups as "racial," ethnic or religious ones (resting on status ascription) are, on *those* grounds, singled out for categorically unequal or differential treatment, then *in such societies*, they *do* constitute minority groups, and their treatment is regarded as discriminatory and anti-democratic.

These, we believe, crucially important observations thus pose the seeming incongruity, that minority groups and racial or ethnic discrimination *can occur only in democratic societies* — to the extent that such societies reflect discrepancies between their enlightened principles and their operant practices.

References

Asbury, Herbert. *The Gangs of New York*. New York: Alfred A. Knopf, 1927.

Ash, Roberta. *Social Movements in America*. New York: Markham, 1972.

Atkinson, Dick. *Orthodox Consensus and Radical Alternative: A Study in Sociological Theory*. New York: Basic Books, 1972.

Baltzell, E. Digby. *The Protestant Establishment: Aristocracy and Caste in America*. New York: Random House, 1964.

Banton, Michael. *Race Relations*. New York: Basic Books, 1967.

———— and Jonathan Harwood. *The Race Concept*. New York: Praeger, 1975.

Barnes, Harry Elmer and Howard Becker. *Social Thought from Lore to Science*. Boston: D. C. Heath, 1938.

Barron, Milton L., ed. *Contemporary Sociology*. New York: Dodd, Mead, 1964.

Bash, Harry H. *American and German Sociologies: An Inquiry into the Development of Contrasting Methodological Orientations*. Unpublished Masters thesis, Indiana University, 1957.

———— "Conflict Intervention and Social Change: Sociological and Ideological Aspects of Professional Social Meddling," *Journal of Intergroup Relations*, 7 (December, 1978), in press.

———— "Counterculture: Some Problems in the Quest for Sociological Theory," in Seymour Leventman, ed. *Counterculture and Social Change*. Springfield, Illinois: Charles C. Thomas, 1979 (forthcoming).

———— "Determinism and Avoidability in Sociohistorical Analysis," *Ethics*, 74 (April, 1964), pp. 186-200.

———— "Review Essay: Orthodox Consensus and Radical Alternative," *Contemporary Sociology*, 3 (November, 1974), pp. 483-487.

Becker, Carl L. *The Heavenly City of the Eighteenth Century Philosophers*. New Haven: Yale University Press, 1932.

Bell, Daniel. "Crime as an American Way of Life," *The Antioch Review*, 13 (June, 1953), pp. 131-154.

Bendix, Reinhard and Bennett Berger. "Images of Society and Problems of Concept Formation in Sociology," in Llewellyn Gross, ed. *Symposium on Sociological Theory*. Evanston, Illinois: Row, Peterson, 1959, pp. 92-118.

Benedict, Ruth. *Patterns of Culture*. New York: New American Library, 1959.

Berger, Peter L. *Invitation to Sociology: A Humanistic Perspective.* Garden City, N.Y.: Doubleday, 1963.

_____ and Thomas Luckmann. *The Social Construction of Reality.* Garden City, N.Y.: Doubleday, 1966.

Bernard, Jessie. "The Conceptualization of Intergroup Relations with Special Reference to Conflict," *Social Forces,* 29 (March, 1951), pp. 243-251.

_____ "Some Current Conceptualizations in the Field of Conflict," *American Journal of Sociology,* 70 (January, 1965), pp. 442-454.

_____ "Where is the Modern Sociology of Conflict?" *American Journal of Sociology,* 56 (July, 1950), pp. 11-16.

Berry, Brewton. *Race and Ethnic Relations.* Third edition. Boston: Houghton Mifflin, 1965.

Bierstedt, Robert. "A Critique of Empiricism in Sociology," in Robert Bierstedt, *Power and Progress: Essays on Sociological Theory.* New York: McGraw-Hill, 1974, pp. 133-149.

_____ "Nominal and Real Definitions in Sociological Theory," in Llewellyn Gross, ed. *Symposium on Sociological Theory.* Evanston, Illinois: Row, Peterson, 1959, pp. 121-144.

Blalock, Hubert M., Jr. *Toward a Theory of Minority-Group Relations.* New York: John Wiley, 1957.

Blumer, Herbert. "The Problem of Concepts in Social Psychology," *American Journal of Sociology,* 45 (March, 1940), pp. 707-719.

_____ "Science Without Concepts," *American Journal of Sociology,* 36 (January, 1931), pp. 515-533.

_____ "What is Wrong with Social Theory?" *American Sociological Review,* 19 (February, 1954), pp. 3-10.

Bogardus, Emory S. "Measuring Social Distance," *Journal of Applied Sociology,* 9 (March-April, 1925), pp. 299-308.

_____ "Social Distance and its Origins," *Journal of Applied Sociology,* 9 (January-February, 1925), pp. 216-226.

Bramson, Leon. *The Political Context of Sociology.* Princeton, N.J.: Princeton University Press, 1961.

Bridgman, P.W. *The Logic of Modern Physics.* New York: Macmillan, 1927.

Butterfield, Herbert. *The Origins of Modern Science.* New York: Macmillan, 1961.

Cahnman, Werner, J. "Weber and the Methodological Controversy," in Werner J. Cahnman and Alvin Boskoff, eds. *Sociology and History.* New York: Free Press, 1964, pp. 103-127.

Catton, William R., Jr. *From Animistic to Naturalistic Sociology.* New York: McGraw-Hill, 1966.

Cooley, Charles Horton. *Human Nature and the Social Order.* New York: Scribner's, 1902.

_____ *Social Organization.* New York: Scribner's, 1912.

_____ *Social Process.* Carbondale: Southern Illinois University Press, 1966.

Coser, Lewis. *The Functions of Social Conflict.* Glencoe, Illinois: Free Press, 1956.

———. "Karl Marx and Contemporary Sociology," in *Continuities in the Study of Social Conflict.* New York: Free Press, 1967, pp. 137-151.

Cox, Oliver Cromwell. *Caste, Class and Race: A Study in Social Dynamics.* New York: Doubleday, 1948.

———. "Leadership Among Negroes in the United States," in Alvin W. Gouldner, ed. *Studies in Leadership.* New York: Russell and Russell, 1965, pp. 228-271.

Dahrendorf, Ralf. "Out of Utopia: Toward a Reorientation of Sociological Analysis," *American Journal of Sociology,* 64 (September, 1958), pp. 115-127.

Davidson, James D., Jr. and Joseph A. Schlangen. "Cultural and Structural Assimilation Among Catholics in the Southwest," in William T. Liu and Nathaniel J. Pallone, eds. *Catholics U.S.A.* New York: John Wiley, 1970, pp. 435-455.

Davis, Kingsley and Wilbert E. Moore. "Some Principles of Stratification," *American Sociological Review,* 10 (April, 1945), pp. 242-249.

Demerath, N. J., III. "Synecdoche and Structural-Functionalism," *Social Forces,* 44 (March, 1966), pp. 390-401.

Deutscher, Irwin. *What We Say/What We Do.* Glenview, Illinois: Scott, Foresman, 1973.

DiRenzo, Gordon J. "Conceptual Definition in the Behavioral Sciences," in Gordon DiRenzo, ed. *Concepts, Theory, and Explanation in the Behavioral Sciences.* New York: Random House, 1966, pp. 6-18.

Dore, Ronald Philip. "Function and Cause," *American Sociological Review,* 26 (December, 1961), pp. 843-853.

Driver, Harold E. *Indians of North America.* Chicago: University of Chicago Press, 1961.

Duke, James T. "Theoretical Alternatives and Social Research," *Social Forces,* 45 (June, 1967), pp. 571-582.

Durkheim, Emile. *The Rules of Sociological Method.* Glencoe: Free Press, 1938.

Edel, Abraham. "The Concepts of Levels in Social Theory," in Llewellyn Gross, ed. *Symposium on Sociological Theory.* Evanston, Illinois: Row, Peterson, 1959, pp. 167-195.

Elmer, M.C. *Contemporary Social Thought: Contributors and Trends.* Pittsburgh: University of Pittsburgh Press, 1956.

Essien-Udom, E. U. *Black Nationalism: A Search for an Identity in America.* Chicago: University of Chicago Press, 1962.

"Exchange." *The American Sociologist,* 12 (May, 1977), pp. 56-80.

Fairchild, Henry Pratt. *Dictionary of Sociology.* New York: Philosophical Library, n.d.

Faris, Ellsworth. "Are Instincts Data or Hypotheses?" *American Journal of Sociology,* 27 (September, 1921), pp. 184-196.

Faris, Robert E. L. "Assimilation," in Julius Gould and William L.

Kolb, eds. *A Dictionary of the Social Sciences.* New York: Free Press, 1964, pp. 38-39.

Fitzhugh, George. *Sociology for the South: Or the Failure of Free Society.* Richmond, Virginia: A. Morris, 1854.

Foss, Daniel. "The World View of Talcott Parsons," in Maurice Stein and Arthur Vidich, eds. *Sociology on Trial.* Englewood Cliffs, N.J.: Prentice-Hall, 1963, pp. 96-126.

Francis, E. K. *Interethnic Relations: An Essay in Sociological Theory.* New York: Elsevier, 1976.

_____ "The Nature of the Ethnic Group," *American Journal of Sociology,* 52 (March, 1947), pp. 393-400.

Francis, Roy G. *The Rhetoric of Science.* Minneapolis: University of Minnesota Press, 1961.

Frazier, E. Franklin. "Sociological Theory and Race Relations," *American Sociological Review,* 12 (June, 1947), pp. 265-271.

Freedman, Maurice. "Some Recent Work on Race Relations: A Critique," *British Journal of Sociology,* 5 (December, 1954), pp. 342-354.

Friedrichs, Robert W. *A Sociology of Sociology.* New York: Free Press, 1970.

Gellner, Ernest. "Holism versus Individualism in History and Sociology," in Patrick Gardiner, ed. *Theories of History.* Glencoe: Free Press, 1959, pp. 489-504.

Giddens, Anthony. "Classical Social Theory and the Origins of Modern Sociology," *American Journal of Sociology,* 81 (January, 1976), pp. 703-729.

Goffman, Erving. *Stigma: Notes on the Management of Spoiled Identity.* Englewood Cliffs, N.J.: Prentice-Hall, 1963.

Goode, William J. "A Theory of Role Strain," *American Sociological Review,* 25 (August, 1960), pp. 483-496.

Gordon, Milton M. *Assimilation in American Life.* New York: Oxford University Press, 1964.

_____ *Social Class in American Sociology.* New York: McGraw-Hill, 1963.

Gossett, Thomas F. *Race: The History of an Idea in America.* Dallas: Southern Methodist University Press, 1963.

Gouldner, Alvin W. "Anti-Minotaur: The Myth of a Value-Free Sociology," *Social Problems,* 9 (Winter, 1962), pp. 199-213.

_____ *The Coming Crisis of Western Sociology.* New York: Basic Books, 1970.

_____ "The Sociologist as Partisan: Sociology and the Welfare State," *The American Sociologist,* 3 (May, 1968), pp. 103-116.

Gumplowicz, Ludwig. *The Outlines of Sociology,* translated by Frederick W. Moore. Philadelphia: American Academy of Political and Social Science, 1899.

_____ *Der Rassenkampf.* Innsbruck: Maguerische Universitäts-Buchhandlung, 1883.

Hacker, Andrew. *Political Theory: Philosophy, Ideology, Science.* New York: Macmillan, 1961.

———— "Sociology and Ideology," in Max Black, ed. *The Social Theories of Talcott Parsons.* Englewood Cliffs, N.J.: Prentice-Hall, 1961, pp. 289-310.

Harding, John, Bernard Kutner, Harold Proshansky and Isidor Chein. "Prejudice and Ethnic Relations," in Gardner Lindzey, ed. *Handbook of Social Psychology,* Volume II. Cambridge: Addison-Wesley, 1954, pp. 1021-1061.

Hart, Hornell. "Some Methods for Improving Sociological Definitions: An Abridged Report of the Sub-Committee on Definition of Definition of the Committee on Conceptual Integration," *American Sociological Review,* 8 (June, 1943), pp. 333-342.

Hayakawa, S. I. *Language in Thought and Action.* New York: Harcourt, Brace, 1949.

Hays, Edward Cary. "Some Social Relations Restated," *American Journal of Sociology,* 31 (November, 1925), pp. 333-346.

Hempel, Carl G. *Fundamentals of Concept Formation in Empirical Science.* Chicago: University of Chicago Press, 1952.

Higham, John. "The Cult of the 'American Consensus'," *Commentary,* 27 (February, 1959), pp. 93-100.

Hinkle, Roscoe C., Jr. "Introduction," in Charles Horton Cooley, *Social Process.* Carbondale: Southern Illinois University Press, 1966, pp. xi-lxiv.

———— and Gisela J. Hinkle. *The Development of Modern Sociology.* New York: Random House, 1954.

Hochberg, Herbert. "Axiomatic Systems, Formalization, and Scientific Theories," in Llewellyn Gross, ed. *Symposium on Sociological Theory.* Evanston, Illinois: Row, Peterson, 1959, pp. 407-436.

Hofstadter, Richard. *Social Darwinism in American Thought.* New York: George Braziller, 1959.

Holmes, Oliver Wendell. *Speeches.* Boston: Little, Brown, 1913.

Holzner, Burkart. *Reality Construction in Society.* Cambridge, Mass.: Schenkman, 1968.

Horowitz, Irving Louis. "Consensus, Conflict and Cooperation: A Sociological Inventory," *Social Forces,* 41 (December, 1962), pp. 177-188.

———— ed. *The New Sociology.* New York: Oxford University Press, 1965.

———— ed. *The Rise and Fall of Project Camelot: Studies in the Relationship Between Social Science and Practical Politics.* Cambridge: The M.I.T. Press, 1967.

Horton, John. "The Dehumanization of Anomie and Alienation: A Problem in the Ideology of Sociology," *British Journal of Sociology,* 15 (December, 1964), pp. 283-300.

———— "Order and Conflict Theories of Social Problems as Competing Ideologies," *American Journal of Sociology,* 71 (May, 1966), pp.

701-713.

Horton, Paul B. and Gerald R. Leslie. *The Sociology of Social Problems.* Third edition. New York: Appleton-Century-Crofts, 1965.

House, Floyd Nelson. *The Development of Sociology.* New York: McGraw-Hill, 1936.

_____ "Social Relations and Social Interaction," *American Journal of Sociology,* 31 (March, 1926), pp. 617-633.

Hughes, Everett C. "Race Relations and the Sociological Imagination," *American Sociological Review,* 28 (December, 1963), pp. 879-890.

_____ and Helen MacGill Hughes. *Where Peoples Meet: Racial and Ethnic Frontiers.* Glencoe, Illinois: Free Press, 1950.

Inkeles, Alex. *What is Sociology?* Englewood Cliffs, N.J.: Prentice-Hall, 1964.

Kaplan, Abraham. *The Conduct of Inquiry.* San Francisco: Chandler, 1964.

Katz, Daniel and Kenneth Braly. "Racial Stereotypes of One Hundred College Students," *Journal of Abnormal and Social Psychology,* 28 (October-December, 1933), pp. 280-290.

Killian, Lewis, M. *The Impossible Revolution, Phase 2: Black Power and the American Dream.* New York: Random House, 1975.

_____ and Charles Grigg. *Racial Crisis in America: Leadership in Conflict.* Englewood Cliffs, N.J.: Prentice-Hall, 1964.

Kuhn, Thomas S. *The Structure of Scientific Revolutions.* Chicago: University of Chicago Press, 1962.

Lachenmeyer, Charles. *The Language of Sociology.* New York: Columbia University Press, 1971.

LaPiere, Richard T. "Attitudes vs. Actions," *Social Forces,* 13 (December, 1934), pp. 230-237.

Lazarsfeld, Paul F. "The Sociology of Empirical Social Research," *American Sociological Review,* 27 (December, 1962), pp. 757-767.

_____ William H. Sewell and Harold L. Wilensky, eds. *The Uses of Sociology.* New York: Basic Books, 1967.

Lenski, Gerhard. *Power and Privilege: A Theory of Social Stratification.* New York: McGraw-Hill, 1966.

Lindesmith, Alfred R. and Anselm L. Strauss. *Social Psychology.* New York: Holt, Rinehart and Winston, 1956.

Linton, Ralph. *The Study of Man.* New York: Appleton-Century, 1936.

Lockwood, David. "Race, Conflict and Plural Society," in Sami Zubaida, ed. *Race and Racialism.* London: Tavistock Publications, 1970, pp. 57-72.

Lowie, Robert H. *Social Organization.* New York: Holt, Rinehart, 1948.

Lukács, Georg. *History and Class Consciousness.* Cambridge, M.I.T., 1971.

Lynd, Robert S. *Knowledge for What?* New York: Grove Press, 1964.

Mandelbaum, Maurice. "Social Facts," *British Journal of Sociology,* 6 (December, 1955), pp. 305-317.

Mannheim, Karl. *Essays on Sociology and Social Psychology*. London: Routledge and Kegan Paul, 1953.

_____ "German Sociology, 1918-33," *Politica*, 1 (February, 1934), pp. 12-33.

_____ *Ideology and Utopia*. New York: Harcourt, Brace, 1936.

Marden, Charles F. and Gladys Meyer. *Minorities in American Society*. Third edition. New York: American Book, 1968.

Martindale, Don. *The Nature and Types of Sociological Theory*. Boston: Houghton Mifflin, 1960.

_____ "Social Disorganization: The Conflict of Normative and Empirical Approaches," in Howard Becker and Alvin Boskoff, eds. *Modern Sociological Theory*. New York: Dryden Press, 1959, pp. 340-367.

Marx, Karl. "Theses on Feuerbach," in Lewis S. Feuer, ed. *Marx and Engels: Basic Writings on Politics and Philosophy*. Garden City: Doubleday, 1959, pp. 243-245.

_____ and Friedrich Engels, "Manifesto of the Communist Party," in Lewis S. Feuer, ed. *Marx and Engels: Basic Writings on Politics and Philosophy*. Garden City: Doubleday, 1959, pp. 1-41.

McGee, Reece. *Social Disorganization in America*. San Francisco: Chandler, 1962.

Mead, George Herbert. *Mind, Self, and Society*. Chicago: University of Chicago Press, 1934.

Merton, Robert K. "Discrimination and the American Creed," in Robert M. MacIver, ed. *Discrimination and National Welfare*. New York: Harper Brothers, 1949, pp. 99-126.

_____ "Notes on Problem Finding in Sociology," in Robert K. Merton, Leonard Broom and Leonard S. Cottrell, Jr., eds. *Sociology Today*. New York: Basic Books, 1959, pp. ix-xxxiv.

_____ "The Role-Set: Problems in Sociological Theory," *British Journal of Sociology*, 8 (June, 1957), pp. 106-120.

_____ *Social Theory and Social Structure*. Enlarged edition. New York: Free Press, 1968.

Metzger, L. Paul. "American Sociology and Black Assimilation: Conflicting Perspectives," *American Journal of Sociology*, 76 (January, 1971), pp. 627-647.

Mills, C. Wright. "The Professional Ideology of the Social Pathologists," *American Journal of Sociology*, 49 (September, 1942), pp. 165-180.

_____ *The Sociological Imagination*. New York: Oxford, 1959.

Montagu, Ashley. *Man's Most Dangerous Myth*. New York: Oxford, 1974.

Myrdal, Gunnar. *An American Dilemma*. New York: Harper Brothers, 1944.

Nagel, Ernest. *Logic Without Metaphysics*. Glencoe: Free Press, 1956.

_____ *The Structure of Science*. New York: Harcourt, Brace, 1961.

Nicholaus, Martin. "Remarks at ASA Convention," *American Socio-*

logist, 4 (May, 1969), pp. 154-156.

Nisbet, Robert A. "The Coming Problem of Assimilation," *American Journal of Sociology*, 50 (January, 1945), pp. 261-270.

――― "Conservatism and Sociology," *American Journal of Sociology*, 58 (September, 1952), pp. 167-175.

――― "The French Revolution and the Rise of Sociology in France," *American Journal of Sociology*, 49 (September, 1943), pp. 156-164.

――― *The Sociological Tradition*. New York: Basic Books, 1966.

Northrop, F. S. C. *The Logic of the Sciences and the Humanities*. New York: Macmillan, 1947.

Novicow, J. *Les Luttes entre Sociétés Humaines*. Paris: Felix Alcan, 1893.

Oberschall, Anthony. *Social Conflict and Social Movements*. Englewood Cliffs, N.J.: Prentice-Hall, 1973.

Park, Robert E. "Assimilation," *Encyclopedia of the Social Sciences*, Volume II. New York: Macmillan, 1930, pp. 281-283.

――― "The Concept of Social Distance," *Journal of Applied Sociology*, 8 (July-August, 1924), pp. 339-344.

――― *Race and Culture*. Glencoe: Free Press, 1950.

――― "The Social Function of War," *American Journal of Sociology*, 46 (January, 1941), pp. 551-570.

――― and Ernest W. Burgess. *Introduction to the Science of Sociology*. Chicago: University of Chicago Press, 1921.

Parsons, Talcott. *The Structure of Social Action*. New York: McGraw-Hill, 1937.

Pease, John, William H. Form and Joan Huber Rytina. "Ideological Currents in American Stratification Literature," *The American Sociologist*, 5 (May, 1970), pp. 127-137.

Poll, Solomon. *The Hasidic Community of Williamsburg*. New York: Free Press, 1962.

Rainwater, Lee and William L. Yancey. *The Moynihan Report and the Politics of Controversy*. Cambridge: M.I.T., 1967.

Ransford, H. Edward. *Race and Class in American Society*. Cambridge, Mass.: Schenkman, 1977.

Remmling, Gunter W. *Road to Suspicion*. New York: Appleton-Century, 1967.

Reuter, Edward Byron. *Handbook of Sociology*. New York: Dryden, 1941.

――― "Racial Theory," *American Journal of Sociology*, 50 (May, 1945), pp. 452-461.

Rose, Peter I. *The Subject is Race*. New York: Oxford, 1968.

Ross, Edward A. *Foundations of Sociology*. New York: Macmillan, 1905.

Ross, Ralph. *Symbols and Civilization*. New York: Harcourt, Brace, 1962.

Rudner, Richard S. *Philosophy of Social Science*. Englewood Cliffs, N.J.: Prentice-Hall, 1966.

Schutz, Alfred. *Collected Papers, II: Studies in Social Theory.* The Hague: Martinus Nijhoff, 1964.

_____ "Common-Sense and Scientific Interpretation of Human Action," *Philosophy and Phenomenological Research,* 14 (September, 1953), pp. 1-37.

_____ "Concept and Theory Formation in the Social Sciences," *Journal of Philosophy,* 51 (April, 1954), pp. 257-273.

Scott, Joseph W. *The Black Revolts: Racial Stratification in the U.S.A.* Cambridge, Mass.: Schenkman, 1976.

Selznick, Philip. *The Organizational Weapon.* Glencoe: Free Press, 1960.

Shibutani, Tamotsu and Kian M. Kwan. *Ethnic Stratification.* New York: Macmillan, 1965.

Simmel, Georg. *Conflict and the Web of Group-Affiliations,* translated by Kurt H. Wolff and Reinhard Bendix. New York: Free Press, 1964.

_____ "The Sociology of Conflict," *American Journal of Sociology,* 9 (January, March and May, 1904), pp. 490-525, 672-689, and 798-811.

_____ "Superiority and Subordination as Subject-Matter of Sociology," *American Journal of Sociology,* 2 (September, and November, 1896), pp. 167-189, and 392-415.

Simons, Sarah E. "Social Assimilation," Parts I-V, *American Journal of Sociology,* 6 (May, 1901), pp. 790-822; 7 (July, 1901), pp. 53-79; (September, 1901), pp. 234-248; (November, 1901), pp. 286-404; (January, 1902), pp. 539-556.

Simpson, George Eaton and J. Milton Yinger. *Racial and Cultural Minorities.* Third edition. New York: Harper and Row, 1965.

_____ George Eaton and J. Milton Yinger. "The Sociology of Race and Ethnic Relations," in Robert K. Merton, Leonard Broom and Leonard S. Cottrell, Jr., eds. *Sociology Today.* New York: Basic Books, 1959, pp. 376-399.

Small, Albion W. *General Sociology.* Chicago: University of Chicago Press, 1905.

_____ *Origins of Sociology.* Chicago: University of Chicago Press, 1924.

_____ "The Present Outlook of Social Science," *American Journal of Sociology,* 18 (January, 1913), pp. 433-469.

Spencer, Herbert. *The Study of Sociology.* Ann Arbor: University of Michigan Press, 1966.

Spykman, Nicholas J. *The Social Theory of Georg Simmel.* New York: Atherton Press, 1965.

Stanton, William. *The Leopard's Spots: Scientific Attitudes Toward Race in America, 1815-1859.* Chicago: University of Chicago Press, 1960.

Stein, Maurice and Arthur Vidich, eds. *Sociology on Trial.* Englewood Cliffs, N.J.: Prentice-Hall, 1963.

Strasser, Hermann. *The Normative Structure of Sociology: Conservative and Emancipatory Themes in Social Thought.* London: Routledge and Kegan Paul, 1976.

Sumner, William Graham. *Folkways.* Boston: Ginn, 1907.

Unger, Irwin. "The 'New Left' and American History: Some Recent Trends in United States Historiography," *American Historical Review,* 72 (July, 1967), pp. 1237-1263.

van den Berghe, Pierre L. "Dialectic and Functionalism: Toward a Theoretical Synthesis," *American Sociological Review,* 28 (October, 1963), pp. 695-705.

—— *Man in Society: A Biosocial View.* New York; Elsevier, 1975.

—— *Race and Ethnicity: Essays in Comparative Sociology.* New York: Basic Books, 1970.

—— *Race and Racism.* New York: John Wiley, 1967.

Vander Zanden, James W. *American Minority Relations.* Second edition. New York: Ronald Press, 1966.

Vine, Margaret Wilson. *An Introduction to Sociological Theory.* New York: Longmans, Green, 1959.

Ward, Lester F. *Pure Sociology.* New York: Macmillan, 1903.

Warren, Roland L. "The Naval Reserve Officer: A Study in Assimilation," *American Sociological Review,* 11 (April, 1946), pp. 202-211.

Warriner, Charles K. "Groups are Real: A Reaffirmation," *American Sociological Review,* 21 (October, 1956), pp. 549-554.

Weatherly, Ulysses G. "The Racial Element in Social Assimilation," *American Journal of Sociology,* 16 (March, 1911), pp. 593-612.

Weber, Max. *The Methodology of the Social Sciences,* translated and edited by Edward A. Shils and Henry A. Finch. Glencoe: Free Press, 1949.

—— *The Theory of Social and Economic Organization,* translated by A. R. Henderson and Talcott Parsons. London: William Hodge, 1947.

Westie, Frank R. "Race and Ethnic Relations," in Robert E. L. Faris, ed. *Handbook of Modern Sociology.* Chicago: Rand McNally, 1964, pp. 576-618.

Whitehead, Alfred North. *Science and the Modern World.* New York: Macmillan, 1925.

Wiatr, Jerzy J. "Sociology-Marxism-Reality," in Peter L. Berger, ed. *Marxism and Sociology: Views from Eastern Europe.* New York: Appleton-Century, 1969, pp. 18-36.

Wiley, Norbert F. "The Ethnic Mobility Trap and Stratification Theory," *Social Problems,* 15 (Fall, 1967), pp. 147-159.

Willer, Judith. *The Social Determination of Knowledge.* Engelwood Cliffs, N.J.: Prentice-Hall, 1971.

Williams, Robin M., Jr. "Racial and Cultural Relations," in Joseph B. Gittler, ed. *Review of Sociology: Analysis of a Decade.* New York:

John Wiley, 1957, pp. 423-464.

_____ *The Reduction of Intergroup Tensions: A Survey of Research on Problems of Ethnic, Racial and Religious Group Relations.* New York: Social Science Research Council, 1947.

_____ "Some Further Comments on Chronic Controversies," *American Journal of Sociology,* 71 (May, 1966), pp. 717-721.

Wilson, Edward O. *Sociobiology: The New Synthesis.* Cambridge: Belknap Press, 1975.

Wilson, Everett K. *Sociology.* Homewood, Illinois: Dorsey, 1966.

Wilson, William J. *Power, Racism and Privilege.* New York: Macmillan, 1973.

Wilson, William Julius. *The Declining Significance of Race: Blacks and Changing American Institutions.* Chicago: University of Chicago Press, 1978.

Wirth, Louis. "Comment" (on G. Ichheiser), *American Journal of Sociology,* 54 (March, 1949), pp. 399-400.

_____ "Problems and Orientations of Research in Race Relations in the United States," *British Journal of Sociology,* 1 (June, 1950), pp. 117-125.

Wissler, Clark. *The American Indian.* Gloucester: Peter Smith, 1957.

Woolston, Howard. "The Process of Assimilation," *Social Forces,* 23 (May, 1945), pp. 416-424.

Young, Donald. *American Minority Peoples.* New York: Harper Brothers, 1932.

Zangwill, Israel. *The Melting Pot.* New York: Macmillan, 1909.

Zeitlin, Irving M. *Ideology and the Development of Sociological Theory.* Englewood Cliffs, N.J.: Prentice-Hall, 1968.

Zetterberg, Hans L. *On Theory and Verification in Sociology.* Totowa, N.J.: Bedminster Press, 1965.

Zubaida, Sami. "Introduction," in Sami Zubaida, ed. *Race and Racialism.* London: Tavistock Publications, 1970, pp. 1-16.

Name Index

Subject Index